Governing Partners

TRANSFORMING AMERICAN POLITICS

Lawrence C. Dodd, Series Editor

Dramatic changes in political institutions and behavior over the past three decades have underscored the dynamic nature of American politics, confronting political scientists with a new and pressing intellectual agenda. The pioneering work of early postwar scholars, while laying a firm empirical foundation for contemporary scholarship, failed to consider how American politics might change or recognize the forces that would make fundamental change inevitable. In reassessing the static interpretations fostered by these classic studies, political scientists are now examining the underlying dynamics that generate transformational change.

Transforming American Politics brings together texts and monographs that address four closely related aspects of change. A first concern is documenting and explaining recent changes in American politics—in institutions, processes, behavior, and policymaking. A second is reinterpreting classic studies and theories to provide a more accurate perspective on postwar politics. The series looks at historical change to identify recurring patterns of political transformation within and across the distinctive eras of American politics. Last and perhaps most important, the series presents new theories and interpretations that explain the dynamic processes at work and thus clarify the direction of contemporary politics. All of the books focus on the central theme of transformation—transformation in both the conduct of American politics and in the way we study and understand its many aspects.

FORTHCOMING TITLES

Masters of the House,
Roger H. Davidson, Susan Webb Hammond, and Raymond Smock

Governing Partners

STATE-LOCAL RELATIONS IN THE UNITED STATES

edited by

Russell L. Hanson
INDIANA UNIVERSITY

WestviewPress
A Division of HarperCollinsPublishers

Transforming American Politics

Copyright © 1998 by Westview Press, A Division of HarperCollins Publishers, Inc.

Published in 1998 in the United States of America by Westview Press, 5500 Central Avenue, Boulder, Colorado 80301-2877, and in the United Kingdom by Westview Press, 12 Hid's Copse Road, Cumnor Hill, Oxford OX2 9JJ

A CIP catalog record for this book is available from the Library of Congress.
ISBN 0-8133-2600-1 (hc)—ISBN 0-8133-2601-X (pb)

10   9   8   7   6   5   4   3   2   1

Contents

Tables and Figures

Preface

This volume has been several years in the making, and I have incurred several debts that should be acknowledged here. The contributors to this volume waited patiently for their work to appear in print, and I am grateful for their unwavering commitment to *Governing Partners*. I also want to thank Larry Dodd, editor of the Transforming American Politics series for Westview Press, for his encouragement of this project.

Governing Partners began its life at Westview Press under the able direction of Jennifer Knerr. When Jennifer left the press, Leo Wiegman assumed responsibility for the volume and skillfully brought it to completion. Under Leo's direction, Ryan Goldberg and Scott Horst produced the final version of the manuscript, which benefited greatly from the copyediting advice of Jennifer Swearingen.

At Indiana University in Bloomington, Eve Alexander patiently and carefully assembled the essays and prepared them for submission in electronic form. Mike Baumgartner traced several elusive references and improved the bibliography. Tim Tilton freely shared his insights on the interactions between state and county governments in Indiana. All of these people did their best to improve *Governing Partners*; any remaining errors or defects are my responsibility.

Russell L. Hanson
Bloomington, Indiana

1

The Interaction of State and Local Governments

Russell L. Hanson

State and local governments have always been important in American politics. Even when the national government assumed a leading role in domestic policymaking during the 1960s and 1970s it did not act on its own, except in the area of civil rights. Instead, Congress and the president pursued their objectives through grants-in-aid, which created powerful incentives for state and local governments to expand the range of goods and services they provided to citizens. Hence, many "national" policies actually involved a partnership of national, state, and local governments. The national government was undoubtedly the senior partner in these programs, but state and local governments enjoyed policymaking powers, too. They were not silent partners so much as they were powerful members of the board of directors advising the CEO.

Indeed, that is precisely why critics of "big government" want to return policymaking responsibilities to states and localities. Devolution is attractive only if state and local governments are capable of exercising power effectively and fairly. This capacity varies from state to state and from place to place within states. Nevertheless, there has been a general increase in the political, administrative, and financial capacity of subnational governments in the United States over the past three decades. This process of development was originally spurred by grants from the national government, but it now has considerable momentum of its own. In fact, state and local governments are at the forefront of efforts to "reinvent government" in the 1990s.

We will soon know if the development of state and local governments is self-sustaining because financial problems are causing the national government to limit its role in domestic policymaking. The social responsibilities of the national government are no longer expanding; expensive new initiatives, for example, comprehensive public health insurance, are out of the question and have been for some time. In fact, national power is waning as Washington tries to make ends meet. The deficit has been a serious problem for more than a decade, and both political parties have pledged to eliminate it by 2002. This will require spending cuts since both parties have promised tax relief, too. The cuts will fall disproportionately on "discretionary spending" in the budget; defense spending will probably not be reduced by much, and retirement benefits will almost certainly be spared for political reasons. Since these two items account for the lion's share of the budget, cuts will be concentrated in grant programs that benefit state and local governments.

Retrenchment at the national level is not merely a fiscal imperative; it is also a function of recent political developments. Congressional Republicans are in the ascendance, and their Contract with America envisions much less government overall. The Contract further stipulates that functions remaining in government hands should be devolved to the states whenever possible. New Democrats such as President Bill Clinton share this inclination, though not to the same degree or with the same fervor as their conservative counterparts. Because of this bipartisan sentiment, states are likely to become even more important in years to come. Welfare reform, the first truly significant devolution of power, will certainly not be the last transfer of policymaking control. We can expect the states to assume primary responsibility for a number of key problems, including economic development, educational reform, and environmental regulation. Indeed, states have already asserted themselves in these areas.

Mandates from the national government have added further to the work of subnational governments. As the deficit grew, Congress had fewer resources to give states and localities, but this did not prevent national lawmakers from assigning new responsibilities to subnational governments. New programs were created in a host of areas, including environmental regulation, education, and welfare. As a result, there was a proliferation of unfunded mandates until a very significant backlash occurred in the late 1980s. Congress is now showing greater restraint, but the political pressures behind mandating are almost irresistible; how else can national legislators show they are addressing the concerns of their constituents, if not by making laws and authorizing regulations that invariably affect state and local governments? The fact that Congress's resources are limited necessarily means that many of these mandates will be unfunded.

Although state governments have always been prominent political actors, they now occupy a central position in domestic policymaking under the New Federalism. Yet in most areas of the country, state governments do not work alone. They work with, through, and around units of local government in providing public goods and services. Because of this connection, any change in the role of state governments affects relations with their local governments. The increasing responsibilities of state governments have therefore produced a more intricate and complicated partnership between state and local governments.

In that respect, state-local relations are becoming a very prominent sector of intergovernmental relations—a trend that is likely to continue for decades to come. Even if gridlock is overcome at the national level, the deficit will limit the activities of the governing party or coalition for the foreseeable future. Furthermore, the desire of state and local governments to control their own affairs makes them reluctant to return to the more centralized mode of policymaking that characterized the "creative federalism" of the Great Society. Unless there is an economic crisis of great proportions, the center of political gravity in the United States is likely to be at the subnational level of government in many significant areas of domestic policy.

Until recently, researchers were unprepared to grasp this realignment of domestic politics and policymaking, largely because they neglected subnational government. That has changed with the completion of a multitude of new studies of state politics, governance, and policymaking. However, the renaissance has not yet reached the vital area of state-local relations. Relatively few scholars know much about the constitutional, political, and fiscal ties that bind states and localities, and even fewer have much information about the complex interactions between state and local governments engaged in the delivery of public goods and services. Research continues to suffer from this blind spot on state-local relations and, of course, so does the teaching of subnational politics.

Governing Partners: State-Local Relations in the United States remedies both defects. This volume presents a compact introduction to state-local relations as they have been, as they are now, and as they are likely to be in the near future. In each chapter, leading experts review key aspects of state-local relations. Thus, in Chapter 2 David Nice puts state-local relations in context, showing how they fit into the larger scheme of intergovernmental relations in the United States. That scheme includes relations between national and state governments, interactions between states, relations between states and localities, and the connections between national and local governments. Because the system of governance is so complex, it cannot be reduced to models of federalism that focus exclusively on relations between national and state governments.

As Nice shows, models of federalism can be divided into three classes: competitive, cooperative, and functional. Competitive models focus on the political contest between national power and states' rights; in so doing these models neglect local governments, which play a very important role in domestic politics. Because local governments do not figure in competitive models of federalism, relations between local and state governments, and between local and national governments, do not receive the attention they deserve. Whole sectors of intergovernmental relations are thereby omitted from consideration.

Cooperative models of federalism do a better job of analytically incorporating local governments. This is particularly evident in treatments of various forms of New Federalism that have been tried or proposed in the past three decades. The interdependence of governments in New Federalism is captured nicely in the metaphor of a rowboat with three oarsmen who must coordinate their actions in order to make progress. The three oarsmen correspond to our three levels of government, which must cooperate in order to provide public goods and services efficiently and fairly. This highlights the politics of intergovernmental undertakings, since the coordination of national, state, and local activities is seen as the key to successful domestic policymaking.

The extent of intergovernmental cooperation varies across policy areas; it is high in social welfare policy but low in regulatory policies dominated by national agencies. Scholars use "picket fence" and "bamboo fence" metaphors to capture these differences. These functional models of federalism stress the vertical integration of federal, state, and local agencies within distinct policy areas. The areas are said to be isolated from each other, with little coordination across areas. Moreover, within each policy area there are bureaucratic specialists who are not elected, but who are nevertheless treated as key actors in functional models. According to this perspective, specialists from national and state agencies make policies, which are then implemented by local administrators. The determination and skill of these administrators ultimately determines the success or failure of policies at the street level, where public goods and services are actually provided.

Cooperative and functional models of federalism are particularly useful in understanding certain aspects of state-local relations. Constitutionally speaking, local governments are the creatures of state government; indeed U.S. law treats states as unitary political systems. As Nice observes, this may explain why local governments do not appear in competitive models of federalism. Such models implicitly assume that state governments impose their will on local governments, so the only relevant question is how much power states enjoy vis-à-vis the national government. Reinforcing this way of thinking is the undeniable centralization of administrative control and financial leverage, a tendency that is growing in all states, although it is particularly pronounced in some. On the surface, it seems as if local governments are powerless in the face of state governments in the late twentieth century.

The appearance is deceiving. State policy makers depend on local governments to provide essential goods and services, which militates against "command and control" policymaking. Moreover, the political process makes state officials sensitive to the policy preferences of county and city governments. State legislators are elected on a local basis and often have experience as mayors, commissioners, council members, or school board representatives. To insure that legislators remember their roots, local governments engage in lobbying, individually and collectively. Indeed, associations of local governments are one of the most formidable political lobbies in state politics, as Nice observes. Thus, the political power of local governments partially offsets their inferior constitutional, administrative, and financial status.

The power of towns, cities, and counties is deeply rooted in American politics. There is a long tradition of local control in the United States, stretching back to the colonial period, as Daniel Elazar reminds us in Chapter 3. In fact, some of the first states formed as federations of local government, giving rise to the notion that local governments are not constitutionally inferior to state government. This view rejects the characterization of states as unitary political systems and is therefore regarded as a form of heresy in most constitutional circles. However, the mid-nineteenth-century movement to charter or incorporate local governments can be seen as an effort to provide a legal basis for local control. The same is true of the somewhat later movement in favor of home rule, which gave localities substantially more autonomy than they enjoyed under Dillon's Rule (which held that local governments only enjoy powers expressly delegated by state government, or powers that are clearly implied in expressly granted powers, or powers that are essential for the functioning of local government).

Home rule was popular with reformers who wanted to give local governments all powers not specifically denied by state governments. These hopes have only been partially realized. Not all states favor home rule, and states that extend home rule may bestow it only upon certain kinds of local government or cities of a certain size. Moreover, home rule provisions are not inviolable. They can be overridden when there is an important state interest at stake. As Elazar notes, governors and legislatures can usually find a state interest to justify interventions that are popular with voters or powerful constituents. This makes it impossible to think of a strict separation of powers between state and local governments, each with its own sphere of responsibilities.

In light of the interdependence of governments, Elazar urges us to think of states as unions of their civil communities. The states are not unitary systems in which local governments are "mere tenants at the will of the legislature," as Judge Dillon argued. Neither are they federations of local governments, as the "constitutional heretics" claim and as the advocates of home rule want. Between these extremes is an intermediate po-

sition, one that reflects the fact that state and local governments each de-
rive their powers from the people. It is the people in each state who ultimately determine the balance of power between state and local governments. The location of this balance will vary from state to state, and it
may change over time as the union evolves. In that respect, the development of state-local relations within states bears a strong resemblance to
the development of the Union itself (which is, of course, Elazar's point).

The term "union" is evocative and reminds us that the *system* of governance is more important than any single government today. This is
Beverly Cigler's conclusion in Chapter 4. State and local governments
face enormously complex problems stemming from demographic
changes, technological developments, and broad economic trends.
Citizens expect their leaders to address these problems, but there is a
shortage of resources needed to solve them. National laws and regulations also limit the remedies that may be pursued by state and local officials. In this context, state and local governments cannot stand apart; they
must cooperate, not only with each other, but with the private sector.
Otherwise, problems will go unsolved and essential needs will be unmet.

Cigler identifies twelve desiderata that ought to define state-local relations in the twenty-first century. In her view, the governing partners must
promote greater self-reliance among citizens. This will allow state and
local governments to concentrate on people, organizations, and places
that are unable to meet basic needs through their own efforts. Even then,
policy makers must try to prevent problems from occurring, or at least
keep them from growing worse once they arise; they should not merely
respond to problems when they reach crisis proportions. In the long run,
preventive action is more efficient than amelioration, Cigler avers.

Whatever policies are pursued by state and local governments, the delivery of goods and services must be reorganized. Cigler advocates a
holistic approach to problem solving. The rigid differentiation of policy
along functional lines must be overcome to achieve greater coordination,
and the scale of operations must be extended beyond local borders. Many
of today's problems, for example, land-use planning or environmental
regulation, must be attacked at the regional level within states; these
problems are beyond the capacity of any single local government. On the
other hand, the actual delivery of goods and services should be decentralized so as to maximize responsiveness to the public. Thus, different
aspects of policymaking require different scales of operation.

Within this complex system of governance, no government enjoys a monopoly on power. For that matter, the system includes nonprofit organizations and profit-seeking service providers, not just public agencies. Instead
of providing goods and services themselves, many state agencies coordinate the activities of local governments and private actors, who provide

goods and services to citizens. One result is greater flexibility for local governments and the private sector, as state policy makers relax their grip and begin to function as facilitators. Another result is closer integration of the public and private sectors as service provision becomes "privatized."

The system will not work well unless policy makers are held accountable for their actions. This requires greater attention to measures of performance and a willingness to experiment with different modes of organization and service delivery. It depends, too, on the will of the people. As Cigler notes, deliberative democracy must be the basis for policy decisions or citizens will not seek the reinvention of state and local government, nor will they accept its outcomes. Institutions that encourage participation by citizens are essential for effective governance.

Public goods and services cost money, and an elaborate system of government finance has developed since the New Deal. A few local governments are financially self-sufficient, but most depend heavily on subsidies from state and national governments to make ends meet. Partly this reflects limitations on the taxing power of local governments. Partly it is because state and national governments rely on the income tax, which produces more revenue than property taxes, the staple of most local governments. And partly it is due to the fact that state and national governments use grants-in-aid to reduce or even eliminate disparities in public goods and services. Local governments' capacity for raising revenue varies tremendously within states; wealthy suburbs can afford the best schools, for example, but rural or inner-city school districts cannot provide a decent education without help from the states. Governors and legislatures are willing to provide assistance for equalizing goods and services and for fulfilling popular functions, but this necessarily breeds financial dependency on state governments, as Jeffrey Stonecash demonstrates in Chapter 5.

The national government has also subsidized local governments, particularly during the administration of Lyndon Johnson, whose Great Society programs funneled a lot of money to cities engaged in the War on Poverty. Richard Nixon's New Federalism brought new money to localities in the form of block grants, but the funds began to dry up as the national government's deficit increased. As Stonecash notes, the reduction in national grants-in-aid led many localities to seek additional aid from state governments, so that service levels could be maintained. By and large, states complied with this request. They assumed an increasingly larger share of the financial burden of providing "local" goods and services, and as a result the system of intergovernmental financing became noticeably more centralized.

Of course, the degree of fiscal centralization varies from state to state. Texas does not have an income tax, so the state cannot offer as much assistance to local governments (including school corporations) as other states. This will not change until there is political support at the state level for increasing taxes. Stonecash shows how support for tax increases materialized when Democrats gained control in New Jersey, which now contributes more than a third of local governments' general revenue. A similar pattern of dependency unfolded in Connecticut after moderate Republicans (and an independent governor) joined Democrats in raising taxes. Thus, the increasing centralization of finances is a function of state governments' willingness and ability to raise revenue—a function of politics and economics, in other words.

State and local revenues are strongly affected by economic conditions. This gives both levels of government a strong fiscal incentive to promote economic development. (Obviously, there are political incentives, too.) In Chapter 6 Peter Eisinger recounts the evolution of development policy. After World War II capital and labor began migrating to the south and west. Some of the shifts were induced by state and local governments in those regions, which recruited industries by offering tax abatements and other enticements. To protect their economic base, states in the north and east began to offer incentives, too, and the First Wave of development policy was characterized by "smokestack chasing," with states competing against each other.

Smokestack chasing was costly and not very effective, economically speaking. In the Second Wave of development policy states became proactive. As Eisinger explains, state governments began to think strategically, identifying general goals for economic development. Taking note of national and international trends, policy makers cultivated specific industries for development. They also tried to generate a "business climate" conducive to those industries through favorable tax and regulatory policies. Within this framework, state and local governments then pursued firms and investors in the private sector, offering them an attractive place to do business.

Local governments played one of four roles in this partnership, according to Eisinger. In some cases, they were merely the passive beneficiary of state programs promoting exports or high technology development. In other cases, local governments were a conduit, passing requests from businesses to state officials, who then gave local officials resources to distribute to private firms and individuals. Often, though, local officials played a more active role, serving as junior partners in a coordinated effort to attract businesses. Some localities took this a step further, becoming independent economic developers by offering incentives and adjusting the "micro" business climate in their area.

The economic impact of Second Wave policies is hard to measure, and some politicians have reverted to smokestack chasing in hopes of making a big score. However, more and more states are adopting Third Wave policies for the next century. These policies are designed to empower local governments, increasing their capacity to attract businesses favored by residents of a community. Examples include job training and worker education programs, initiatives to enhance local planning, the establishment of community development corporations, and so forth. Obviously, this represents a new pattern of interaction between state and local governments, one that is consonant with Beverly Cigler's recommendations for effective governance in a rapidly changing environment.

Businesses need workers who are well educated, and many state policy makers view effective public schools as the key to long-term economic development. Hence governors and state legislatures devote considerable attention to educational matters, hoping to improve the skills of their state's workforce. They also spend a great deal of money on primary, secondary, and higher education. Outlays for education represent the largest item in most states' budgets, and state policy makers understandably want some say in how this money is used by local school boards, public vocational schools, community colleges, and public universities.

The state-local partnership in education is reviewed by Daniel DiLeo in Chapter 7. As economic development policy became important, state officials became more interested in education, which had long been dominated by local school boards. State agencies concerned with education also became more knowledgeable about finance, personnel, and curriculum issues in public schools. State policy makers began to reform education from the top down, so to speak. They established policies for hiring and rewarding teachers. They emphasized economically relevant subjects in the curriculum (and regulated others, for example, sex education). They changed the length of school years and redefined graduation requirements. In so doing, states brought greater standardization to public schooling, often at the expense of local control.

This first wave of reforms has been followed by a second, which aims to improve the quality of education and the range of choices open to parents of school children. Quality improvements include programs designed for "at risk" populations and the disabled. Outcomes-based education is part of this movement, too, insofar as it stresses the need to organize schools and classrooms in accordance with specific pedagogical objectives in mind. Entrenched interests sometimes oppose these reforms, and there are sharp disagreements about which outcomes should be pursued. Thus, school politics can be very contentious, indeed.

In some states parents have a broad range of educational choices. Neighborhood public schools still do most of the work, but some states, for example, Minnesota, allow parents to send their children to a local school of their own choosing. As DiLeo explains, the choice may extend across district lines, as well as within district boundaries. Charter schools are also becoming popular in states that want to eliminate regulations they imposed a decade or two earlier. Home schooling is more common, too, particularly in states with substantial numbers of parents who are religious conservatives. Such groups are politically well organized and can be a potent force in the legislature, which defines the overall framework of educational possibilities in a state.

As the range of providers becomes more diverse, considerations of equity become more prominent. A few states provide educational funds to localities on a per pupil basis. However, these flat grants are giving way to formulas that award proportionately more funds to poor school districts. DiLeo mentions four methods of achieving greater equality in funding across localities. One is the use of school foundation programs, which guarantee a minimum level of funding per pupil but place no restrictions on local spending. A second is percentage equalizing, which makes state aid inversely proportional to a school district's wealth. A third and even more radical approach is district power equalizing, which redistributes revenues from wealthy to poor school districts. The fourth method involves the complete takeover of educational funding by the state, which Hawaii has done to insure that school spending is truly equal.

Local school boards are still important administrative bodies, although school superintendents exercise day-to-day control (under guidelines established by the state). However, school boards no longer dominate the partnership of public education. Their political power has been reduced over the past twenty-five years, first by national courts concerned about racial segregation, and then by state policy makers who wanted to reform education. To a very significant extent local school boards now operate under the watchful eye of state officials who may even "take over" a local school system that becomes academically or financially bankrupt. The junior partner has been promoted to senior manager, and the one-time senior partner has been marginalized as state officials begin to operate directly on schools and foster arrangements with other suppliers of education.

A new partnership between state and local governments is being forged in environmental regulation, the subject of Chapter 8. James Lester and Emmett Lombard describe the emergence of programs to protect air and water quality. Originally, these programs were the responsibility of local governments; state governments played a relatively small role in early efforts to combat pollution. That changed when the Water Quality Act and Clear Air Act were passed by Congress. Under this legislation, the national government became the dominant force in environmental policymaking in the 1970s and 1980s.

Although environmental regulation was spearheaded by the Environmental Protection Agency, the EPA was not the only important actor. As

Lester and Lombard note, corresponding agencies at the state level exerted influence, too, at least in some parts of the country. Indeed, many states acquired substantial experience in regulating air and water quality, usually in conjunction with local officials who were in position to monitor the sources of pollution. This interest and expertise in regulation will become very important if Congress devolves environmental policymaking to the state level and limits the resources that are available to the EPA.

In the future, states are likely to rely heavily on regional policymaking bodies, just as they have in the past. Because pollution spills over local boundaries, larger geographic jurisdictions are needed to protect air and water quality. They are also useful in dealing with common problems, such as the disposal of hazardous waste. Hence states have created substate regional authorities to cope with many environmental problems. Most of these authorities take the form of special districts; unlike general purpose governments, they have a single function to perform. Thus, there has been a proliferation of soil conservation districts, watershed authorities, pollution control districts, and so forth. Such agencies are particularly common in large states, but even small states employ them, as Lester and Lombard report.

Some states rely exclusively on regional authorities when it comes to environmental regulation. However, most assign at least some responsibilities to existing local governments. County and city governments monitor air and water quality and help make rules governing land use, conservation of resources, preservation of wetlands and other habitats, and waste disposal. As these responsibilities have grown, so have the staffs of local regulatory agencies. The local staffs are linked to state agencies, which have grown in size, too.

Although they share the same responsibility, there are important differences between state and local agencies, especially in local agencies that are part of county and city government. Lester and Lombard observe that state agencies are often most concerned about the impact of environmental regulation on economic development. They do not want to harm the state's business climate, so they rely on self-monitoring by industries instead of sanctions-based or enforcement-based strategies of pollution control. Local officials, by contrast, face pressure from citizens who seek environmental protection. They want to stop pollution, or better yet, prevent it from occurring in the first place. The division of interests means the partnership between state and local governments does not always operate smoothly (a phenomenon that Eisinger notices in economic development policy, too).

In discussing the Southeast Michigan Council of Governments, Lester and Lombard show how the partnership works in practice. Timothy Tilton provides another example in Chapter 9. He recounts the protracted negotiations between Monroe County officials in Indiana and the Indiana Department of Environmental Management. While Tilton was a county commissioner, state regulators pressed the county to upgrade its landfill operations. The county's solid waste landfill was publicly owned but operated by a private contractor in a joint venture of the sort Cigler advocates. Leaching from the landfill was a problem, however, and the state threatened to close the landfill if operations did not improve. Yet county officials were reluctant to impose stringent controls on the landfill operator because that might have forced the business into bankruptcy or required the county to pay substantially more for services.

Then the county entered into an arrangement with the city of Bloomington, the largest user of the landfill. A recycling program was started, and fees to use the landfill were increased. Soon a solid waste district was created, with the county ceding responsibility to the new authority. The district was governed by a bipartisan board, which hired skilled administrators to run the landfill. In turn, public employees replaced private workers at the landfill, and the operation became a model of efficiency. State officials then backed away, having achieved their original objective (with minimal costs to the state, it should be added).

Tilton shows that local compliance with state mandates is not automatic and often involves a great deal of politicking. Metaphors commonly used to describe state-local relations do not capture this process very well. Neither do they do justice to the differentiation of those relations along functional lines. For this reason, it is misleading to say that state governments interact with local governments, as if the two governments are unitary actors. It is more accurate to say that on any given issue, officials from specific state agencies work with, or sometimes against, their counterparts in local agencies. The missions of these agencies and the people who staff them are important and may affect the outcome of negotiations or the success of policymaking.

Moreover, almost every issue or problem spawns its own distinctive pattern of interaction. At any given time, several county agencies may be contacting state agencies about different issues. Elected officials from general purpose governments are aware of this, and their response to one issue may be affected by their experiences in other issue areas. In that sense, there is a political linkage between issues even when the functional differentiation of policymaking activity is fairly advanced. There is also a political linkage spanning levels of government, insofar as city and county officials rely on area legislators to represent their interests in the state capital.

Tilton also mentions an important phenomenon that he calls "mandating by dereliction." State governments frequently issue mandates to local government, and the mandates are often unfunded. Local officials complain about these expensive orders or commands, but inaction by states can present even greater problems for county and city governments. When states fail to address significant social problems or public health concerns, local governments are faced with the consequences of that failure: poverty, disease, and crime. These problems require local action just as surely as mandates from the legislature or some other state agency, and the fiscal consequences can be very serious.

Charles Barrilleaux makes this point well in Chapter 10, which examines health and welfare policy. All three levels of government are active in this area, sometimes on their own, but more often in conjunction with each other. On its own the national government provides cash benefits and medical services to most of the aged population. States maintain institutions for the deaf and blind, those who are afflicted with incurable diseases, and the mentally incapacitated. Counties and townships supply general assistance to the indigent and operate medical facilities that aid the poor. None of these programs involves intergovernmental decision-making, but two of the most important programs do. Public assistance and Medicaid require the coordinated efforts of all three levels of government. As such, they are quintessentially federal social welfare programs.

Until 1996 these programs were administered by local governments in most states. Counties and cities assisted the poor, under the supervision of the states, who provided financial resources. In turn, the states acted under guidelines established by the national government, which made grants-in-aid available for this purpose. That pattern still holds for Medicaid, but the replacement of Aid to Families with Dependent Children by Temporary Assistance for Needy Families in 1996 reduced the role of national policy makers and significantly expanded the power of states. A few states will probably assume complete responsibility for assisting poor children, and some others may assign it to local governments, exercising their constitutional prerogatives. However, most states will share responsibility, which means that state-local relations will be at the center of governmental efforts to assist America's poor children in the future.

Barrilleaux analyzes the politics surrounding programs in aid of the poor, noting a substantial decline in states' support for poor children between 1980 and 1990. This is not because states are poorer than they once were, and it is not because economic considerations are more important in the 1990s. Neither is it because policy makers have become more conservative, nor does it mean that political considerations have become more important with the passage of time. The decline in efforts to assist children seems to be associated with the rising costs of providing medical treatment to the poor, including the aged and disabled, whose need for long-term institutional care accounts for the lion's share of Medicaid spending. In short, policy makers in many states have decided to help some, but not all, of the poor. Perhaps not surprisingly, they favor assistance for poor people who are themselves old enough to vote, and whose children are old enough to support candidates committed to programs that care for their parents.

The pattern is unlikely to change in the future; indeed, it may become more pronounced now that states have more freedom to shape Temporary Assistance for Needy Families. The consequences for local governments are great, as Barrilleaux recognizes. If states are unwilling to assist poor children and their families, the burden will fall on local governments. Local governments will have to supply assistance on their own, which will be expensive and politically contentious, or they will have to deal with the consequences of poverty within their jurisdictions. These include higher rates of juvenile delinquency, an increase in the size of "at risk" populations in local schools, and a workforce that is not as healthy or well trained as it must be to attract business investors. Either way, the costs of "mandating by dereliction" will be high.

From this brief review of the contents of this volume, four themes stand out. First, the authors agree that state-local relations in the United States will become more important in the coming years. As the national government reduces its role in domestic politics, state governments will become the focal point of citizens' demands for public goods and services. Since most state governments work through local governments, any increase in the power of states necessarily means a larger role for local governments, too. The partnership will develop on both sides, and relations between the partners will become more complex and differentiated over time.

The second theme is that the form of interaction between state and local government is changing. The "wave" metaphor is frequently invoked to explain the evolution of policy and, by implication, the development of state-local relations. In most, but not all, policy areas the trend is toward greater assistance for local governments. States are not taking over the functions of local government; they are trying to increase local governments' capacity for supplying public goods and services. Financial assistance is crucial to this endeavor, but so is technical advice on difficult policy issues. States are supplying both, and they are simultaneously increasing the power of local governments. All of this underscores the enabling role of states and the reassertion of the political preference for localized problem solving in American politics.

The need for effective forms of popular control is a third theme in the following chapters. The distinction between state and local government is likely to blur as the system of governance evolves in the twenty-first century. The line between public and private sectors will become less distinct, too, as the provision and delivery of goods and services become selectively privatized. This is bound to raise troubling issues of accountability and equity. Issues of accountability will arise because it will become harder for citizens to identify those who are responsible for failures in the delivery of goods and services: Is it the fault of a local agency, or its partners in state government and the private sector? Or is it perhaps the whole system that is to blame? In that case, elections, which are the usual means of making officials respond to citizens' demands, may not be very effective.

Issues of equity will emerge, too. The "devolution revolution" is predicated on the notion that states should take the lead in domestic policymaking, but not every state government is willing or able to play that role. Some states lack the political will or the financial resources needed to promote economic development, protect the environment, improve schools, and assist the poor. Local governments will be left to their own devices in these states. However, the problem-solving capacity of local governments varies enormously: Wealthy school districts can improve education much more easily than poor districts, for example. Thus, in the absence of strong leadership on the part of state government, differences in the capacities of local governments could lead to the unequal provision of goods and services and corresponding complaints about the unfairness of political decisionmaking. One way of addressing these complaints is through new forms of political participation, forms that are appropriate for the newly emerging system of governance.

In that sense, relations between state and local governments are themselves becoming a policy issue. This is the fourth theme of *Governing Partners.* In the past, intergovernmental relations developed incrementally and without much discussion between state and local authorities. Now intergovernmental relations are planned; they are the product of considerable discussion about the advantages and disadvantages of alternative forms of partnership. The so-called reinvention of government has become a conscious, even self-conscious, exercise as we enter the next millennium. It is also a highly experimental process, so we should expect great variation in the form of state-local relations across the United States. That has always been true, but the range of variation may increase and its political significance will undoubtedly become more pronounced as the "devolution revolution" unfolds. The following essays make this point very well; in almost every policy area the governing partnership between state and local governments varies from place to place and from time to time. Making sense of that variation is the central task of *Governing Partners.*

2

The Intergovernmental Setting of State-Local Relations

David C. Nice

State-local relations in the United States take place within our federal system. Although federalism has been defined in many ways over the years, for present purposes federalism is a system of government that includes a national government and one or more levels of subnational governments (states, cantons, local governments) and that allows each level to make some significant decisions independently of the other(s). Independence is not absolute; each level may influence the others in various ways. Nonetheless, a federal system enables each level to make some decisions without the approval (formal or informal) of the other level (see Macmahon 1972: 3; Riker 1964: 5; Wheare 1964: chapter 1).

Federalism is an intermediate type of political system. In a unitary system, all decisionmaking power belongs to the national government, and subnational governments do not exist or serve only to implement policies established by the national government.[1] The United Kingdom is a relatively unitary system. At the other extreme, no national government exists and the "subunits" are independent countries. Federalism falls between the two extremes.

Federal systems distribute power and responsibilities in many ways, from systems in which the national government is relatively weak and the subunits are dominant, systems that are often called confederations, to systems placing most of the authority in the national government and leaving the subunits with a relatively minor role. The allocation of powers and duties in a system can change, as it has in the United States, and can vary from one program to another. Responsibilities can be divided, with some given to the national government and others to the subunits, or responsibilities can be shared.

Many observers over the years have argued about how the American federal system operates and how it should operate. The status of local governments in the federal system has been a frequent source of disagreement. Scholars and politicians have developed a number of interpretations of what federalism is or should be. We will refer to these interpretations as models, which are simplified versions of reality or images of an ideal situation stripped of unnecessary detail.

Models of Federalism

Models of federalism emphasize important aspects of how a federal system operates.[2] Competitive models, including nation-centered federalism, state-centered federalism, and dual federalism, focus on competition between national and state levels of government. Local governments typically receive little attention in these models. Interdependent models, such as cooperative federalism, creative federalism, the various New Federalisms, and rowboat federalism, emphasize shared responsibilities and give more attention to local governments, although in varying degrees. Finally, functional models of federalism, including picket fence and bamboo fence federalism, emphasize divisions among different policy specialists, such as conservation officers or transportation administrators at all levels of government, including local.

Competitive Models

Some observers believe that federalism is a zero-sum game—that is, a game in which there is a fixed amount of some commodity and in which one player can increase his or her share of the commodity only by taking some from another player. Competitive models of federalism, which are among the older models, generally regard federalism as a zero-sum game with two levels of government, national and state, competing for power. One level can gain power only at the expense of the other. Local governments receive little attention, if any. The various competitive models disagree, however, on the outcome (real or desired) of the competition.

Nation-Centered Federalism.   According to nation-centered federalism, the national government is (or should be) the dominant force in a federal system. The national government has a broader perspective on issues, and the states are poorly equipped to deal with difficult problems (a criticism that is certainly less valid today than it once was). Adherents to this model generally advocate extensive national government activity, prefer a broad in-

terpretation of national government powers, and fear that leaving problems to the states results in inaction or an ineffective response, with different states adopting different strategies without a coherent plan of action.

However, nation-centered federalism is sometimes associated with a
fear or dislike of national government power. In this case, national dominance is criticized as undesirable or even dangerous. National dominance produces red tape, bureaucratic inefficiency, and government that
is inaccessible to ordinary citizens and out of touch with local conditions.
Adherents of this perspective usually have a second competitive model
as their ideal.

State-Centered Federalism. With state-centered federalism, the states are de-
picted as the dominant force in the federal system. Adherents of this model
contend that state dominance is preferable because of the risks of concen-
trating too much power in the national government. The states are seen as
closer to people and better able to respond to varying needs or preferences
from one state to another. In addition, individual states can try different
programs in order to develop improved policies. Adherents of this view
often contend that the national government was created by the states and
is therefore inferior to them, a contention that is rather controversial (see
Anderson 1955: chapters 3–4; Nice and Fredericksen 1995: 93–94).

State-centered federalism is usually not regarded as a valid description
of American federalism in recent years because of the size and importance
of the national government. However, many observers emphasize the importance of the states in our governmental system. States governments
participate in most major public policies, have grown dramatically since
1900, and often exert substantial influence on other levels of government.
As discussed in this volume, the states play a critical role in local government (although most of the writing on state-centered federalism does not
consider local governments as participants in federalism). The states have
also shown that they are often able to effectively resist pressures from
other levels of government when the inclination is present.

Dual Federalism. The third and best-known competitive model is dual federalism, which is sometimes called layer-cake federalism. According to
dual federalism, each level of government, national and state, is supreme
within its defined responsibilities. Neither level is dominant over the other,
and neither level should interfere in the other's operations. Dual federalism emphasizes balance; we sometimes need the flexibility that national
policies cannot provide and sometimes need the broad perspective and
concerted action that states acting individually cannot provide. Since tasks
are clearly divided, with the national government handling national functions and the states handling state functions, voters can easily determine

where credit and blame belong. Dual federalism gives a fairly accurate picture of America's early years (though it is perhaps not totally accurate; see Elazar 1962). The Supreme Court delineated boundaries between national and state functions, and sharing of tasks between national and state levels was relatively limited in the nineteenth century.

Dual federalism presents several problems, however. In drawing boundaries between national and state functions, some problems may end up on the boundary; consequently, neither level can resolve these problems. Dual federalism also ignores the possibility that a national and state partnership may sometimes be more effective than either level acting individually. It assumes that responsibilities and powers can be divided so that decisions made in one policy area do not affect other policy areas, a dubious assumption at best. Last, how do we decide whether a problem should be handled nationally or at the state level? If civil rights for blacks had remained a state responsibility through the 1950s and 1960s, fewer blacks would have voted or attended integrated schools in the late 1970s.

Overall, the competitive models are pretty clearly flawed by overlooking the possibility that both levels of government could gain power simultaneously. The competitive models also share a serious omission: Local governments are typically ignored, although there are some exceptions (see Dye 1990). That omission is particularly noteworthy because, during the era when the competitive models were most influential, local governments were the largest level of government in terms of financial and labor resources. The competitive models omitted local governments because the U.S. Constitution did not mention them and because state constitutions and courts tended to treat local governments as creatures of the states and legally subordinate to them. In practice, however, local governments often have considerable freedom to maneuver. The competitive models have value in emphasizing that conflicts do arise between levels of government in a federal system. Those conflicts may result in a victory for one side over the other, but sometimes the result is a stalemate or truce, with neither level triumphing. Some of the conflicts are partly for public relations purposes, as when a governor dramatically opposes a national government action, but many times the conflict is genuine and represents differing beliefs about what should be done about some problem.

Interdependent Models

In contrast to competitive models of federalism, interdependent models emphasize shared powers and responsibilities, with the various governments working toward shared objectives. Power is not a zero-sum game; all may gain simultaneously. In addition, local governments are typically included as relevant actors in these models. The best-known interdependent model is cooperative federalism (Grodzins 1983).

Cooperative Federalism. Cooperative federalism (sometimes called marble-cake federalism) encourages cooperation among levels of government because working as partners may produce better results than any one level acting alone. Most major public policies have national effects but also have localized consequences that may vary from place to place. The multiple effects of policies are most likely to be handled effectively if all levels of government are involved, including local governments. The national government and the states are often unable to keep track of numerous variations in local needs and preferences, but local governments may be unable to cope with their problems alone. A partnership is a reasonable solution. No level of government has all the answers to our problems: Sharing responsibilities enables the best ideas to emerge, regardless of where they originated.

Cooperative federalism calls attention to the substantial amount of interaction among different levels of government in the United States. A great deal of cooperative activity in pursuit of shared goals does occur, and responsibilities for most major programs are shared among all three levels of government. Note, however, that cooperation is not automatic, nor is it always or easily achieved. When tasks are shared, how is cooperation achieved, and what happens if it cannot be brought about?

Creative Federalism. Creative federalism, a cousin of cooperative federalism, emerged in the late 1950s and 1960s. Advocates of creative federalism believed that many traditional public policies designed to combat poverty and urban decay had failed and that new ideas and solutions were needed. Creative federalism called for an enlarged partnership of national, state, and local governments and the private sector. Together they would develop and test new strategies to attack major social problems. Bringing in the private sector would provide new ideas and additional resources, and if current governmental organizations proved to be inadequate, new governmental or quasi-governmental bodies should be created.

Creative federalism is a reasonably accurate description of the Great Society era of the mid-1960s, when officials tried to apply the model to actual policy problems. The Clinton administration's emphasis on developing new policy strategies is also in the spirit of creative federalism. The results in the 1960s were somewhat disappointing. Progress was made on some problems, but high expectations made the progress appear small. Many new grant programs were enacted to foster development of new strategies, but the result was sometimes confusion over what money was available and how to apply for it. Established government agencies did not always welcome the new governmental and quasi-governmental bodies that were created, particularly when some of them became controversial. These problems led to the creation of yet another cooperative model.

The New Federalism I.   The New Federalism I, a major initiative of the
Nixon and Ford administrations, was a version of cooperative federalism
with some dual or state-centered federalism mixed in. The New
Federalism I recognized and approved of shared responsibilities but
charged that the national programs had become too large and intrusive,
particularly because of the many categorical grant programs and the regulations that accompanied them. Federal regulation of state and local
programs was too cumbersome, and public management at all levels was
weak. State and local officials needed greater flexibility to deal with state-
local needs. The New Federalism I advocated having fewer grants but
giving states and local governments more flexibility over their use; that
in turn was supposed to produce better coordination in dealing with
problems such as crime and community development. The New
Federalism I was consistent with the attempts made by Presidents Nixon
and Ford to reduce federal restrictions and to give states and localities
more leeway in using federal grant funds. Both presidents generally favored a partnership among levels of government and shared responsibilities but with a smaller role for the national government and more state-
local flexibility.

The New Federalism II.   The New Federalism II[3] of Ronald Reagan re-
sembled the New Federalism I but attached more importance to separating national and state functions. In addition, the New Federalism II called
for reducing national grants to states and especially to localities, in contrast to the growth of those grants during the Nixon and Ford years, and
for greatly reducing direct contacts between the national government and
local governments. The Reagan administration also proposed less national involvement in domestic policymaking generally. In all these respects the New Federalism II was closer to dual or state-centered federalism than the Nixon-Ford version, although Reagan did not always
follow the model consistently. Congressional Republicans in 1995 also followed the guidelines of the New Federalism II in a number of their proposals. If followed consistently, the New Federalism II would have given
states considerably more freedom in dealing with localities and would
have given local governments fewer choices in seeking assistance for
solving local problems.

Rowboat Federalism.   The last interdependent model to be discussed here
is rowboat federalism, which depicts the federal system as resembling
three people in a boat. If they work together, they can make more rapid
progress. If they quarrel or one or more persons fail to exert much effort,
they will make little progress and may possibly sink (Sanford 1967: 97).
This model clearly conveys a sense of shared fate and mutual reliance but

does not make many assumptions about the nature of the relationships among those involved. Although the participants may agree on some things, such as the need to survive, they may not agree on their destination, the appropriate level of exertion, or the allocation of drinking water. Cooperation is possible, but so is conflict. Power is not always a zero-sum game, for cooperation may help all of them achieve mutual goals more readily than individual action. If the participants disagree about goals, however, then one participant's gain may be another participant's loss.

Taken together the interdependent models call attention to several problems, particularly in the matter of governmental accountability. If all levels of government are involved in a program that fails, who deserves the blame? Who deserves credit when a program succeeds? If a program is designed on the premise that all three levels will work together harmoniously, deadlock or waste may result if cooperation is not achieved. Sharing of tasks creates opportunities for scapegoating; officials in one level of government will be tempted to blame their mistakes on officials at other levels. Shared responsibilities can slow program operations when action requires consultation with many officials in many different units of government. Negotiations to develop a plan of action acceptable to all may take months or even years. Meanwhile people who want action on a problem may grow angry about the delay, and the problem may grow larger or cause considerable damage.

On the positive side, the interdependent models do call attention to genuine benefits that cooperative action can sometimes produce. In addition, interdependence clearly exists in our federal system, and that situation is almost certain to continue. Shared responsibilities may encourage officials at each level to keep an eye on officials at other levels to avoid being blamed for the results of their failures. If a task is entirely assigned to one level of government, what incentive would officials at other levels have to monitor the handling of that task?

The interdependent models provide a valuable correction by including local governments as part of the federal system. That change is partly an outgrowth of evidence local governments do not simply function as servants of state governments but instead manage to make some decisions locally and also exert significant influence in state politics. In addition, as political scientists begin to place more emphasis on actual activities instead of confining their attention to legal provisions and formal arrangements, the importance of local governments becomes increasingly clear.

Functional Models

Some analysts believe that the significant divisions in the federal system are not the horizontal divisions between levels of government but rather the vertical divisions among government programs such as education, environmental protection, and law enforcement. A valid model of the system must include these vertical divisions.

Picket Fence Federalism.   Adherents to picket fence federalism contend that the most important components of the federal system are the various functional bureaucracies, not the national, state, or local governments. Program specialists, such as public health officials, have more in common with their counterparts in other levels of government than with other officials in the same level of government but not in the same specialty. The bonds among agencies in a particular policy area but at different levels of government (national, state, and local) are created by personnel who have similar training, attend the same professional meetings, and sometimes have careers that span two or more levels of government. Additional bonds are created by shared goals and tasks and by grants channeling funds to a specific program that are legally unavailable for any other use. Structures of local government that create separate governments for particular programs encourage people who work in those programs to think of themselves as separate from people who work for other local governments. Finally, the functional emphasis is strengthened by alliances among a bureaucratic agency, interest groups that care strongly about the agency's activities, and the legislative committees that govern agency operations. These alliances, sometimes called subgovernments or "iron triangles," form a mutual benefit society that is often resistant to outside control (see Cater 1964: 17–48; Freeman 1965).

According to picket fence federalism, the horizontal components of the fence (the national, state, and local governments) have a difficult time coordinating the various functional specialists. Congress and the state legislatures, with committee systems organized along functional lines and with highly fragmented power, are poorly equipped to serve as coordinators. Presidents and governors often believe that program implementation and coordination are unrewarding and uninteresting activities and therefore give them limited attention. State and local bureaucracies are often too fragmented to coordinate different programs.

The picket fence model very appropriately draws attention to the important divisions that exist within levels of government in a federal system. It also highlights some potential problems: First, what will happen if the program specialists who administer a grant program have less loyalty to the level of government that employs them than to the program specialists in another level of government that receives the grant? Will the recipients obey regulations they oppose, or will the regulations be watered down or even ignored? A number of studies find that program specialists are not always very vigorous enforcers when others members of their profession are concerned.

The picket fence model also highlights the problems of setting priorities and coordinating among different programs. The picket fence model holds that power is largely held by program specialists, most of whom believe that their programs are vital, and the interest groups that benefit from those programs. The major players believe that each of their programs should be a high priority, and proposals to reduce funding or revise regulations often succumb to strong opposition.

The picket fence model probably overstates the power of functional specialists, however, and probably understates the importance of national, state, and local governments. First of all, the picket fence model implies considerable uniformity in a particular program, regardless of the jurisdiction. In fact many programs vary substantially from one part of the country to another; evidently the functional specialists are unable or unwilling to create a uniform program everywhere. The picket fence model also implies substantial unity within program specialties. That unity is far from consistent, though, as clashes between teachers and school administrators illustrate.

Bamboo Fence Federalism.   A more moderate functional model, bamboo fence federalism, emphasizes both vertical and horizontal relationships in the federal system. Vertical ties among bureaucratic subspecialists, such as highway transportation officials (as opposed to transportation officials in general), are very strong, regardless of the level of government employing those subspecialists. Broad groups of specialists, however, such as transportation officials or educators of all types, often disagree among themselves. Program administrators and interest groups are joined by academic researchers, policy analysts from think tanks, and other participants. Horizontal linkages are more important than they are in picket fence federalism. National officials have significant influence over national program specialists; state officials influence state program specialists, and so forth. Bamboo fence federalism contends that functional program specialists are often more accommodating than the picket fence model implies and are responsive to pressures exerted by national, state, and local officials.

In this perspective, the education profession, for example, is internally fragmented along a number of lines: level of instruction (primary and secondary schools versus colleges and universities), clientele served (vocational students, exceptionally gifted students, and so forth), and sector (public versus private, religious versus secular). Also there are numerous differences of opinion on all sorts of issues. Administrative reforms, especially at the state level, have increased capabilities for horizontal coordination.

Bamboo fence federalism has some similarities to issue networks (Heclo 1977), in contrast to iron triangles or subgovernments. Issue networks include an agency, interest groups concerned with agency activities, and legislative committees, but the networks are less stable and more permeable than are subgovernments. Outsiders, such as political appointees of a new governor or academic researchers, may join an issue network and bring in new ideas. Changing public attitudes or a major crisis may disrupt the established relationships within an issue network; external forces can shape agency behavior. The functional models appropriately call attention to the role of bureaucratic specialists in making policies. Those specialists and their interest group allies may resist outside control. A number of studies of policy implementation find that coordination among different programs is sometimes very difficult, a finding consistent with the functional models. Moreover, they remind us of the considerable differences of opinion that exist within levels of government, a perspective that is particularly different from the competitive models, which tend to suggest that there is a relatively united national point of view and a relatively united state point of view on any given issue.

The functional models, particularly picket fence federalism, probably overstate the extent of consensus that exists within some functional specialties, however. The picket fence version also seems to underplay the importance of national, state, and local governments. The functional models are valuable in drawing attention to the importance of bureaucratic politics and offer a valuable corrective to the exclusive focus of the competitive and interdependent models on levels of government.

The different models of federalism are all useful in calling attention to important issues and concerns. In addition, knowing which model of federalism is held by public officials or scholars can help an observer interpret what they mean. The phrase "appropriate role of the national government" means one thing if uttered by an advocate of state-centered federalism but means something quite different if stated by someone who believes in cooperative federalism.

Familiarity with several different models is helpful when a federal system changes. As noted earlier, a model that accurately depicts the operation of a system at one point may be inaccurate if the system changes substantially. Finally, when people are unhappy with governmental performance, a common phenomenon in many countries, the different models of federalism suggest some potential sources of problems and present some ideas for improving performance.

State-Local Relations: Are They Unitary or Federal?

The older, competitive models of federalism excluded local governments at least in part because those models often assumed, sometimes implicitly, that state-local relations were unitary rather than federal. In a formal sense that perspective had considerable validity for much of our history, although the informal picture looks considerably different.

The Legal Status of Local Governments

The U.S. Constitution makes no mention of local governments, and state constitutions have traditionally held that local governments receive their authority from the state government rather than directly from the public. For many years, the most influential legal doctrine regarding state-local relations has been Dillon's Rule, which holds that local governments have only those powers that are

1. expressly granted to them;
2. clearly implied by the expressly granted powers;
3. essential for the functioning of the local government.

Traditionally, Dillon's Rule meant that if there was substantial doubt regarding whether a local government had the authority to do something, then it did not have the authority. Over the years, the courts have tended to become somewhat more lenient in interpreting local powers, though not consistently (Adrian and Fine 1991: 82–83; Marks and Cooper 1988: 193–198; Zimmerman 1992: 166–169).

One result of Dillon's Rule is that local governments are frequently vulnerable to legal challenges when they try to do something new. The fear of litigation, with its delays and expense, not to mention possible defeat, is sometimes a powerful deterrent to local initiative (Adrian and Fine 1991: 82–83; McCarthy 1990: 40). Although state and national governments also face legal challenges at times, Dillon's Rule makes legal opposition especially potent at the local level.

Dillon's Rule, especially if interpreted strictly, also enhances state government's role in local policymaking. When local officials do not have clear authority to enact a policy, they may have to seek a grant of authority from the governor and state legislature. Seeking that authority can be difficult and time consuming and may prove fruitless; local authorities often resent having to ask for state approval. The importance of state authority was underscored by a 1982 U.S. Supreme Court decision holding that local governments are not immune to antitrust suits unless they are acting under a specific state law (Blair 1986: 27; McCarthy 1990: 30, 231–232). In some cases, however, the need for state approval can be politically useful to local officials who face a controversial problem. Their lack of authority can be used to deflect the controversy onto state officials.

Dillon's Rule has probably helped contribute to the long-term expansion of national and state government power. If local officials cannot respond to public demands because local authority is inadequate, citizens are likely to take their demands elsewhere. The comparatively slow growth of local government revenues and spending in this century, relative to national and state governments, is consistent with this perspective, although a variety of other forces have also been at work.

The impact of Dillon's Rule has been undercut in about half of the states by the devolution of authority to local governments. Devolution gives local governments the authority to exercise all powers that have not been forbidden to them (Advisory Commission on Intergovernmental Relations 1982: 156; Elazar 1984: 203). Devolution gives local officials greater ability to respond to demands than is the case if local action requires a specific grant of authority from the state. One must bear in mind that the authority granted in a devolution statute may be significantly narrowed by restrictions in that statute or other state laws. When state and local statutes conflict, state policies typically prevail.

The historically weak legal status of local governments also grew from the tendency for federal courts to regard local governments as having no legal rights as far as the U.S. Constitution is concerned. Localities have, however, sometimes been able to use federal laws to defend local initiatives from state opposition. In addition, some state courts in recent years have granted local governments legal standing to challenge state actions, a dramatic reversal of the traditional practice (see McCarthy 1990: 28–29, 45; Pagano 1990: 101). The overall result has been some strengthening of the legal status of local governments, although the full implications may not be known for some time.

The Historical Development of State-Local Relations

When the U.S. Constitution was ratified, the United States was an overwhelmingly rural nation. Only about 5 percent of the population lived in cities, and most cities were quite small by today's standards: Only one had more than 30,000 residents. The tasks of government were few, and the system of local government was relatively simple, with an emphasis on general-purpose governments, such as cities, counties, and towns. During the late 1800s and the 1900s, the proportion of the population living in urban areas rose dramatically. The responsibilities of local government grew considerably, and systems of local government grew increasingly complex. By 1942, the United States had 155,067 local governments, including more than 100,000 school districts. General-purpose governments now had a sometime partner, sometime rival in local governments created to handle only one task or at most a few tasks (see Blair 1986: 9; Glaab and Brown 1983; Martin 1965: 2–4).

Local governments now take many forms, but the major types are as follows (see Blair 1986: 13–15). Bear in mind that each type comes in many varieties. Municipalities typically provide more services and have more powers than other types of local government, though the responsibilities and powers of municipalities vary considerably from state to state and often within individual states. Municipalities are typically responsible for implementing a variety of state policies but also have responsibilities that are primarily of interest to the individual communities served.

Counties are found in every state except Connecticut and Rhode Island (Alaska uses the term "borough" and Louisiana, "parish," but the organizations are essentially the same). Counties traditionally administered state programs and services, but over the years counties have become involved in many programs, particularly in urban areas, to the point that the types of services and programs offered by some counties are virtually identical to those offered by municipalities.

Special districts are now the most numerous form of local government. Most were created to provide a single service—school districts being the best-known example. Some, however, offer two or more services, though the range of offerings is generally limited. Some special districts were created to insulate their programs from "politics"; other special districts were formed to overcome limits on city and/or county authority or because problems did not correspond to the boundaries of existing local governments.

Towns and townships are found primarily in New England (towns) and the upper Midwest (townships). New England towns are the major general-purpose local governments in much of New England. Townships in rural areas today usually provide relatively few services, but some townships in urban areas have taken on increased responsibilities.

Establishing Local Governments: Charters and Other Approaches

Local governments can be established and given authority in a variety of ways. Most of the literature on this topic involves municipalities, but comparable issues arise for other types of local governments, particularly in recent years. The following discussion primarily addresses municipalities but where noted other local governments follow similar lines.

Charters. Municipal government authority is established by a charter, which is similar to a constitution at the state or national level. The charter defines the powers of a city government and its structure. The charter may also include limitations on what the city government may do, although those limitations are often found in state laws that are separate from the charter. The states have used a variety of methods for providing city charters (see Adrian and Fine 1991: 84–97; Nice and Fredericksen 1995: 148–153; Zimmerman 1992: 170–173).

The special act charter system, which is one of the older approaches to providing charters, requires the state legislature to draft a specific charter for each municipality. This system, at least in theory, permits each city to have a charter that is tailored to the community's specific needs and wants. In a similar fashion, state legislation may create a single special district government in order to handle an unusual task, such as operating the only major port in the state; in this case a charter is not generally used, but a single statute creates a single local government.

The special act charter may suffer from the fact that it is adopted by the state legislature, not the city. A city with many friends in the state capital may be given powers and flexibility that are denied to another city. If charter revisions are needed at a later date, the city must go again to the legislature for approval of the changes, and that approval may be difficult to gain. If a state has many cities, charter revisions are likely to generate a considerable amount of work for state officials under the special act approach. In addition, those revisions may drag state officials into local controversies they would rather avoid. Those same officials may sometimes appreciate the opportunities for involvement in local affairs, however.

A second, relatively old, approach to chartering is the general act charter. A state using this approach adopts one charter that applies to all cities in the state. The state government is relieved of the burden of drafting and updating individual charters, and the problem of favoritism is reduced, at least in the sense that no city can be singled out for limitations that are not applied to other cities. Counties and many special district governments were created under an analogous procedure, with a general statute granting all counties in the state the same powers and providing the same structure of government; traditionally this was not a charter, but the mechanism had much in common with the general act charter.

Critics of the general act charter charge that it gives no flexibility to adapt to different needs or wants from one locality to another. All cities are given the same structure of government and the same powers, regardless of local conditions. Moreover, although all cities are given the same charter, some cities' residents may get exactly the charter they want, whereas others do not. Any changes in the charter affects all cities in the state, whether they desire the changes or not. The classified charter system is a sort of compromise between the special act and general act charter systems. The cities of a state are divided into classes, typically according to population, and the state drafts a charter for all of the cities in a particular class. All cities with fewer than 100,000 residents will have one charter; all cities with 100,000 to 999,999 will have a second charter, and so forth. The classified system limits the opportunities for preferential treatment of cities but also provides some flexibility to accommodate differences in the needs and problems faced by different cities.

A potential difficulty with the classified system arises from the possibility that cities with similar populations may have significantly different problems or desires. In some states, too, legislators have created classes of cities that include only a single city. When that is done, the city in a one-city class is vulnerable to the same sort of unequal treatment that can occur under the special act charter system. The classified system can also create complications when a city population shifts enough to put the city into a different class and, therefore, causes a change in the city charter.

A common feature of the special act, general act, and classified charter systems is that they all involve charters that are drafted by the state. Cities have no official role in choosing their charters, although city officials and residents may try to influence state decisions regarding the initial drafting and later revisions of city charters. If a city has relatively little influence in the state capital, those efforts may not be successful.

Efforts to give cities more of a choice in their charters have yielded two other approaches to providing charters. Under the optional charter system, the state establishes several different charters. Cities can then select from the various charters offered by the state. This system reduces the ability of the state to target individual cities for special restrictions or limitations, at least as far as the charters are concerned. Cities are given some degree of flexibility, although the amount depends on the number and variety of charter options that the state chooses to make available.

A basic difficulty with the optional charter system arises when a city needs revisions in the charter. Those revisions must be adopted by the state and will affect all the cities that have chosen that charter option, whether they want the revision or not (assuming that the revision is adopted by the state). The available options may not include the charter most desired by residents of a city.

Home Rule.   The chartering system that provides the greatest responsiveness to local preferences and minimizes the risk of preferential treatment, home rule, was first adopted in Iowa just before the Civil War and has long been advocated by municipal reformers (see Marks and Cooper 1988: 203–207; McCarthy 1990: 19–20, 37–43). With home rule, a city drafts and adopts its own charter, a process that usually requires voter approval and sometimes requires state approval as well. A city can draft a charter tailored to its particular preferences, and the city can amend the charter to meet changing conditions, generally without state approval. Forty-eight states have now adopted home rule provisions for at least some of their cities, and thirty-seven states authorize home rule for counties (Advisory Commission on Intergovernmental Relations 1993: 20–23).

Reformers hoped that home rule would give local governments greater control over local decisions and reduce state influence over local affairs, but those hopes have been only partially fulfilled. Home rule has enhanced local autonomy and flexibility somewhat and helped reduce the amount of local legislation passed in the typical state legislative session. However, home rule has not been as effective as many reformers expected.

The impact of home rule has been limited by the fact that state laws continue to override local laws, even under home rule, whenever a genuine state interest exists. In the event of a disagreement, the courts have usually sided with state governments in deciding whether a state interest exists. State laws providing for home rule may also limit its use to cities or counties above a certain population, and state laws may require state approval before a city or county may exercise home rule powers. Moreover, home rule provisions vary considerably; in some states, home rule includes the ability to change the structures of city (or county) government and the ability to alter its substantive authority. In other states, home rule can be used to alter the structure of local government but not to give it additional authority to deal with a problem or, at most, home rule can only be used to alter local authority in limited ways. In the latter states, a city or county in need of additional authority to tackle a major problem must seek that authority from the state government.

To the extent that it increases local autonomy, home rule may be criticized for causing undue parochialism and discouraging needed cooperation among localities. In a related vein, home rule may hinder necessary state involvement in problems that have a significant local component but also have larger aspects. Home rule also brings the risk that voters in some communities may be repeatedly bombarded with proposals to revise the charter, a situation that may destabilize program operations and annoy or bore the electorate (Zimmerman 1992: 172–173).

The fact that home rule has not created fully independent cities and counties is not surprising in view of the history of American federalism. Given that we have never been able to clearly delineate the powers or responsibilities of the national government and the states, the prospects for clearly delineating state and local powers are no better. Moreover, many local decisions affect people who are not residents of the locality and who would have little or no voice in the local decision. Too much local autonomy can create serious problems, as can too little local autonomy (see Elazar 1984: 205–206; Grodzins 1983: 363).

The success of the home rule movement has varied considerably across the country. In general, states that were admitted to the Union well before the home rule movement became a substantial political force (using the first adoption by Iowa in 1858 as a rough benchmark) generally have been less receptive to home rule than states admitted more recently (see Table 2.1). Less than one-third of the states admitted by 1791 have adopted municipal home rule provisions that permit structural reforms

TABLE 2.1 State Receptivity to Home Rule: The Legacy of History

Year State Joined Union	Percentage of States with Both Structural and Broad Functional Home Rules
1787–1791	29% (n=14)
1796–1837	50% (n=12)
1845–1899	63% (n=19)
1907–1959	40% (n=5)

SOURCE: Advisory Commission on Intergovernmental Relations, *State Laws Governing Local Governments Structure and Administration* (Washington, D.C.: USGPO, 1993), pp. 20–21.

and provide broad functional authority. By contrast, nearly two-thirds of the states admitted between 1845 and 1900 have adopted such home rule provisions. Those states may have been more receptive to home rule because they had not had time to develop long-standing patterns of state-local relations before the home rule movement became effective.

Although the number of cases is small, states admitted during the twentieth century seem to be less receptive to broad home rule, a pattern that may reflect the tendency for modern governmental problems to exceed the capabilities of local governments (on the latter point, see Graves 1964: 705).

Centralization in State-Local Relations

One of the most important trends in state-local relations during the twentieth century is the growth of state government relative to local government (Stephens 1974). Although advocates of home rule have worked to improve the legal status of localities, other trends have worked to the advantage of state governments. The relative growth of state government and the causes and consequences of that growth cast considerable light on the changing nature of state-local relations.

The Trends

Around 1900, local government revenue and spending exceeded the revenue and spending of the states and national government combined. Local government employment also exceeded combined national and state government employment (Stephens 1974: 49). Comparing localities with just the states, local revenue, spending, and employment exceeded their state counterparts by roughly five to one. Moreover, local governments at that time were almost entirely self-sufficient financially (Maxwell

TABLE 2.2   Change in State Centralization

Indicator	State	Local
Own-Source General Revenues		
1902	17%	83%
1988	57%	43%
Direct General Expenditures		
1902	13%	87%
1988	40%	60%
Personnel		
1901	14%	86%
1989	29%	71%

SOURCE: Council of State Governments 1992; Mosher and Poland 1964; Stephens 1974; and Advisory Commission on Intergovernmental Relations 1990.

and Aronson 1977: 85). Local governments were on weak legal ground much of the time in those days, but they had significant financial and labor resources.

Since that time, the situation has changed dramatically (see Table 2.2). Although state and local governments have both grown, growth in state revenue, spending, and employment has been considerably more rapid than local growth. The local share of state-local revenue declined from 83 percent in 1902 to less than half in recent years. The state share of state-local spending has tripled. In addition, local governments have grown heavily dependent on financial assistance from the states and, to a lesser degree, the national government. In 1902, local governments raised almost 95 percent of their revenue themselves, but in recent years local governments have received approximately one-third of their revenue from the states and the national government, with the states providing the lion's share (Advisory Commission on Intergovernmental Relations 1990: 64).

Although the state share of state-local employment has grown less dramatically, it has virtually doubled since 1900. That growth has given the states much greater capacity for providing services directly and for overseeing the operations of local governments.

One other potential sign of state centralization is the formation of state departments of community affairs (Stephens 1974: 72–73). They are now found in all states and usually take the form of a cabinet department, although some are part of a larger department or a component of the governor's office (Advisory Commission on Intergovernmental Relations 1982: 153, 192). Although state departments of community affairs might be an instrument of state control over localities, in practice those departments usually function as service agencies for local governments rather than as regulatory agents (Advisory Commission on Intergovernmental Relations 1982: 153). Provision of services can, of course, generate opportunities for state oversight at times, but the primary emphasis seems to be on helping localities rather than controlling them. Most state regulation of localities is, instead, carried out by individual functional agencies, for example, state public health agencies overseeing local public health programs(Blair 1986: 29; Graves 1964: 719–724). That pattern is consistent with picket fence federalism, with its emphasis on program specialists.

Causes of State Centralization

A number of factors have contributed to the growing state role in state and local government. One factor is greater social and economic complexity. When the United States was largely a rural, agrarian country, local governments were nearly all quite small, and many were very isolated from one another. As a result, an individual local government could often make decisions without having much impact on people outside that locality. As the nation grew more urbanized and industrial and as the population grew, decisions made in one locality were more likely to affect people in other localities, a situation that created pressure for state involvement.

The shortcomings of local governments have also helped encourage state centralization. Most of America's county governments were created when transportation technologies were relatively primitive; those counties were made small enough to enable people to travel from their homes to the county seat and back within a day (probably traveling by horse). The result has been counties that, with some exceptions, are too small to handle major programs without assistance. Many counties have also failed to establish coherent administrative structures and attract well-trained personnel (Grant and Nixon 1982: 343–348). Most metropolitan areas have dozens of local governments, many of which overlap with one another, with no local government able to deal with major problems that affect the entire area. Local governments' legal and financial powers are also restricted by the states in many ways, a circumstance that gives the states considerable advantages in the quest for resources. When local governments are unable to act, state governments may fill the void (Graves 1964: 705).

State centralization has also been encouraged by the national grant system (Stephens 1974: 69). Many state grants to local governments are financed in part by national grants to the states. National grants have also helped the states to provide services directly. The national grant system, which has been widely regarded as increasing national government power, has also helped the states gain additional power over their local units.

The growing cost of many government services, due in part to technological changes and in part to changing public expectations, has also increased state centralization. Modern transportation systems, educational and social services, and environmental protection programs are vastly more expensive than most local governments can afford on their own. The result has been a growing state role, both in helping to finance local programs and in providing services directly (Graves 1964: 705).

NOTES

1. A purely unitary system is a theoretical concept. In practice, national governments face many obstacles to exerting effective control over subnational governments, even in officially unitary systems.

2. For discussions of models of federalism and intergovernmental relations, see Dye 1990: 6–13; Elazar 1984: chapter 3; Grodzins 1983; Leach 1970: 10–17; Nice and Fredericksen 1995: 4–15; Walker 1981: 46–65, 123–128, and chapters 3–4; and Wright 1988: 36–111.

3. For discussion of the two New Federalisms, see Conlan 1988; Nathan 1983: 59–68; and Zimmerman 1991.

3

State-Local Relations: Union and Home Rule

Daniel J. Elazar

Constitutional home rule, initiated in 1875, is an idea as American as the proverbial apple pie.[1] It was designed to introduce by contract what the English tradition of government denies in principle, namely, the right to local governmental autonomy.[2] Under English law, all powers not explicitly granted to local government by the states are ultra vires, that is to say, denied them. The American states rejected the ultra vires theory from the first but had to find another to put in its place. They did so through several devices. A number of the original British colonies were founded as federations of local governments. Many of the new states included provisions in their constitutions that required local consent for changes in their boundaries or governmental structures. Still others accepted a new version of ultra vires promulgated by the state courts, later known as "Dillon's Rule" after Judge John Dillon of the Iowa Supreme Court. The rule denied powers to local governments that were not conferred on them by state governments.

Shortly after the Civil War, the state of Missouri was the first to respond to what was becoming the increasingly ironclad grip of Dillon's Rule by changing its fundamental law with the intention of bypassing the rule's restrictions. Since then, thirty-six states have added home rule provisions for counties to their constitutions, a thirty-seventh (Florida) has adopted home rule by statute, and the world has turned itself over two or three times. The velocity of government on all planes—but particularly on the federal one—has taken a quantum leap forward, and complexity has become the principal feature of our time. In the process, the realities of the local position in the constellation of American governments have changed drastically from the relatively simple conditions of the last century. If home rule remains a desired goal for many, it has become clear that the original premises of constitutional home rule—that local self-government can be achieved by a clear demarcation of structures and functions between local and state governments with significant powers entrusted to the former—are no longer within the realm of possibility, if they ever were. In place of neatly separated spheres, we are faced with the problem of unending externalities, "spillovers" whose consequences surface in unexpected places.

If home rule has not brought all the benefits its champions sought, it did represent a major step in the transformation (or restoration) of local government as a recognized partner in its own right within the federal system. The ways of American politics have done the rest, enabling local governments to retain substantial powers of self-government through less formal means (Grodzins 1966). We can build upon the successes of home rule and learn from its limitations to further enhance local self-government and state-local relations in the American system.

The principal strength of home rule has been its ability to guarantee the residents of a particular locality substantial freedom to shape the structures of the local governments serving them. This was no mean contribution to strengthening local government's ability to play a partnership role in the federal system by enabling first cities (including towns and boroughs in some states) and then counties to better pay their "ante" to sit in on the great game of government—something that the states can do with their plenary powers and that the federal government can do with its great powers of the purse.

The principal limitation of home rule has been the inability of its underlying premises to come to grips with the close intergovernmental relationships that characterize the American governmental scene; the complexities of a civil society in which separation of tasks by plane of government is extremely difficult; the American tendency to divide local government powers among a number of different governments; and the great problem of externalities, particularly in a metropolitan society. This limitation has manifested itself at every turn, as events have drawn the states and their localities into every-closer relationships under ever-tighter state umbrellas, home rule provisions notwithstanding.

The Quest for Realignment

Paradoxically, despite academic analyses of all these problems, in recent years the old demand for separation of functions by plane of government—the traditional basis for home rule—has surfaced once again. After approximately two generations of emphasis on the intermixture of governmental functions and actors in the United States (cooperative federalism), the idea has reemerged among those concerned with such matters that an effective federal system and, in particular, effective state and local governments depend upon a realignment of functions and actors, effectively a redivision of responsibilities by governmental plane (or "level"—the term generally but erroneously used in the public discussion). In part, the impetus for this renewed consideration of functional separation of governmental planes arose out of the states' interest in transferring welfare costs to the federal government and the localities' interest in transferring educational costs to their state governments.[3]

In both cases, the contemporary quest for realignment differs radically from earlier conceptions of dual federalism. The earlier view emphasized the independence and separate responsibilities of state and local governments and advocated a separation of functions on the grounds that the federal government should not "meddle" in the affairs of the states, and that the states should not "meddle" in local matters.[4] The present argument has the distinct flavor of passing the buck. The states and localities want the federal government or the states, respectively, to assume costs for services that have been traditionally provided by the smaller arena because they do not want to be burdened with those costs. In both cases, the argument tends to be: Let the larger governmental arena pay for the service and let the smaller one run it. Thus, it is not an argument for dual federalism, but for a separation between paying the piper and calling the tune. Unfunded mandates, federal and state, are the flip side of this. Governments of larger arenas want the credit for doing something but have no money so they mandate smaller arenas of government to do something and to pay for it.

As it has become clear to the states and localities that the federal government is not likely to assume any additional costs in the spirit of the times, it has also become clear that Congress has found in unfunded mandates a very convenient way to seem to be acting. Unfunded mandates became possible when the constitutional barriers separating the federal and state governments had fallen to the point where it appeared that the federal government could act toward the states in a hierarchical manner, ordering them to do this or that rather than bribing them through the grant-in-aid system. The states had the constitutional powers to do the same to the localities even before but were constrained by the political culture and climate from doing so until very recently.

For those who see American federalism in constitutional terms, the rapid spread of unfunded federal mandates was at the very least astounding and in most cases frightening. Since the 1994 congressional elections and the capture of both houses of Congress by the Republicans, a bill to limit future unfunded mandates of very modest strength was enacted and signed into law by President Clinton, while at the same time, in 1995 the United States Supreme Court for the first time seemed to place limits on the interpretation of the federal commerce power that might prohibit the federal government from entering fields traditionally thought to belong to the states.

The debate over the separation of functions began to return to its earlier path of transferring functions from the federal government back to the states and from the states back to localities. As of this writing, nothing much has changed except the terms of the discussion, but that change may be important for the future. Still, after fifteen years of efforts to "turn things back to the states" and separate functions, careful observers are beginning to conclude that dual federalism, which had never existed as the myth would have it, is even less possible today. At the same time, a certain separation of functions has its place if only to make it possible for the states to exist as authentic polities with real powers.

Curiously enough, the arguments for this kind of realignment were first advanced by governmental reformers (once considered to be among the strongest partisans of local home rule) and only later by elected officials. For the reformers, the problem was not one of realigning functions so as to strengthen the states and localities, but, rather, realigning responsibility for payment so as to better match revenue resources with costs and thereby ensure greater equality of treatment for all citizens. Ostensibly at least, the reformers did not seek to eliminate state or local powers per se, but rather to transform the structure of intergovernmental cooperation in certain fields in such a way that more uniform national (or state)—or at least nationwide (or statewide)—standards would be set for the provision of certain governmental services.

The elected officials got into the act only after the idea had been suggested to them by the reformers, and they came to perceive that such realignment would help them balance their budgets and even leave them with funds for other activities that would allow them to build records. For them, realignment was also primarily a matter of funding (albeit in a different sense); they were not particularly interested in transferring responsibility for implementing programs funded elsewhere. This was particularly true in the case of education, where localities have consistently sought "no strings" aid combined with maximum local control. Many of the reformers, on the other hand, saw in a realignment of funding the first step toward a realignment of administration as well, something which they took to be desirable, since their goal was professionalization, equalization, and uniformity on the basis of standards more to their liking.

Since the issue of realignment was first raised, it has spread to a whole host of issues other than welfare and education—in some cases stimulated by leaders in the smaller governmental arenas seeking to transfer onerous responsibilities to some larger arena, in some cases by leaders in the larger arenas who feel that in order to do the job right they must have increased responsibility, and in some cases by reformers who see in a change the chance to effectuate other goals. In some instances, the realignment is based upon an acceptance of existing governmental structural arrangements. Thus, suggestions that education costs be transferred from local school boards to the state implicitly recognize that the school district consolidation movement essentially has come to an end and that the task now is to work within the existing framework. In other instances, there is a clear commitment to new frameworks as well as to a shift in responsibilities. This is particularly true in matters affecting metropolitan problems, where arguments for the creation of metropolitan-wide authorities, whether full-fledged governmental consolidation (a diminishing demand) or metropolitan agencies with special functions, emphasize structural change first and foremost.

Focusing more specifically on state-local realignment, the Advisory Commission on Intergovernmental Relations and other reform-minded groups have listed fourteen major areas where changes should be made:[5]

growth policy and land use;
housing;
regional governmental structures;
property taxes;
the criminal justice system;
community development;
state-local tax and revenue relations;
transportation;
health planning and service delivery;
environmental protection and energy;
local government management;
rationalizing city and county powers, functions, and structures;
manpower policy; and
elementary and secondary education.

In every one of these areas, reform groups see the states as playing a greater role than heretofore, although the character of the role they suggest differs considerably from problem area to problem area.

To the extent that suggestions for realignment are suggestions for a redivision of functions, it is unlikely that any such realignment would work to favor local autonomy (just as state-federal realignment is not likely to favor state self-government). Once the question as to where a function properly falls is opened in the United States, the overall historical tendency has been to push matters to ever larger arenas, in great measure in a quest for a degree of equality that is not easily definable and even less readily attainable, but that invariably works against the interests of the states and localities as polities or political systems. This is likely to be just as true of suggestions to transfer funding responsibility in one direction while holding operational responsibility within smaller arenas as it is for suggestions to make major transfers of both in one direction or another.

It has been demonstrated by Morton Grodzins and others that he who pays the piper does not automatically get to call the tune; when payment is shared among so many bodies that the payers cannot get together they must rely upon the original caller to continue to do so.[6] That has been the secret of the successful maintenance of substantial state and local autonomy to date within a highly integrated federal system. The varied "mess" of grants-in-aid and other forms of transfers of payments from larger to smaller arenas has enabled those responsible for the smaller arenas to maintain their autonomy by picking and choosing from a variety of offers, many even contradictory, in ways that suit local ends. Any "rationalization" of this system might make matters more pleasing to the eye, by satisfying Americans' aesthetic penchant for neat organization, but would make local self-government much more difficult since it would then be much easier for those supplying the funds to control programs as well. Consequently, for those interested in maintaining local autonomy and, by extension, state self-government, questions of realignment should be approached very cautiously indeed. Ostensible immediate advantages should be carefully examined to see whether they are likely to be offset by future disadvantages of far greater magnitude.

This is not to suggest that no realignment need take place. Quite to the contrary, realignments take place constantly and are a regular feature of any dynamic political system. What is required for the American system is that such realignments should be made within a framework of sharing that seeks to preserve a role for every plane of government in the making and execution of policy. Directing change in this manner requires a social basis for judging and evaluating particular forms of intergovernmental collaboration and realignment. This basis can be developed only by avoiding prior commitment to shibboleths and myths, on the one hand, and having a firmly grounded philosophy and policy, on the other.

Philosophy and Policy

A word is in order here about the philosophy within which the states and localities must operate to fulfill their roles in the American system and about the policy dimensions of that philosophy. The element of American political philosophy that most concerns us here is federalism. Americans have come to define federalism as simply a matter of intergovernmental relations. In fact, it is a broad philosophy having to do with the linkage of partners, whether people or political units, in systems that combine self-rule and shared rule, with one another in such a way as to preserve their respective integrities while making possible action as a common whole.

As a philosophy, federalism has many ramifications, revolving around a particular understanding of what constitutes good social and political relations. The philosophy of federalism suggests that partnership among people and polities is the proper mode of political organization. Abstract philosophy must be translated into theory in order to become politically meaningful in a concrete way. Basic to the theory of federalism is compactual noncentralization—the location and maintenance of a dispersion of power among several centers within a common moral-constitutional framework. Although a good theory of federalism suggests the means for organizing political power, it is necessary to have a proper doctrine in order to effectuate the theory. For our purposes here, a proper doctrine is one of balanced decisionmaking, whereby decisions are made so as to reflect and protect the noncentralized character of the political order by involving all relevant actors in every decision or by dividing up decisions among the actors in such a way that each has important ones to make, upon which all the others are in some respect dependent.

Proper application of this theory and doctrine of federalism should lead to a policy of substantial local control of governmental activities within every locality.[7] According to this policy, the goals of federalism are best achieved when local control is maximized on the assumption that it can best promote involvement of political units and of people (in their individual and collective capacities) as partners.

The effectuation of a policy depends upon the strategy and tactics employed. The basic strategy for the states must be one of selective intervention, no more, designed to ensure that standards are maintained without undue interference with local control. The specific tactics—which include legislative enactment of statewide standards; provisions for transfers of payments through revenue sharing, grants-in-aid, or joint taxes; and technical assistance—must be adjusted to each particular situation.

This approach can be schematized as follows:

Philosophy: Federalism
Theory: Compactual noncentralization (the location and maintenance of a dispersion of power among several centers within a common moral-constitutional framework)
Doctrine: Balanced decisionmaking
Policy: Local control
Strategy: Selective intervention on the part of larger arenas
Tactics: Minimum standards, transfers of payments, technical assistance

In general, those faced with making political decisions are constrained by time and circumstance to considering alternative tactics based upon certain implicit policy assumptions that are, in turn, based upon philosophical premises that have become part of the common political culture

and are accepted uncritically. This is natural enough and sufficiently effective for normal policymaking purposes. When, however, changes
whose consequences clearly have long-range implications are contem-
plated, it is necessary to reflect more fully upon them, to consider strategies as well as tactics, and, more than that, to choose among strategic and
tactical options on the basis of proper doctrine and theory.

Moreover, there are moments in history when there is a need to revive
concern with the philosophic underpinnings of the whole. At present, we
are at one of those moments. The subtle accretion of myths and habits derived from nineteenth- and twentieth-century ideologies has substantially weakened our understanding of the authentic meaning of American
federalism. Because these accretions have been added subconsciously for
the most part, not as a result of philosophic reflection, the changes they
have wrought do not reflect some rationally derived consensus but simply an uncritical acceptance of new styles. Nevertheless, their impact on
the theory and doctrine of intergovernmental relations has been as great
as it has been unreflective. Thus any discussion of realignment of functions and actors today must also seek to restore a concern with philosophy in order to regenerate good theory and doctrine and, ultimately, appropriate strategy and tactics.

The States as Polities and Political Systems

We begin by seeking to clarify the character of the states as polities and
political systems within the context of the American federal republic. This
is a necessary prerequisite for determination of what constitutes appropriate state-local relationships.

According to the conventional theory of the states as unitary polities,
the state governments should be able to make unilateral decisions regarding state-local relations and the allocation of functions within their
boundaries. The Supreme Court of the United States has held that the
states are unitary systems and that all local governments are simply their
creatures, subject to alteration in structure or function by legislative action.[8] The Court has reaffirmed this position whenever the issue has been
raised. Indeed, its stand from the reapportionment cases onward rests in
great measure on this understanding of the nature of the states as unitary
polities. Moreover, commonly accepted legal doctrines have tended to reinforce the unitary view of state government by emphasizing the plenary
powers of the states. Dillon's Rule, the dominant legal doctrine defining
state-local relations, holds:

> Municipal corporations owe their origin to, and derive their powers and
> rights wholly from, the legislature. It breathes into them the breath of life,

without which they cannot exist. As it creates, so it may destroy. If it may destroy, it may abridge and control. Unless there is some constitutional limitation on the right, the legislature might, by a single act, if we can suppose it capable of so great a folly and so great a wrong, sweep from existence all of the municipal corporations of the state, and the corporations could not prevent it. We know of no limitation on this right so far as the corporations themselves are concerned. They are, so to phrase it, the mere tenants at will of the legislature.[9]

Moreover, in any case of state-local conflict, the presumption is that state powers are preemptive and local powers are limited to the express terms of the state grant. Thus constitutionally and legally the prevailing doctrine holds that the states are unitary and potentially highly centralized polities.

Although the unitary doctrine is the recognized one, throughout American history there are those who have argued—or assumed—that the states are at least quasi federations of their localities (Syed 1966, chapter 3). Under this view the relationship between state and local governments should be the same as that between the federal government and the states, with local governments having inherent rights and the states having only those powers delegated to them specifically by their constitutions. This federal theory had its origins in the colonial period, when the idea of the people's inherent right to local self-government was widespread and was confirmed by the historical reality that several of the states-to-be were actually formed by the constitutional coming together of preexisting counties or towns to establish larger polities.

Delaware, for example, by the terms of its own constitutional history was founded when its three counties came together to establish the state. Both Rhode Island and Connecticut were initially created by the union of their original towns. Similar constitutional traditions can be found in New Hampshire, New Jersey, Tennessee, and Vermont.

Nearly half of the states whose settlement began before the Revolution see themselves as having a federal origin. Moreover, the American Revolution was to no little extent organized in the towns and counties of the colonies which, in taking matters into their own hands, essentially reassumed their inherent rights of self-government and then collectively reconstituted their colonies as states. Nevertheless, the federal theory of state founding has remained no more than a "legitimate constitutional heresy," that is to say, a doctrine with a certain historical legitimacy that has never gained proper recognition in constitutional law.

Until the mid-nineteenth century, champions of local autonomy, even if they did not accept the federalist "heresy," relied upon this constitutional tradition of the inherent right of local self-government to protect local liberties (McBain 1916a, 1916b). This tradition was embodied in the early municipal charters granted by the middle colonies (New York and Pennsylvania) which were, in the words of Howard Lee McBain (1918), "brief and simple instruments" conferring broad powers of local self-government on cities as public corporations. It is not unfair to say that incorporation was conceived to be a means to constitutionalize this inherent local right, to give it concrete expression in law instead of simply relying on tradition. In certain respects, incorporation was the home rule of its day.

Like home rule, the ostensible autonomy conferred by incorporation was progressively eroded by state intervention which had the added twist of periodic state-initiated charter revision or replacement. Since charters represented unilateral grants by the legislatures, the latter could rewrite them at will, provided they had the political backing to do so. By introducing the elements of local initiative and consent to local constitutional change, home rule was instituted in no small measure to remedy this glaring defect in the effort to protect local liberties through chartering.

Once the constitutional tradition was replaced by court decisions with a well-nigh-uniform definition of the states as unitary polities, the states had to develop another means to protect those liberties. It was then that the home rule movement was born, to reinforce the by-then eroded powers of municipal corporations by adding yet another constitutional guarantee of local liberty.[10] Guarantees of local autonomy were sought, first through legislative enactment and then by the incorporation of home rule provisions in state constitutions.

The principle behind home rule was very much attuned to the then-dominant theory of dual federalism, namely, that the only way to assure the autonomy of the several political units within a political system was to separate their operations as completely as possible. Thus home rule was an attempt to demarcate certain spheres of activity as exclusively local in character. Dvorin and Misner (1966) summarized the matter as follows: "The underlying assumption of home rule is that the municipality, not the state legislature, makes policies concerning the form or pattern of municipal organization, the authority or powers the municipality may exercise, and the methods by which such authority is enforced." Constitutional home rule represented an attempt to alter the theory that local governments are merely the creatures of their states by accepting the theory on its face and then writing into the state constitutions provisions whereby the people of the state irrevocably delegate substantial autonomy to their localities, or at least to those localities which the legislature endows with the powers of municipal corporations.

In the well over a century since the state of Missouri first adopted constitutional home rule in 1875, home rule provisions have served to strengthen local structural autonomy but have not given municipalities much functional independence. Thus the net effect of home rule, even in its most comprehensive constitutional form, has been far less than its advocates had hoped. Part of the problem is the hostility of state legislatures toward the surrender of any of their claimed prerogatives. The legislatures of some states have simply ignored the constitutional provisions for home rule. In other states, few municipalities have taken advantage of the opportunities ostensibly provided by home rule, whereas in most, the necessary escape clauses written into the constitution, which normally provide that the state legislature can still declare any matter to be of statewide concern and thus act even preemptively with regard to it, are used with impunity (Cole 1976).

Another factor limiting the utility of home rule is that its theoretical grounding was based on a faulty perception of the realities of American government. Even at the time the first states were adopting home rule, dual federalism, or the separation of functions by plane of government, was far less widespread in practice than the theory would have it. In a dynamic developing society like the United States, it was impossible to neatly separate governmental operations in that way. Rather, citizens turned to governments indiscriminately, and their governments, sensitive as always to citizen demands and interests, responded accordingly, seeking means to collaborate with one another rather than emphasizing their separateness. Hence a system of local autonomy based upon the need for separation of functions could not be expected to take hold. By the twentieth century, it had become substantially anachronistic in every sphere but the structural one.

Nevertheless, even structural home rule came to represent an important gain for local liberties in some states, in quite unanticipated ways, because of the character of American politics. So much of American politics revolves around who has the ante to sit in on the game. Home rule strengthened the localities' ability to ante in and play. For example, even where the state legislature handles the details of local legislation, it was generally the practice to defer to the legislative delegation from the locality affected, making it, in effect, a super city council. When the same powers were transferred to the municipalities through home rule, the locus of power was shifted accordingly. Rather than strengthening the localities by isolating their governmental processes, home rule more often served to provide a better basis from which the localities could negotiate with their state counterparts.

An Alternate Theory: The States as Unions

In fact, neither the unitary nor the federal theorists of state-local relations satisfactorily account for the realities of these relations or for the common aspirations of both planes. The struggle over home rule and its inadequacies as a solution to the problem are reflections of this larger inadequacy. It is clear that the states are not federations of localities. Even those states whose historical origins were based upon the coming together of counties or towns rarely if ever introduced federal arrangements into their constitutions. On the other hand, given the continuing American concern for local liberty and the very real degree of local autonomy that exists within the system by custom and practice, the unitary theory also fails to explain the realities of state-local relations or to provide a proper model upon which to develop a strategy for that relationship. The unitary state theory is a product of modern nationalism, a European import that may be suitable for France or Portugal but one that totally ignores American ideas and experience.

An alternate theory is available that is authentically American and that reflects British precedents as well. It is a theory that was at one time widely recognized, implicitly if not always explicitly, whose terminology is familiar to us all, and that was applied in the course of state building as Americans settled the continent. I would suggest that the states should be considered neither unitary nor federal, but rather unions of their civil communities. In some respects, a union can be seen as a form of government that combines elements of the unitary and federal forms. Unlike those of a unitary system, its component parts do not exist simply at the discretion of some central authority, and power within it tends to be dispersed rather than concentrated. On the other hand, unlike a federal system, its constituent units exist only by virtue of being part of the larger whole and have only those powers authorized by the common constitution. From another perspective, a union more closely resembles a federation than it does a unitary state, but a very consolidated one.

Perhaps the most famous union of the Anglo-American world is the United Kingdom—the union of England, Scotland, Wales, and Northern Ireland. Under that union, all four countries (for that is how the original units are known in the British Isles) preserve their respective integrities as countries without possessing the powers of separate states. Each country preserves its boundaries intact. Scotland, under the Act of Union of 1707, preserves its own legal, administrative, and banking system and has its own established church. In return for giving up its separate legislature, it has a guaranteed minimum representation in the common parliament. Both Scotland and Wales have been granted their own administrative systems by the common parliament under the terms of the union, while by act of Parliament Northern Ireland has been granted its own legislature (suspended during the civil war), which possesses something more than municipal powers (Elazar 1994, 262–274).

A federation may be considered a partial union. What is clear is that both are species of a common genus—the compound polity or, in the

United States, the compound republic—a genus that is quite different from that of the unitary state (Ostrom 1987). For the unitary state, central power and hierarchical organization are of the essence, whereas for compound republics, the dispersion of power among different centers and the consequent sharing of power within common institutions on the basis of that initial dispersion is of the essence. The salient feature of both is the existence of concurrent political systems—in federal polities concurrent regimes and in unions what might be called concurrent authorities.

The constitutional status of local government and the state-local relationship as it has evolved have given most states all the attributes of the union form. Every unitary state is essentially an undivided whole whose central authorities are free to establish and abolish subsidiary agencies, either functional or territorial, and to assign them only those purposes specified by their creators. In fact, experience has shown us that local governments, even counties which until recently did not even have the potential of acquiring municipal powers and were considered by law to be simply agents of the state to carry out state-assigned tasks, cannot be abolished without the consent of their residents. Over time, many states have written explicit provisions into their constitutions to that effect. In most states, even local boundaries cannot be changed without local consent. Moreover, whatever the formal conditions of home rule, state legislatures and state constitutions both have tended in the direction of guaranteeing wide-ranging concurrent powers to local governments of all kinds. None of this represents the stuff of which unitary states are made.

Moreover, the history of American state building outside the South tends to support the theory that states are unions of their respective civil communities. We have already mentioned several classic examples: the four original towns of Connecticut coming together in 1639 to establish through union a common colonial government; the union of the towns of Rhode Island and Providence Plantations (still the official name of that state) that same decade; the revolutionary era unions of East and West Jersey to form New Jersey and of Delaware's three counties to form that state. All represent a coming together of local entities to form a larger body, not by federating but by uniting, albeit in such a way that the original founding bodies preserved their respective integrities as political units and were able to add or establish other political units within the state on the same basis.

Fundamentally the same pattern held true as Americans moved westward. New settlers founded local communities in what was considered uninhabited territory. Sometimes they received recognition as counties or even municipalities from a territorial government; sometimes there was no territorial government to extend them that recognition. Ultimately they would be cut loose as the territory to the east of them attained statehood, and then they would assemble together to secure first territorial status and then statehood for themselves, meeting as representatives of counties, towns, boroughs, or cities to do so.

If Dillon's Rule emphasized the unitary nature of the states, Thomas M. Cooley, the great Michigan jurist, systematically formulated a doctrine that implicitly recognized the states as unions. Arguing along the lines of New England tradition, Cooley held that although a state could shape local institutions to accord with state policies, local self-government was an absolute right, had to be recognized as such by the state, and could serve as an implied restriction on state government activity.[11] Cooley, in the true fashion of theorists of the compound republic, saw sovereignty as reposing in the people and simply delegated by them to their political institutions. Hence, he concluded, state legislatures could not have sovereign power but only delegated powers. Moreover, the usages and values of the people in their local communities represent a form of delegation of the sovereign powers of the people as a whole no less than the constitutional delegation of powers to state institutions.

Although the supreme courts of no more than a fifth of the states even recognized the Cooley doctrine as determinative (today it is recognized as such only in Alaska and Texas), it remains a more accurate description of the realities of American state-local relations and a more appropriate American theory of that relationship.[12] Whatever their formal constitutional positions, most states treat such basic functions as education, land-use control, and law enforcement as inherently local prerogatives. Increasingly, state constitutions are being written or rewritten to include a de facto acceptance of the Cooley doctrine, at least partially through home rule. It can be argued that nearly four-fifths of the states today can be understood to be unions on the basis of the provisions in their own constitutions. Even the southern states, long the best examples of truly unitary systems, seem to be moving in that direction.

Equally important, if not more so, is the American intellectual and cultural commitment to the principle of local self-government, or at least local control of those functions that directly affect local residents. Americans operate on the assumption that these are inherent rights in a democratic society. Thus the union theory has strong support in the country's political culture as well.[13]

What is lacking is an enunciation of the proper doctrine of state-local relations within the context of the union theory and the development of appropriate strategies and tactics for the implementation of that doctrine. All too often, even friends of local self-government are so indoctrinated with the notion that every big problem requires a big solution—usually expressed in terms of more centralization and new hierarchical organization—that they opt automatically for the kind of realignment of functions and actors that, in the end, is self-defeating. What is needed instead is a willingness to be inventive in finding imaginative solutions that are in keeping with the doctrine. This is a joint state-local task of first magnitude, but a task that is definitely possible.

Notes

1. Editor's note: In 1858 the Iowa legislature extended home rule to cities that were formally incorporated before statehood (McBain 1916b). Missouri's provisions for home rule were the first to appear in a state constitution. Constitutional home rule is more secure than legislative home rule, for obvious reasons.

2. The history of home rule is best reflected in the pages of the *National Civic Review* (originally the *National Municipal Review*), published by the National Municipal League since 1911.

3. A good discussion of these developments from the perspective of those supporting them can be found in *Striking a Better Balance: Federalism in 1972,* the fourteenth annual report of the Advisory Commission on Intergovernmental Relations (Washington, D.C.: Government Printing Office, January 1973), particularly chapters 1 and 5.

4. For a discussion of dual and cooperative federalism in the past, see Elazar (1962), particularly chapter 1.

5. Adapted from a summary prepared by the National Governors' Conference Center for Policy Research and Analysis, 1975.

6. See, in particular, Grodzins 1966.

7. It should be noted that local control in this sense is not necessarily local self-government on the home rule model; it may involve local power in relation to federal and state agencies as much as local instrumentalities.

8. The key case is *Hunter v. City of Pittsburgh,* 207 U.S. 161 (1907).

9. *City of Clinton v. Cedar Rapids and Missouri River R.R. Co.,* 24 Iowa 455, 475. See also Dillon 1911.

10. Unlike the original corporation charters, however, it did not deal with the problem of local representation in the governing bodies of the state. In an era of ideological commitment to dual federalism, perhaps this could have been expected.

11. See, for example, *People v. Hurlbut,* 24 Mich. 24 (1871).

12. It should be noted that Dillon himself indicated his personal preference for endowing local government with real autonomy, and virtually says so in the passage quoted previously, even though his legal judgment was otherwise (erroneously, in this writer's opinion).

13. The comments of Alexis de Tocqueville on this question, while in places outdated on specifics, remain the best analysis of this attitude. See, in particular, *Democracy in America,* volume 1, part 1, chapter 5. De Tocqueville himself subscribes to views similar to those of Cooley.

4

Emerging Trends in
State-Local Relations

Beverly A. Cigler

State and local governments are the major service providers in the American political system and play important policymaking roles. The state and local portion of the public sector grew considerably in recent decades as its contribution to the social and economic well-being of the nation increased. The current challenge is to forge a system of governance across all sectors (public, private, and nonprofit) and levels (national, regional, state, local) that can respond creatively to the intertwined challenges of interdependence, fiscal uncertainty, and accelerated economic, technological, social, and political change.[1]

"Government" is less important today than the overall "system of governance" that results from the interaction of organizations in policy development and implementation and service delivery across economic regions. Because problems spill over the boundaries of geographic-based local governments, solutions must be sought on a regional basis; watersheds, laborsheds, rural commutersheds, and ecosystems are the new units of organization in which state-local relations often occur. Strong suburbs help cities, but strong cities make suburbs even stronger (e.g., Barnes and Ledebur 1994; Rusk 1993). Intergovernmental relations have shifted substantially toward improving intergovernmental management and intersector relations and management (Cigler 1996a).

The continuing devolution of responsibilities from the national to state governments is important, as is national devolution's impact on local communities. Changes in state-local relations have received less scrutiny, but may be the overall key to devolution's success. The forces that generate new demands on subnational (state and local) governments and their wide-ranging institutional renewal also merit more attention.

This chapter highlights the macrotrends affecting the state-local governance system and its reshaping. Included are crosscutting concerns such as mandates and other regulations, capacity-building activities such as technical assistance, the provision of financial and other incentives, and structural reform of local government (Cigler 1993b). Background information that suggests varying capabilities of local governments is provided to enhance the discussion of state-local interaction. Emphasis is given to key principles and assumptions that are guiding the direction of state-local interaction at the approach of the twenty-first century.

Formal State-Local Relationships

The formal nature of the state-local relationship is unitary and hierarchical (i.e., vertical). Local governments—whether general purpose towns, boroughs, townships, cities, or counties—are creatures of the states; they are treated legally as municipal corporations. States curb their superiority by providing for some limited municipal immunity through home rule, but state government remains superior and home rule makes no claims about separate spheres of state and local authority. Home rule is, instead, an umbrella of policies and understandings between a state and its local governments.

Local governments generally possess substantial power in the regulatory arena and have extensive regulatory and service delivery responsibilities. The most significant constraint on municipal power is in fiscal matters (Cigler 1996b). Mixed with the great diversity of local governments—in type, function, size, wealth, and demographics (age, race, income, and class)—is interjurisdictional competition that results in a pattern of fiscal disparities in service delivery and social inequities across metropolitan areas and between rural and urban places. Local land-use and growth-management practices, often of an exclusionary nature, deepen the extent of local fiscal disparities.

Preemption is the most common form of state control over municipal taxing power, that is, state legislatures often deny their municipalities the power either to impose a particular tax or to impose a tax on a particular class of taxpayers. Extensive state legislative limits on revenue raising and expenditure powers, along with tight limits on alternative sources of revenue, are usually more restrictive than state restraints on local regulatory powers.

Macrotrends Affecting State-Local Relations

The current environment for state-local relations is complex, involving demographic, economic, social, political, and technological dynamics, as well as increased demands for service in a time of uneven resources, regionalization, and disintegration of the civic infrastructure (Cigler 1996a; 1993a).

Demographic and Social Trends

A changing population that includes more elderly in need of long-term care, more youth in schools and prone to crime, and a more diverse workforce lacking in basic skills are key demographic trends influencing intergovernmental relations. The number of senior citizens in the United States will increase by more than 60 percent over the next two decades; the population of seniors 85 years and older will more than double. School enrollment is growing more rapidly than at any time since the baby boom of the 1950s and 1960s, with growth generally concentrated in outer-ring metropolitan suburbs where new classroom construction is required.

Costly government programs for health care, primary and secondary schools, and colleges have strained government budgets. National and state mandates and preemptions increase government costs, as do rising public salaries and employee benefits. High standards for performance challenge the balancing of quality and affordability. Infrastructure costs—for aging schools, highways, and bridges, as well as for expansion to the suburbs—must include funding for an expansion of the telecommunications infrastructure. Future financing for two national programs, Social Security and Medicare, influences all governmental budgets.

By the end of the 1980s, 90 percent of U.S. population growth and 87 percent of employment growth occurred in metropolitan areas (that is, cities and suburbs). Half of all Americans now live in thirty-nine metropolitan areas; 80 million (30 percent of the population) live in central cities. The U.S. population is becoming more diverse in its racial and ethnic composition, with many individuals often lacking the skills necessary for the increasingly service- and information-based economy. What lacks diversity is the spatial location of minorities, who are now majorities in the largest central cities (Cigler 1996a).

Telecommunications, Technology, and the Global Economy

State and local governments operate in a globalized economy that requires dramatic changes in the ways that governments operate. Connections are easier to make across large distances; the Internet and other communication technologies have a leveling effect by making it possible for more to compete as equals. The emergence of so many new actors suggests that organizations (including governments) that traditionally were competitors must now work as partners and form working alliances.

Advances in technology, especially the ability to collect, store, and retrieve information from a central data base, have a significant impact on government operations (Kost 1996). Such advances enable states to monitor local use of state funding allocations, assess local performance, and transfer technology to local governments. Technology holds promise for cost savings across a wide variety of policy and service delivery areas. It is a catalyst for procurement reform, which enhances the possibility for more state-local piggybacking of governmental purchases. Resources can be catalogued and linked, and "paperless" offices can facilitate the use of single applications for state-local and other transactions. Business assistance applications can be consolidated and transferred through electronic mail; information clearinghouses are more accessible. Prefabricated prisons reduce costs, as does prefabricated housing for the poor. Travel costs and time are saved by judges who conduct video arraignments; schools use distance learning technologies; telemedicine provides quality consultations in rural areas; and local and state employees have increased access to training, information, and each other. Costly geographic information systems (GIS) and computer-assisted design graphics can be developed jointly via state resources for a wide variety of local planning functions.

Technology also poses problems for state-local relations. There are questions about the constitutionality of witness testimony by video, currently limiting the use of such technology to pretrial, administrative proceedings and appeals. Gambling on the Internet (cybergambling) increases the likelihood of new types of tax shelters, greater gambling addiction by the young, and possible state regulation. These have impacts on local governments—their tax bases, spending for social problems, and compliance with regulations. The costs of providing the full array of telecommunications to rural areas are often prohibitive, widening the gaps in service availability between rural and urban areas. Oklahoma, for example, recently eliminated its telemedicine program to remote areas. An information-based economy that is fueled by advanced telecommunications may mean that small cities and rural areas—many already with declining population and job bases—lose locational advantages derived from proximity to railroads or water. These "places without purpose" (in an economic sense) struggle for survival, with states sometimes forced to provide bailouts.

Increased Problem Complexity

Old problems seldom die; they change form and/or grow worse. Crime rates are driven by drugs. The feminization of poverty places large numbers of women and children at risk. Entire families face homelessness. As technology improves, health care and education costs rise.

In dealing with complex problems, state bureaucracies and lawmakers struggle with ways to integrate services, including linkages to appropriate local officials and agencies. Policy options must necessarily be clustered and linked: Workfare and daycare, education and job training, child and maternal health—all go together in effective welfare reform. Natural resource management, economic development, and environmental problems require regional solutions involving many government entities, too. However, this can blur lines of responsibility, leaving the sense that "when everyone is in charge, no one is in charge" (Cigler 1990). The challenges of moving toward decentralized, cooperative, and collaborative problem solving are immense in the working partnerships between states and their local governments. Strategies, structures, and systems for each policy area must be reshaped.

Serious imbalances exist between local fiscal needs and resources; income inequalities continue to escalate. In 1990, the wealthiest fifth of the nation's citizens made more than the other four-fifths combined. According to Robert Reich (1991), the rich retreat into their own self-sufficient communities: the "secession of the successful." Local fiscal disparities, and their effects on school financing and land-use patterns, however, are driving the states to take a greater role in these local policy areas.

Increased Demand for Services

Local governments provide traditional and basic services but cannot borrow their way out of problems. Public demands for activism, growth, and innovation continue unabated despite contemporary antigovernment rhetoric and aversion to taxes. Growing service demand; the increasing scope, range, and cost of services; and the tax limitation movement have pushed state and local governments to reconsider what they do, how, and with what resources. Local government structural reform is receiving wide attention, including tax-base and revenue-base sharing options (Cigler 1995a; 1996b). In addition, a skeptical citizenry has pushed elected officials to embrace new management paradigms, alternate policy tools, and service delivery options. This changes the mix of service deliverers and modifies governments' relationships with service recipients.

Increased Activism by Citizens, Groups, and Elected Officials

Citizen and interest group empowerment brings social and economic concerns to state and local officials in new ways. Access is afforded to every phase of the policy cycle: problem identification, agenda setting, policy formulation, policy and program implementation, and evaluation (Cigler 1990). Citizen activism pushes elected officials to demand greater accountability from service bureaucracies, sometimes leading to micromanagement. Similarly, state legislators are prone to view local governments as "just another interest group" (Cigler 1994; 1995b) and to tighten their regulatory grip in some matters, especially fiscal. Institutional responsibilities are fragmented, blurred, and diffused, making access easier for special interests. The media have amassed enormous influence in designing agendas. Citizen customers (of government services) have redefined their wants as "needs" and their needs as "rights." In that milieu, governments must work harder to educate citizens and to balance everyone's rights with their responsibilities (Cigler 1996a).

Regionalization and Regionalism

The future of local government is regional. It is not a question of whether local areas will be regionalized, but who or what will be the driving force in promoting regionalism, including pressure from state governments. Regionalization of services is driven by economies of scale and prodded by national and state mandates (e.g., solid waste management). Regionalization of police forces, solid waste disposal, and emergency service is becoming commonplace nationwide (Cigler 1994). In some cases, only the funding is shifted to another level, such as state funding for jails. In other cases, funding, planning, and delivery responsibilities shift upward to counties, regional authorities, or the state. State regulatory functions (e.g., environmental regulations) may also be downloaded to regions. Municipal functions (e.g., firefighting) may be consolidated within regions. State legislation may direct planning to the regional level, too.

Public sector efficiency has a significant impact on the total efficiency of the U.S. economy. Differences in telecommunications costs and in regulations among states, for example, are becoming more important in business locational decisions that affect local economies. Harmonizing regulations across a region requires multistate and state-local cooperation with the private sector.

With an increasingly dynamic, open, and competitive world economy, governments have developed new ways of working with the private sector to improve economic performance. Companies think in terms of economic regions, not archaic political-geographic jurisdictions. States and local governments are challenged to develop regional relationships within a political system organized around individual places—towns, townships, boroughs, cities, and counties—to achieve sustainable community and economic development. The challenge is to develop a regional citizenry without destroying the strong feelings of community at the local level.

Looming Structural Budget Gaps

Municipal governments deal with issues of life (police, corrections, fire protection, public health, emergency management) and lifestyle (housing, land use, zoning, schools), and they provide other basic services (streets, lights) and amenities (libraries, parks). Counties are the major providers of human services in the political system, serving as the administrative arms of states to implement many state and national programs. Special districts and public authorities play important roles in providing water and sewer systems, parking garages, housing, parks, and other technical services.

By the end of the 1980s, however, the national deficit was hampering the ability of governments at all levels to create jobs, protect the social safety net, and counter the detrimental effects of deindustrialization that are transforming many metropolitan areas. The cities' fiscal ills transcend class, racial, and jurisdictional boundaries; rural areas mirror the metropolitan problems, with additional obstacles posed by isolation, low population density, and less revenue flexibility, among other differences.

At the end of fiscal 1995, the states were financially healthy, with an aggregate balance of $20 billion, or 5.7 percent of spending. The positive budget picture is a result of a strong national economy and decreased state spending in anticipation of national aid cuts (Gold 1995). Current budget trends indicate only short-term stability for most state and local governments, however.

The states will face a large and growing cumulative deficit early in the next century if current demographic and spending trends continue unchecked. That is because costs are escalating rapidly in the major areas of state government spending. This includes health care (driven by Medicaid costs); corrections (rising incarceration rates, mandatory sentencing, court mandates on overcrowding); primary and secondary education (due to a baby "boomlet"); higher education (new technology, the growing need for financial aid); and local government aid, especially after devolution (Cigler 1993a). Without significant changes in government operations, state governments and local communities will enter the twenty-first century with a broad pattern of budget deficits. Without better control of spending, funds cannot be freed to handle many of the challenges of the global economy.

If current demographic trends hold, there will be slower income growth and an increase in the number of youth, elderly, and others using government services. The size of the budget gap will be determined in part by the level of national government funding cuts in the near future, whether a major recession occurs, whether the states continue to spend existing surpluses on tax cuts or develop new surpluses and rainy day funds. The gap will also be affected by whether state and local governments pursue new revenue options (by eliminating unproductive business incentive programs, requiring sales taxes on mail order and Internet sales, revising tax exemption laws, increasing user fees, uncoupling from the Internal Revenue Code) and by other state and local responses to dramatic changes in their environment. Already, state aid to local governments is growing more slowly than other areas of state spending. In 1992, state aid amounted to 32.3 percent of state spending, which is the lowest proportion since the U.S. Census Bureau began reporting the statistic in 1956 (Gold 1995).

National Devolution and Regulatory Flexibility

States will determine the success of national block grant devolution, especially in the treatment of cities and counties. The transition to block grants may lead to substantial reductions in financial resources, fueling concern for the efficiency of state and local service delivery. In times of economic downturn, demands for welfare and Medicaid increase; state finances could be altered dramatically if a move is made to state block grants for these programs. Growth in spending due to rising costs, demographic shifts, or economic changes would challenge state revenue systems since block grants remove the countercyclical thrust of traditional welfare programs. (Block grants are fixed in size, whereas entitlement spending increases with demand, which typically rises in economic recessions.)

Decentralized decisionmaking requires changes in how states work with local governments to provide financial and technical assistance and evaluate programs. States will play the central role in being the forum for discussion, and they will need to develop more analytical and higher-quality information for making and evaluating decisions regarding the block grant devolution.

One major new block grant is already in effect. The Personal Responsibility and Work Opportunity Reconciliation Act of 1996 ended the national government's 61-year-old practice of providing assistance to eligible low-income mothers and children. The legislation is expected to save the national government nearly $55 billion through federal fiscal year 2002, but the financial effects on subnational governments are not fully known. The number of poor people in the United States has declined in the mid-1990s but could increase with any national economic downturn. Block grant funds ($16.4 billion annually from fiscal year 1996 through 2001) will be given to states, which will have nearly complete control over eligibility and benefits and thus will create their own welfare programs.

Some fear a "race to the bottom" whereas others look forward to cost savings from increased programmatic flexibility. The change in public assistance programs to concerns with workfare and cost containment involves private companies (IBM, EDS, Lockheed Martin IMS) as part of the potentially multibillion dollar new industry. Already, these private companies are working with state human service agencies to administer and operate eligibility determination functions and work-related programs for public assistance recipients. Such activity also will change how states work with counties on human services, perhaps reducing the county role in favor of the private sector.

Future population changes across the states will mean differential outcomes for many programs. National aid for family assistance and child care block grants will be appropriated through state legislatures and not controlled exclusively by a state's executive branch. This creates additional uncertainty for local governments.

Other block grants (such as some part of Medicaid reform), federal tax cuts, or a massive overhaul of the federal tax system would all have significant impacts on state-local relations. State taxes are linked to the federal tax code so state revenues decline when there is a national tax cut (unless a state chooses to uncouple from the system). A national flat tax would eliminate individual deductions for state and local taxes and for home mortgages, depressing home prices while aiding businesses in the local economy.

The national government has also begun to shift from a heavy hand in regulating state and local actions toward greater flexibility. (State government mandates on local governments follow the same pattern but not at the same pace as the national changes.) The U.S. Environmental Protection Agency's (EPA) "Policy on Flexible State Enforcement Responses to Small Community Violations" is an example of how the national government grants flexibility to subnational governments. States continue to enforce EPA regulations on communities of less than 2,500, but state enforcement compliance schedules that show progress within a specified time period receive waivers of penalties in noncriminal cases. The Federal Emergency Management Agency (FEMA) follows a similar path with its Community Rating System within the National Flood Insurance Program (NFIP). In shifting away from command and control through the heavy hand of regulation, there is also greater use of incentives in national and state policies (for example, Empowerment and Enterprise Zone funding encourages community collaboration, as does the Youth Environmental Services program).

States have been successfully seeking waivers that relax federal rules and increase flexibility for mandated programs. If the Intermodal Surface Transportation Efficiency Act (ISTEA), originally passed in 1991, is reauthorized in 1997 with little change in concept, it will signal that the national government is relinquishing a one-size-fits-all approach and is moving to an outcome-based approach to problem solving. ISTEA links air, energy, and access issues together in a system of long-range and strategic planning. The current legislation grants local flexibility to spend as much as half of local funds on options other than highways. Economic

efficiency, cost-benefit analysis, risk assessment, measurement, and accountability are all part of the package.

Increased State Judicial Activism

Judicial activism at the state level regarding local fiscal disparities has led
to court orders regarding prison overcrowding. Child welfare programs
operate under court supervision in more than twenty states because of
deficiencies in their systems. The U.S. juvenile justice system also is in
disrepair. Despite the legal right to counsel in juvenile court, access to
counsel and quality of representation are major problems. An increasing
number of juvenile cases are going to adult courts, which increasingly use
adult jails and prisons to punish offenders. County governments, feeling
the pressures of the changes in the juvenile justice system, are seeking financial relief from the states.

After many years of favoring local autonomy in cases of school finance
inequities, recent state court decisions in Montana, Kentucky, and Texas
have invalidated local school financing systems, with lawsuits pending in
a number of other states. A similar narrowing of local autonomy has occurred through recent state court cases involving charges of exclusionary
zoning. Courts in California, New York, New Jersey, and Pennsylvania,
for example, have dealt with differences in interlocal wealth by linking
housing policies to the regional general welfare concept. Fair share affordable housing is promoted in some states.

The school finance and exclusionary zoning cases exemplify the call for
a greater state role (including supervision of local governments) and a need
for more local acccountability in projecting "reasonableness" into policies
regarding housing, zoning, land-use, and educational financing issues.
Roger Caves (1992) and Eric Kelly (1993) document the increase in state assertion in the land-use policy and growth management arena, and Barry
Rabe (1994) examines the rise in NIMBY (Not In My Backyard) sentiments
regarding locally unwanted land uses (LULUs) such as hazardous waste
siting. Local property owners charge that zoning ordinances violate the
"takings" clause of the Fifth Amendment and often sue local governments.
To meet state expectations for effective growth management, local officials
must invest in more careful and costly planning practices. The property
rights, wise use, and county supremacy movements consist of those ob-
jecting to "takings" and include many elected local officials.

Civic Disengagement and Collaborative Governance

Citizens, who are the core of the governance system, are often not engaged in meaningful participation thought to be necessary for sustaining

communities, the states, and the nation. As individual and group "wants" are redefined as "needs" and then demanded as "rights," attention must turn to the broader discussion about what is good for society (Cigler 1996a, 1996b). Single-minded advocacy, hostility, confrontation, and a general lack of civility often overshadow the development of what has been called the civic infrastructure, civic culture, or social capital deemed necessary for collectively analyzing, understanding, and responding to public problems (Harwood 1991; Putnam et al. 1993; Peirce 1993; Rusk 1993; Cisneros 1993; Downs 1994). Collaborative processes and other new ways of interacting are a growing part of elected officials' environment. The states play an important role in building local government capacity in the use of collaborative skills and alternative dispute resolution (ADR). It is at the local level where problems are encountered face-to-face.

Policy and Institutional Fragmentation amid Uneven Resources

Public policies and management efforts have developed largely through piecemeal processes, often born of expediency. Multicentered-policy dominance, a multiplicity of governments (including nearly 90,000 local governments), and governmental and institutional fragmentation (including the private and nonprofit sectors) must be met by bold, focused, and accountable political leadership and facilitative styles of management (Cigler 1990; Svara 1994; Chrislip and Larson 1994). An array of formal and informal governance structures collaboratively deal with the problems of achieving coordination at the local level (Gage and Mandell 1990). Attention has shifted from solely vertical relations (e.g., national-state-local) toward horizontal relations among local (intermunicipal) and state (interstate, multistate) governments.

More than 90 percent of municipal governments in the United States serve communities of less than 10,000 people; more than 80 percent of them serve under 5,000 people. More than three-fourths of counties serve populations of less than 50,000 and nearly a third of the population lives in rural areas, in which two-thirds of all local governmental units exist. Thus, although most people live in urban areas, most local governments (whether urban or rural) serve small populations and have limited policymaking and management capacity (Cigler 1989; 1996a).

State Downsizing, Streamlining, and Restructuring

Governments have to do things right, do the right things, and then convince everyone of results. Fueled by the belief that national aid will be cut, by the realities of block grant devolution, and by citizen concerns about waste, mismanagement, and too much taxation, the states are doing things better—and differently. Many states have downsized to control government expenses by consolidating and reorganizing agencies and services, privatizing responsibilities, and limiting eligibility for social services. The changes involve increased attention to results, not just processes; flexibility in generating resources and their allocations; and concern with accountability for performance.

Downsizing and other aspects of state government reinvention have mixed results for state-local relations. Laid-off or terminated state employees may depress local economies, especially in state capital regions. State reorganization can lead to local agency reorganization. State downsizing fuels interest in shifting even more responsibilities to local governments, along with the costs. At the same time, less funding may be available for local financial aid and for technical assistance and other ways to build capacity among widely varying local governments.

Principles and Assumptions
Reshaping State-Local Relations

What are state and local governments doing as working partners to meet their responsibilities in light of these trends? State-local relations are being reshaped by emerging principles that promote competition within public sector agencies and with the private and nonprofit sectors; encourage community empowerment, along with intermunicipal and state-local cooperation; promote cost-effectiveness in government operations and policies; encourage individual risk sharing; demand individual and community responsibility; and promote flexibility, innovation, risk taking, results, and performance accountability. Few state and local officials are unaware of such popular writing on the topic as "reinventing government" (Osborne and Gaebler 1992) or the National Performance Review (1993).

Several underlying and intertwined assumptions shape the principles that I see shaping state-local relations. Each assumption is discussed, along with its impact on state and local interactions.

1. Monopoly government is not necessarily the most appropriate way to meet the needs of society or public responsibilities. Officials at all levels are reassessing the rationale for government action. Health care proposals increasingly promote consumer options—for affordable acute and long-term care programs, managed care, and health maintenance organizations. K–12 education policy options include alternatives such as charter schools, school choice, and vouchers.

Privatization, for both the production and the delivery of services, and outsourcing of government operations (payroll, ticket processing, bill collection, prison administration) are becoming commonplace. Privatization is being used more frequently to deliver, measure, and monitor human services (e.g., juvenile and family services, some welfare activities, home care and nursing homes). Privatization reduces the number of state and local government employees and the ratio of government employees to the total population. It affects county-state relations as former county functions are privatized and shifted upward to the state. The need for improved standards, performance contracts, and monitoring for results is increased. States and counties, especially, must work more closely in developing integrated human service delivery systems. States may need to bolster their roles as information collectors and disseminators to help local governments make informed decisions.

Privatization remains a highly contentious issue, facing frequent opposition by unions and the courts. Privatization itself may be less an issue than increased competition in the public sector. Competitive bidding, for example, is being required for local governments in the provision of public services. Low bids are less important than altering overall costs. When public agencies must compete with the private sector for contracts, cost efficiencies and service effectiveness can be achieved. Many states require local governments to use referenda for deciding whether property tax rates can be increased, putting a check on local government autonomy.

Flexibility, choice, and discretion in the use of policy instruments are also more prevalent than in the past. Market-oriented approaches, such as vouchers, user charges, contracting out, and demand rationing are now part of the policy tool kit used by states, working with their local governments. Centralized, rule-bound, inflexible, and process-oriented approaches have given way to decentralization, flexibility, and cost-effective approaches to allocation and management of finances. The financing and delivery of services is driven more by consumers, not programs, making states and local governments work together to analyze needs.

2. Government should be less of a direct funder, service provider, and regulator and more of a facilitator, catalyst, enabler, convenor, information generator and disseminator, standard setter, broker, and capacity builder in helping to develop new relationships among people and groups across all sectors and government levels.

States are increasingly less likely to offer grant programs to single jurisdictions and more likely to reward jurisdictions that collaborate. Building the managerial, financial, and technical capacity of local governments is an important state function. States can disseminate information on "best practices" or "model" policies to local governments, devise measurement, monitoring, and evaluation systems, and otherwise facilitate continuous learning by partnering with local entities. A well-used capacity-building technique for local governments in some states (e.g., Pennsylvania) is funding for "circuit-riders" who provide assistance to a cluster of local governments in financial management, economic development, or other local functions. These state strategies afford the opportunity to strike an appropriate balance between centralized direction and local discretion, integrating concerns for equity, cost effectiveness, and quality.

School reform presents an interesting example, as many states focus more attention on teacher development, professionalism, and standards. Citizens are sent report cards that offer increased information about schools, teachers, and student accomplishments (National Governors' Association 1996). Financial incentives are sometimes combined with sanctions to change the behavior of local governments. An example is the use of cash rewards to schools that improve students' academic performance, coupled with the imposition of penalties on schools that do not improve. Penalties include teacher probation, firing of principals, or turning control over the school to the state. Southern states, which tend to rank lower in educational achievement standards, are most likely to use such approaches, but Connecticut, Hawaii, and Illinois use some variants as well. Critics complain of gimmicks and seek more direct funds to improve classroom environments; proponents of incentive-sanction approaches cite progress in Kentucky, where most schools have made progress toward their stated goals since the educational system was restructured.

3. Holistic approaches to complex and intertwined problems must be forged, based on the complexity of problems, fiscal constraints, and the accelerated changes in technology and communication.

Global competitiveness has pushed the public sector toward boundary-spanning roles in building relationships for the development of self-sufficient regional economies. This includes holistic approaches to (a) workforce skill development through the use of state-of-the-art technology and innovation; (b) high-quality physical infrastructure development (highways and bridges, water and sewer systems, telecommunications); (c) strategic and visionary collaborative planning; (d) leveraged financial and technical resources; and (e) adequate provision of the basics for quality living (e.g., affordable, quality health care and housing). In all of these areas, intergovernmental and intersector collaboration is necessary.

Traditionally, states have touted the benefits of economic growth and offered extensive tax abatements and other incentive packages to lure businesses. Local governments too have joined the economic development wars, spurring intense interjurisdictional competition. These development policies are based on the belief that growth will reduce local unemployment, build the local tax base, and provide a favorable business climate that will increase prosperity. However, growth often necessitates increased outlays for public infrastructure (roads, sewers, water, schools). This can drain a municipality's finances if the development does not pay the full costs and pits localities (and states) within a region against each other.

A number of states are pursuing new approaches that involve greater participation by the private sector to develop coherent economic development policies and to avoid unproductive jurisdictional competition. These public-private partnerships work to ensure that business needs are understood and met and that long-range strategies are implemented despite turnover among elected officials. The Greensboro, North Carolina, region's twelve-county economic development partnership was entirely initiated by the private sector. Mississippi and Tennessee coordinate a tourism promotion to Europeans that highlights "Blues Alley." The 1996 Summer Olympics sparked interest by Georgia, Tennessee, and North Carolina in multistate tourism promotion. All facilitate local and regional economic development.

State governments are being pushed to facilitate local self-sufficiency and more entrepreneurial economies. In education there is an increased emphasis on cooperation with employers to foster skills needed in the workplace. School-to-work and school-to-career programs link local schools and employers before students reach the workforce. Universities collaborate with businesses to advance cutting-edge technologies. All of these programs must be coordinated with broader community development efforts.

The states play an important role in working with businesses to demonstrate communications applications that can help local areas to thrive. Traditionally low-tech industries, such as the furniture industry, now use robotics, lasers, and scanning and bar codes to improve competitive advantage. Voice mail can give a minimally staffed small business the ability to take orders from customers twenty-four hours per day. Shipping, receiving, accounting, and production can be electronically linked. Electronic data interchange uses digital information transfers to replace paper information transfers in, for example, enrolling college students, the invoicing and payment of bills, and the reporting of data to monitoring agencies. And state and local governments are working together to facilitate the role that communication technologies, such as distance learning and telemedicine, play in improving the quality of rural life.

4. Regional delivery of goods and services is becoming more common, as states position themselves in the global economy. A key question is whether states will mandate regional approaches or develop incentive-based systems. Some existing local entities may not survive. Some states, for example, Massachusetts, are trying to abolish counties and to create regional units, though these efforts have not succeeded thus far. In other states, the push is to strengthen counties, especially their planning authority. Georgia, for example, is considering giving counties the authority to require municipalities to develop service delivery plans and new arrangements for utility districts. New units and boundaries may emerge

for regional entities, such as those based on watersheds. Financing techniques growing in popularity are a regional assets tax and various forms of tax-base and revenue-base sharing. A popular state incentive is to reward municipalities that regionalize services with more points in grant competition for state funding.

Another trend is that states are working with local communities to devise stronger land-use planning in order to counter the negative effects of urban sprawl. Florida has concurrency legislation; that is, no development can take place unless services such as roads, sewer, solid waste, parks and recreation, education, and health are provided at the same time. Local governments are empowered to set standards for each service and to prohibit development unless these requirements are met. Communities can agree to provide the services, or developers can provide them or post bonds to ensure that necessary infrastructure and services are provided as development takes place. The state coordinates and regulates the implementation of the law. Planning and zoning regulations must be coordinated on a regional and statewide basis by the local governments. If coordination is inadequate, a moratorium can be placed by the state on local development (Cigler 1996b).

Washington's concurrency includes provisions relating to land-use and capital facilities planning, transportation planning, and subdivision plat approvals linked to open space, drainage, street, sewer, water, recreation, school, and sidewalk needs. Concurrency, often called "pay as you grow," manages growth with advantages over traditional "pay later" approaches. The policy requires municipal-county fiscal collaboration and the exercise of state regulatory powers.

5. Entities that supply services to the public should operate at the community level, individually or collectively. Improved institutional capacity and revitalized governing boards are high on reform agendas. State governments (and municipal associations) offer training programs for local officials to increase their abilities to handle complex responsibilities and to compete for public office. The assumption that programs are best operated at the community level also fuels interest in regionalism since no one government or organization alone has the capability to deal with complex problems. By combining resources and people across communities, appropriate responses can be developed.

State officials are reassessing state programs, deciding which should be decentralized to the local or regional level, which must be retained by the state in the interest of a broader public interest, and which should be eliminated. Increased attention to issues of accountability, eligibility, and liability may result.

6. Resources should be concentrated on the people, organizations, and places in greatest need, with more self-reliance expected of recipients of

government aid. To ensure accountability, the trend is toward providing aid directly to individuals rather than to bureaucracies. School programs include vouchers for low-income families. Health care programs include benefit packages that reflect ability to pay. Financial assistance is given directly to college students instead of funneled indirectly through institutions. State aid to cities has decreased, but property tax relief for needy people in many cities has been increased by state legislatures. Welfare benefits are trimmed for families with children who quit or skip school. High school dropouts may lose the privilege of having a driver's license. Parents who do not maintain child support obligations may have funds automatically deducted from their paychecks or lottery winnings, or they may be arrested. Welfare recipients are being asked to become more self-reliant; five-year lifetime limits on welfare and requirements to work within two years provide incentives. Eligibility restrictions are reducing the number of individuals receiving food stamps. Major place-specific programs assist those in greatest need, such as state enterprise zones, community development financial institutions, and community development corporations (Galster and Killen 1995; Vidal 1995).

7. Policy options should include an appropriate balance of citizen rights and responsibilities. Many new state laws reflect this emphasis on individual responsibility. Changes in welfare policies were mentioned previously. Citizens can own guns, but gun ownership is denied to anyone convicted of domestic violence, including child and spousal abuse. "Three strikes and you're out" laws, with various levels of harshness, automatically send offenders with a third felony conviction to prison for life. Prison fee programs require prisoners to pay for room and board, medical care, haircuts, and other services. This may include charging fees only to prisoners in work release programs or those with the financial ability to pay.

Genuine self-government requires public institutions to empower citizens to act for themselves by expanding individual choice, decentralizing power, and building competition into the delivery of public goods and services. It requires opportunities for citizens to participate in the full gamut of activities that inform policymaking.

8. Increased mandate, regulatory, and fiscal flexibility should be given to local governments and the private sector. Cities, counties, townships, and school districts spend hundreds of millions of dollars meeting state mandates. (Local and state governments do the same with national mandates.) Conditions are attached to grant-in-aid programs, which offer cash payments to state and local governments for adopting programs that the national or state governments want to promote. Participation is voluntary but the money is enticing. Other mandates are general laws of the land that apply to all public and private sector entities (e.g., environ-

mental and civil rights requirements); they are usually very costly and come with no financial assistance.

The purposes of many mandates are noble, such as ensuring uniform rights for all citizens and consistency in the application of regulations. Mandates, however, are often overly prescriptive. They dictate how activities must be carried out, not only the goals to be accomplished. State mandates on local governments have been especially notorious for their legal and procedural complexity. However, flexibility is taking root as many states seek to improve their business climate, beyond offering tax cuts to corporations. Streamlined facility permitting or integrated permitting and incentive programs improve local economic development (Rabe 1995). "Brownfields" legislation lends flexibility in assessing liability for toxic wastes on old industrial sites turned into "greenfields."

Another trend is to combine state mandates on local governments with a wide variety of capacity-building tools and inducements (e.g., technical assistance, financial aid). Some states require their local governments to prepare comprehensive land-use plans, with noncompliance tied to the withholding of state aid. A state might also reward a local government with a grant-in-aid and/or technical assistance for plan development. State requirements have traditionally been highly prescriptive regarding the content of local plans. Today, some states require certain procedures for plan development but not for content. Less coercive approaches by states may enhance local innovation and the ability to shape solutions for uniquely local circumstances.

Increased flexibility in the state-local regulatory arena also includes regulatory negotiations, which bring together all stakeholders early in the process to design approaches for avoiding later problems. This helps local governments to implement environmental and other regulations legislated by the national and state governments. Alternative dispute resolution techniques encourage intergovernmental cooperation and save money.

Local revenue diversification is the major focus of current reform of state-local fiscal relations. This includes some loosening of rigid restraints upon levying local property taxes and borrowing, in addition to increasing the types of tax and user fee options available to local governments (especially counties). Elsewhere, I have reviewed five categories of state-local fiscal reform (Cigler 1996b). Samuel Nunn and Mark Rosentraub (1996) have examined tax base and revenue sharing plans for fiscal equalization within metropolitan areas. Local taxing and borrowing policies could have disastrous effects upon state interests; taxpayer and bondholder protections against local government abuses are necessary. On the other hand, local autonomy rests on fiscal flexibility. Rigid constitutional limits on the power to tax or borrow and on sources of revenue burden local governments strapped with growing responsibilities, unfunded mandates, and decreasing intergovernmental aid.

9. Accountability for performance, including strategic planning processes, benchmarking, performance monitoring, and consultative processes with citizens, should be stressed over processes, inputs, and bean counting. As local governments are given relief from stringent state regulations, they are required to abide by stringent performance standards. Thus, schemes that are tied to "contract for performance" give local governments stronger roles and flexibility, but demand more accountability. Partnership approaches among national, state, and local governments; between metropolitan and rural areas; and with the private sector are prevalent. Greater attention is being paid to analyzing impacts, risk assessment, user design, and information disclosure to citizens. Devolution of national programs to state governments (including many that will be implemented by local agencies) follows a similar pattern in setting national goals and priorities.

As responsibility, authority, and discretion are devolved to lower levels of government, accountability requirements have also increased through the use of benchmarks, standards, and performance reviews (Ammons 1996). The movement (in at least twenty-nine states) toward making some schools or entire school districts charter schools is an example. Charter schools operate free of most state regulations; they are under performance contracts and different funding formulas than traditional schools. The notion of a performance review is also embodied in the concept of school report cards issued annually to the community and parent surveys of school performance. Educational reform in Kentucky was legislated after the entire system was declared unconstitutional by the state's supreme court for failing to be equitable, adequate, and uniform. The state then required its school systems to meet higher standards but also provided more funds for research and distance learning, new curricula and methods, and technology. Spending was equalized among school districts.

The effort to achieve sustainable development communities (i.e., livable communities that taxpayers can afford and the environment sustain) in many states has led to a variety of flexible approaches in state-local relations. Broad goals are established for guiding state and local plans to achieve sustainability in the use of natural and financial resources, but counties are permitted to choose how and where development occurs in cooperation with other counties and with their own municipalities. Broad, flexible state goals include ways to enhance the economic strength of communities, assurances that new growth pays for itself, and the preservation of areas of local, regional, and statewide significance. A state agency may review county plans to ensure compatibility with the state's long-term goals, but the state also requires its agencies to comply with any county plans that the state approves.

"Let managers manage, but require managers to manage" is the phrase that best expresses the wide-ranging government reinvention themes that tie together good management and necessary accountability. All this is achieved by attention to measurement, monitoring, quality performance, goals and objectives, and strategic processes. Regional indices to gauge the success or failure of regional strategies are yet another example of how states work in cooperation with their local governments. So, too, are the issuance of "community scorecards," which provide indicators of service quality and quality of life, generally based on some type of benchmarking.

10. Deliberative democracy must be the basis for policy decisions. State and national government agencies, along with a number of foundations (the Kettering and Pew Charitable Trusts, for example), newspapers syndicates (such as Knight-Ridder), and a wider array of nonprofit organizations (League of Women Voters, and so forth) are beginning to promote new ways to engage citizens in designing future governance. Study circles, citizen forums, civic journalism, focus groups, citizen juries, and other strategies aim at creating dialogue that is issue- and knowledge-based and nonconfrontational. Such "community conversations" promote collegial learning and dialogue to develop approaches to social and political problems. These strategies aim to build the civic infrastructure by developing greater trust relationships as a basis for increased collaboration with local communities and regions (Putnam et al. 1993).

11. Experimentation, cautious risk taking, and innovation should be encouraged and rewarded, not avoided and penalized. Slowly, the public sector is learning to tolerate failure and copy success. Selective policies and programs are favored over radical change. Voluntary programs are promoted over those imposed on people and communities. Single, comprehensive approaches are giving way to multistaged, experimental approaches based on pacing and sequencing strategies. Public service values, such as accountability and responsiveness, are reinforced, not replaced.

A movement toward child-first systems (placing less emphasis on keeping abused children with their parents and more willingness to place children in foster homes, for example) has significant impact on state-county relations since counties implement the major human service mandates in the political system. Other policy experimentation includes alternatives to institutionalization of the elderly and nonviolent criminals. Corrections policy ideas range from the development of private sector options for incarceration, expanded pretrial intervention and alternative sentencing, and improved use of state and local facilities. State aid to local governments is no longer confined to money; it encompasses a wide array of structural reforms and the granting of revenue flexibility.

Alternatives to building new prisons include expanding the use of community-based penalties, adjusting sentences of nonviolent offenders, stopping the spiral of increasing criminal penalties, and investing in prevention (a long-term strategy). Community policing redirects police from a sole focus on regulation and enforcement toward collaborative community building and facilitation. Results and outcomes—to community, neighborhoods, families, and individuals—are emphasized over programs and services.

12. A focus on prevention results in cost efficiencies. Greater attention to prevention can avoid more complex and costly problems later. Child care, immunizations, Head Start, and other child development programs improve children's health and prepare them for school success. Checkups, screening, and immunization lower Medicaid costs. Integrated human service networks that focus on "families at risk" deal with child abuse and neglect, teen pregnancy, school dropouts, and other problems of children in poverty. Homes for unwed mothers, now called "second chance homes," offer adult supervision to teen mothers and help in early child development.

The Future of State-Local Relations

State and local governments will look different in the future—and there may be fewer general purpose local governments. Smaller, more streamlined, and less involved in direct service provision, governments will probably focus on flexible structures and financing. Results, not process, will be better monitored and evaluated. Rather than a decline in the importance of the public sector, state and local governments, interacting with a host of stakeholders across various sectors, may play more important roles in some policy areas. Public officials and their organizations will be expected to offer innovative approaches to policymaking and service delivery and will be responsible for building enhanced structures for communicating with citizens. Improved decisionmaking and rule setting could enhance governmental performance, and government will likely be better monitored and evaluated than in the past.

The guiding principles and their underlying assumptions herein discussed have far-reaching effects on the overall patterns of intergovernmental and intersector relations and on the relationship between government and citizens as well. Democrats and Republicans, liberals and conservatives differ in some matters of "kind" and differ greatly in matters of "degree" in implementing these ideas. Should "underutilized assets," such as public lands, be sold? How stringent should eligibility be for welfare programs? Should health care be rationed? Are some prison fees double jeopardy? Should metropolitan areas be required to provide "fair share" housing? Should a child's opportunities in life be tied to his or her family's wealth? When, and for what, are enforceable statewide standards necessary? What *is* the core business of government?

The "big questions" of state-local relations involve who should do what, when, where, why, and how. These remain highly contentious. Party is pitted against party, government level against government level, program against program, and so forth. The future of state-local interaction is uncertain. Government is in a long-term trend toward more professionalization and more democracy, although it is trusted less by citizens (Cigler 1990). Much of what will happen in the future is driven by demographics and commitments made previously (Social Security and Medicare are important examples). The reshaping of governments' structures, systems, and processes leads to yet untested relationships with the private sector and uncertain outcomes as far as equity and equality of opportunity are concerned. Regional- or metropolitan-level structures and processes—where most local problems occur and must be handled—are in their infancy (Downs 1996). State-local relations will likely not achieve the success demanded until the window of regional opportunity is fully open.

Notes

1. The framing of issues and assumptions reshaping state-local relations, along with examples used in the chapter, were drawn from research supported by a grant from the United States Department of Agriculture, National Research Initiative (NRICCP Project Number 93–337401–9088).

5

The Politics of State-Local Fiscal Relations

Jeffrey M. Stonecash

The finances of state and local governments are closely connected. The states have legal control of local financial practices and provide much of the revenue of local governments. The states also are responsible for the creation of multiple local governments, which differ greatly in local tax bases that support services. The limited resources of local governments and disparities of tax bases often produce calls for states to do more to help their local governments. These demands have led to a gradual but steady expansion of state involvement in local affairs during the twentieth century. This growth has been accelerated by actions of the national government. However, the rate and timing of expansion varies from state to state, reflecting patterns of party control.

The Entanglement of State and Local Finances

State and local finances are fundamentally intertwined. Legally speaking, local governments depend on state government. State governments create counties, municipalities, towns, villages, school districts, and special districts. The state also grants each of these local governments the power to tax and borrow. This power is used in almost all states to regulate what kinds of taxes may be imposed, maximum levels of taxation and debt, and what kinds of borrowing may occur (ACIR 1978; Stonecash 1981b; Kenyon 1989).

The states also determine which level of government can use various kinds of taxes. States generally reserve the income tax for state use. The sales tax is also a state tax, though many states allow local governments to impose additional percentages of the sales tax for local use. Property taxes are generally reserved for local governments.

States regulate how local property taxes can be applied. There are limits on what properties local governments can tax. Many properties are declared tax exempt because the organization owning land is nonprofit and a political determination has been made that such organizations should not pay taxes. For this reason, state governments grant exemptions to churches, elementary and secondary schools, higher education institutions, neighborhood groups, and a large array of social service groups such as the Red Cross, public television, youth organizations, and religious charities. These exemptions from property taxes limit the ability of local governments to raise money within their boundaries.

States are continually involved with local governments because many state functions are implemented through local governments. States rely on local governments to administer local courts, deliver public education, maintain roads, provide police and fire protection, and so forth. States also rely on local governments for implementation of many federal programs. In 1935 the federal government began the ADC (Aid to Dependent Children) program as a way to provide assistance to poor children. The federal government provided assistance in exchange for states meeting some minimal standards when implementing the program. Many states initially chose to implement the program through local governments (Derthick 1970), a pattern that continued when ADC became Aid to Families with Dependent Children (which has now been replaced by Temporary Assistance to Needy Families). Similar decisions were made when the Medicaid program began in 1965. This program provides medical assistance to those below the poverty level. This usage of local governments for state purposes creates continual demands for state aid to help implement programs. The dependency of local governments on state aid increases the interdependency of state and local governments.

Since the state has legal authority over local governments, there is always a question of how much autonomy local governments should have in choosing policies. Many groups pressure state politicians (governors and legislators) to impose mandates on local governments. Civil rights groups want mandatory procedures for handling local complaints. Education groups want laws that specify the minimal numbers of hours that must be devoted to physical education, music, and other subjects. Teacher unions want laws that require school boards to recognize unions and negotiate with them. Local public employee unions want laws that mandate employee pension contributions and benefits. They also want mandatory job protection provisions. Environmental groups do not trust local governments to be aggressive in monitoring business practices, so they seek mandatory inspection practices. Government employee groups want laws defining local work rules.

All these activities lead to the imposition of state mandates, or rules that apply to all local governments (ACIR 1978). Some states have been very active in imposing a wide array of mandates on local governments. Many of these mandates are unfunded. The state requires that something be done by a local government, but there is no direct state aid to help pay for the cost of this local activity. This leads to persistent lobbying to either relax the mandates or provide state aid to help pay for the required activities.

There are also continuing debates about the responsibility of state governments for the collective situation of local governments. Within every state, local governments differ in their tax bases and racial compositions (Galster and Hill 1992). Local governments and school districts differ dramatically in the services they can provide and in the quality of schools that are provided (Kozol 1991). Local governments also differ in the majoritarian views that dominate in each area. Some areas are heavily conservative, which leads to desires for different policies than in areas that are heavily liberal.

Policy differences prompt debates about their legitimacy. Conservatives tend to see diversity of policies as positive reflections of the diversity of American society. People will cluster together and create communities that reflect common views and can have combinations of services that reflect the preferences of the people in that area (Bish and Ostrom 1973). Of course, people differ in how they want their public life conducted, and this leads to differences in settlement patterns, lifestyles, and service levels (Williams 1971). Economists also argue that these arrangements are more efficient because service packages match local preferences, instead of imposing uniform policies on all local areas (Tiebout 1956).

Liberals differ sharply with this interpretation of diversity among local governments. They argue that local governments use their zoning powers to create expensive housing that excludes low income groups (Danielson 1976). This also results in the exclusion of minorities, who tend to have lower incomes. The consequence has been the evolution of American urban areas that are segregated by class and race (Judd and Swanstrom 1994). Local governments, in this view, do not embody reflections of differing "tastes," but the use of government powers to maintain inequalities in American society. This is why schools vary dramatically in their resource levels and in the opportunities afforded children (Kozol 1991). Segregation in the schools has grown in the last twenty years as more whites moved to suburbs, resulting in many largely minority school districts (Orfield 1993).

These variations in tax bases and resources are the basis for claims that the state should increase intergovernmental aid and provide more money to areas with lower tax bases. The argument is that state government should engage in redistribution to enhance equality of opportunity in our society. Residents of low income areas argue that the state should provide their local governments with more state aid and that their areas should get more aid per person than affluent communities. This creates perpetual battles in state legislatures about whether to raise more revenue to respond to these requests and about how to distribute state aid.

These disputes often culminate in lawsuits against the state. Those areas with poorer tax bases have argued that the state created the system of local governments and is ultimately responsible for the existing inequalities. School districts with lower tax bases have sued to force the state to assume greater responsibility for this situation and distribute more aid to them. In states such as California, Kentucky, New Jersey, and Texas, the courts have ruled that the existing system is unconstitutional and have required state governments to address the issue in some way. In each of these states there was a prolonged battle over how to redistribute state aid. Almost one-half the states face lawsuits concerning the inequality of school finance (Celis 1992b).

All these relationships leave states heavily involved in local finances. States regulate the ability of local governments to raise money, while placing service delivery demands on them that require state aid. At the same time, the proliferation of local governments with varying tax bases has prompted questions of whether services and opportunities are unfairly distributed. Many state decisions involve the issue of whether the state will respond by raising more revenue and how state funds will be distributed among local governments.

The Increasing Role of State Governments

Debates about the proper role of the state have produced considerable change in recent decades. Factors external and internal to states have prompted a greater role for state governments in state and local fiscal affairs. The federal government has initiated many new programs by promising states significant aid if they implement them. If states participate, as almost always happens, they take on new fiscal responsibilities. In recent decades the amount of federal aid to state governments has increased dramatically. Figure 5.1 presents the per capita federal aid to state governments since 1952. The figures are presented in real dollars (adjusted for inflation). Federal aid to states is now about seven times greater than it was during the early 1950s. When states take on new federal programs, there are also decisions about whether to have the state fund and administer programs or whether these activities should be done by local governments (Derthick 1970). When the latter is chosen, state and local finances become more entangled.

FIGURE 5.1   Real per Capita Intergovernmental Aid, 1952–1992

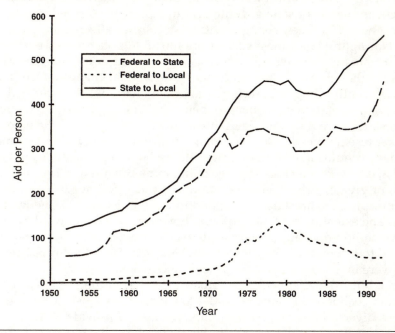

NOTE: The CPI index for 1982–84 = 100 is used to adjust for inflation.
SOURCE: The data on intergovernmental aid are from various editions of Advisory Commission on Intergovernmental Relations, *Significant Features of Fiscal Federalism* and U.S. Census Bureau, *Government Finances*, GF-5 series (Washington, D.C.: USGPO).

The relationship between states and their local governments has also been affected by the direct involvement of the federal government with local governments. By the early 1970s the federal government was providing extensive amounts of direct assistance to local governments. The rise in per capita direct federal aid to local governments is also shown in Figure 5.1. This led to arguments about whether states should be bypassed, and whether state governments shouldn't be financially responsible for their local governments.

This greater federal involvement in local affairs did not please everyone. Many groups argued that the state should have primary responsibility for local affairs. They also argued that a greater federal role leads to mandates imposed from Washington that are intrusive and often out of touch with local preferences. This opposition, plus growing federal budget deficits, resulted in significant cutbacks in direct federal aid beginning in the late 1970s. By 1991 the aggregate amount of direct federal aid to local governments had declined to levels that prevailed in the late 1950s (Farber 1989). This withdrawal of federal aid prompted demands from local governments for state governments to replace the lost federal aid.

There have also been changes within states that affected state fiscal roles. During the 1960s most states were forced to undergo reapportionment. For many years states had resisted changing legislative district lines even though population settlement patterns had changed. Over the twentieth century population shifted to urban areas, but these areas did not get representation equivalent to their numbers. The courts finally required states to redraw their legislative district lines to give urban areas more representatives (O'Rourke 1980). This occurred at the same time that many central cities were experiencing declines in population and tax bases, and poverty in cities was becoming more of an issue. The combination of greater urban representation and increased needs in central cities put pressure on states to respond to the problems of local governments. The extent of the state response, however, was constrained by divisions within urban areas. Central city residents were in favor of greater state aid to respond to poverty and economic decline, but suburban residents were more concerned with schools and general services. States did respond, but aid was spread more broadly because of the need to satisfy a broader coalition of interests in order to get state aid legislation passed.

These diverse pressures have prompted states to provide more assistance to local governments. Since the 1960s states have generally increased their tax-raising efforts. The decline in federal aid beginning in 1978 was met with greater state efforts to raise money and provide aid (Stonecash 1990). A basic indicator of a government's inclination to tax is tax effort. This is the total amount of taxes collected by a state or local government divided by the total personal income of the population. The ratio of these two represents the proportion of the public's income taken in taxes by that government. Figure 5.2 presents state and local tax effort since 1950. State and local tax effort both increased gradually until the late 1960s. In 1969 and 1970 state tax effort increased significantly, whereas local tax effort declined in the late 1970s. Since then local tax effort has been in the 4 to 5 percent range, while state tax effort has gradually increased to around 6.5 percent of personal income.

The increase in state revenue has allowed states to provide much more aid to local governments. Real per capita state aid to local governments, shown as the top line in Figure 5.1, has increased dramatically over the years. States have come to assume a much greater role in state-local finances. The three indicators shown in Figure 5.3 reflect the gradual increase in the state role since 1957 (Stonecash 1981a). The top line indicates the proportion of all state-local taxes raised by state governments. The middle line indicates the proportion of all direct general expenditure (ed-

FIGURE 5.2   State and Local Tax Effort, 1950–1992

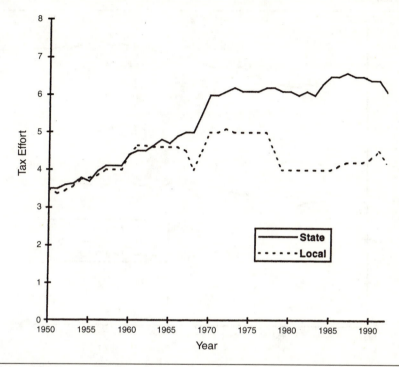

SOURCE: Data is from Advisory Commission on Intergovernmental Relations, *Significant Features of Fiscal Federalism* (Washington, D.C.: U.S. Government Printing Office), various years; and U.S. Bureau of the Census, *Government Finances*, GF-5 Series (Washington, D.C.: U.S. Government Printing Office), various years.

ucation, transportation, fire, police, etc.) conducted by state governments. The bottom line indicates the proportion of all local general revenue supplied by state aid. All three indicators have drifted upward. The state now raises more in the way of taxes and provides more state aid to fund local government activities.

The Politics of Change

The increase in the role of the state has not been a uniform phenomenon across the country. Regions of the country have changed at different times and at different rates. During the Civil War, northern states made significant moves toward state centralization as part of a war mobilization effort (Bensel 1990). Many years later, during the Great Depression, south-

FIGURE 5.3   The Changing State Role in State-Local Fiscal Responsibilities,
1957–1992

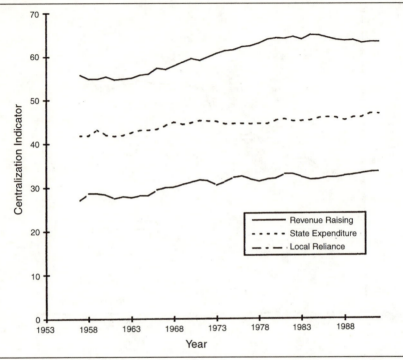

SOURCE: Data is from Advisory Commission on Intergovernmental Relations,
Significant Features of Fiscal Federalism (Washington, D.C.: U.S. Government
Printing Office), various years; and U.S. Bureau of the Census, *Government
Finances,* GF-5 Series (Washington, D.C.: U.S. Government Printing Office),
various years.

ern states emerged from the 1930s relatively more centralized than the
rest of the country. Opposition to local taxes was particularly strong in the
South, and efforts to reduce local taxes were more successful there than
elsewhere in the country (Stonecash 1995a).

There have also been broad differences in change by region over time.
State governments in northern and western states have steadily increased
their role. Figure 5.4 presents averages by region for the state role in raising
tax revenue. Southern states have been relatively centralized since the 1930s,
and they have stayed at that level for some time. Other states have gradually increased the taxes imposed and moved the state into a larger role.

The state has come to play a relatively greater role. This greater role
might come about two ways. Local government may cut back on taxation
and expenditure and leave the state with a relatively greater role. This is

FIGURE 5.4   The State Role in Raising Tax Revenue, by Region, 1957–1992

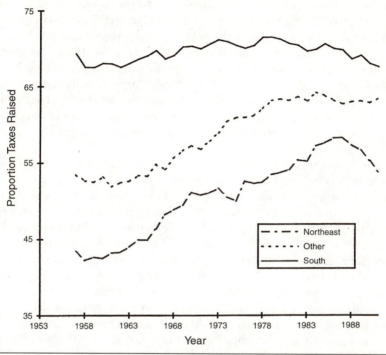

SOURCE: Data is from Advisory Commission on Intergovernmental Relations, *Significant Features of Fiscal Federalism* (Washington, D.C.: U.S. Government Printing Office), various years; and U.S. Bureau of the Census, *Government Finances,* GF-5 Series (Washington, D.C.: U.S. Government Printing Office), various years.

not the usual case, however. The typical pattern is for state government to acquire more revenue. The interesting question is how state government acquires greater revenue. It may occur without an explicit decision to raise revenue. If a state has a progressive income tax and also uses the sales tax, increases in personal income and sales activity in the state will gradually bring in more state revenue without any explicit decision to increase revenue. It just appears, and there may be no significant political issue or battle surrounding the change, aside from conservative grumblings about the growing size of government. Change would be incremental, gradual, and sustained. On the other hand, increasing the role of the state may involve explicit decisions to make a significant change in tax rates. Change may be a product of prominent debate that results in relatively abrupt increases in the state role.

The evidence suggests that the latter explanation prevails. There are few detailed studies of decision processes that alter the role of state governments, but we can track the results of decisions over time to assess what patterns of change have prevailed. That evidence indicates that when a significant increase in the role of state government has occurred since 1950, it has usually come about because of several large single-year increases. Those states that took on a significantly greater role since 1950 are ones that experienced two or three large single-year increases in state tax raising (Stonecash 1986: 195–197). It does not appear that states take on a larger role simply because of an incremental increase of revenue as their economy grows. Something more significant, and politically interesting, occurs.

Case studies provide a means to understand why changes occur. Since 1953, New Jersey and Connecticut have experienced significant change. State government has increased its tax effort relative to local governments. This produced a reversal in the relative roles of the state and local governments. In 1953 the state of New Jersey raised 25.9 percent of tax revenue; by 1992 it was 56.0 percent. Local governments received 8.7 percent of their general revenue from the state in 1953; by 1992 this percent was at 35.8. The same sort of transition took place in Connecticut. These changes came about because state politicians decided to raise state taxes. The important question is why this transition took place.

The decision to raise taxes is a difficult one for politicians. Increased taxes are generally disliked by the public, and enacting them costs votes (Kone and Winters 1993). There must be a reason for advocating tax hikes. Taxes produce revenue, which allows politicians to provide more direct services or more state aid. Who is inclined to impose taxes and want to have the state do more? Our general presumption is that Democrats are more likely to do this. Susan Hansen assessed the adoption of income and sales taxes in the states and found that Democrats were more likely than Republicans to have been in power when taxes were adopted (Hansen 1983: 154–156).

Partisanship is often very important in these decisions, but there are reasons to be careful in forming expectations about the relationship between parties and tax enactments. We generally presume that Democrats have a constituency of middle- to lower-income individuals and communities that need state programs (welfare, Medicaid, job training, subsidies to state universities, etc.) and state aid (for schools and property tax relief). However, Democrats do not always have an electoral base that fits our expectations. Democrats may prefer programs that need revenue, but they may be significantly constrained by fears about the consequences of voting to raise taxes. The inclination to raise taxes is likely to be contingent on several conditions. Democrats must have a clear constituency base that will benefit from any programs funded by the taxes (Key 1949; Jennings 1977, 1979; Stonecash 1987–88). If the electoral base of the Democratic party is diverse and some constituents will be net losers, then the party is less likely to be supportive of greater taxes (Stonecash 1995b: chapter 5). Even if there is an inclination to increase revenue, there often must be some precipitating "crisis" that requires a decision. If state revenue is declining because of a recession, politicians must decide to cut services or raise taxes. Federal programs may be available, but the state may have to provide matching revenue. The courts may have ruled that the existing school finance system is unconstitutional. All these situations create pressure to increase taxes. If Democrats have the relevant constituency base, they are more likely than Republicans to enact taxes that increase the role of the state.

New Jersey provides an example of the diversity of situations that prompt change. The Democrats held power for three periods from 1950 to 1994. Tax increases did not occur every year that Democrats held power. But every tax increase that did occur took place when Democrats were in power. After the 1965 elections, the Democrats held both houses of the legislature and the governorship for the first time since the early 1900s. The Democratic governor claimed that this constituted a mandate for government to do more. After a lengthy battle, a sales tax was enacted. The Democrats next held power from 1974 to 1985. The state supreme court ruled in 1974 that the school financing inequities were unconstitutional. After a prolonged stalemate with the courts about whether the schools could continue with the existing system, the legislature and the governor agreed to adopt a state income tax. Finally, after the 1989 election, the Democrats again gained control over government. The national recession produced declining tax revenues and persistent budget deficits. The courts once again ruled that the school finance situation was unconstitutional. The Democrats responded by increasing the sales tax and imposing a surcharge on the income tax for wealthier individuals.

Figure 5.5 presents the consequences of these decisions. State tax effort (or taxes as a percent of personal income) increased significantly in 1966, 1976, and 1991. Those increases were not repealed, and by 1992 the state was playing a much greater role than forty years prior. Each tax increase was brought about by different circumstances, but in each case it was Democrats who pushed through the changes.

Although Democrats were the enactors of change in New Jersey, that is not always the case. Sometimes coalitions cut across party lines. The role of the state has increased in Connecticut since 1950. The state enacted several significant increases in state taxes while local taxes remained relatively stable over time. That resulted in the state playing a greater role in raising taxes and providing state aid. The changing role of state govern-

FIGURE 5.5   State and Local Tax Effort in New Jersey, 1950–1992

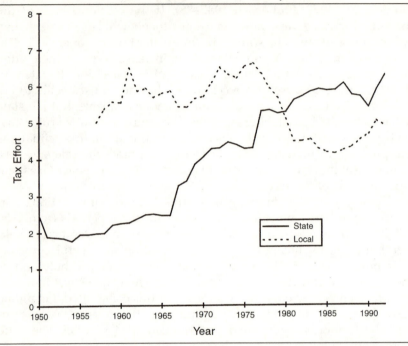

SOURCE: Data is from Advisory Commission on Intergovernmental Relations, *Significant Features of Fiscal Federalism* (Washington, D.C.: U.S. Government Printing Office), various years; and U.S. Bureau of the Census, *Government Finances*, GF-5 Series (Washington, D.C.: U.S. Government Printing Office), various years.

ment in Connecticut is shown in Figure 5.6. The increases in state taxes, however, were not always enacted by Democrats. In 1961 a Republican governor worked with a legislature divided between two parties to enact a small state tax increase. In 1971 a Republican governor facing a budget shortfall worked with a Democratic legislature to enact an increase in the sales tax. In 1991 Lowell Weicker, a Republican elected as an Independent, also faced a budget shortfall. He drew upon Democratic votes in the legislature to enact an income tax (Murphy 1992: 70).

Republicans can play a role in creating a greater state role when their party has a constituency base that will benefit from the programs that require greater funding. In Connecticut some Republican governors did well in moderate, Democratic areas. When faced with budget shortfalls, they found it logical to work with Democrats to enact taxes that allowed them to maintain existing state programs. This also has occurred in New York over the last thirty years (Stonecash 1992).

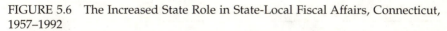

FIGURE 5.6   The Increased State Role in State-Local Fiscal Affairs, Connecticut, 1957–1992

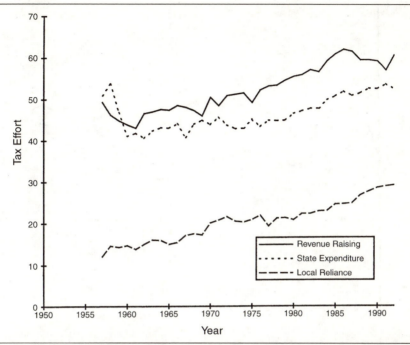

SOURCE: Data is from Advisory Commission on Intergovernmental Relations, *Significant Features of Fiscal Federalism* (Washington, D.C.: U.S. Government Printing Office), various years; and U.S. Bureau of the Census, *Government Finances*, GF-5 Series (Washington, D.C.: U.S. Government Printing Office), various years.

There are many states where change has not occurred over time. In Texas there has been considerable pressure for the state to play a greater role, but that pressure has not resulted in change. Beginning with *San Antonio v. Rodriguez* in 1969, Texas courts have ruled with various degrees of firmness that the school finance situation is unconstitutional. Texas has no state income tax and critics of the system argue that the only way to reach the level of funding necessary to correct the problem is to impose an income tax. The income tax is deeply opposed by many groups in Texas, however, and it has been impossible to put together a coalition in the legislature to enact an income tax. The Democratic party holds the majority in the legislature, but it contains many conservatives who oppose adopting an income tax.

Consequently the role of the state has changed very little in recent decades in Texas. Figure 5.7 presents state and local tax effort in Texas since

FIGURE 5.7   State and Local Tax Effort in Texas, 1957–1992

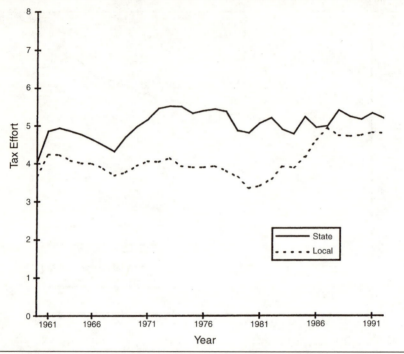

SOURCE: Data is from Advisory Commission on Intergovernmental Relations, *Significant Features of Fiscal Federalism* (Washington, D.C.: U.S. Government Printing Office), various years; and U.S. Bureau of the Census, *Government Finances*, GF-5 Series (Washington, D.C.: U.S. Government Printing Office), various years.

1957. There has been little change over time. Despite considerable pressure for the state to assume a greater role in providing aid for the schools, there is no political coalition cohesive enough to enact the necessary taxes.

Diversity in State Roles Across the Country

States have come to play a greater role across the country. The largest increases have been among states that were once most decentralized. As a result, states are now more alike than they were in 1950. States have not all become the same, however. There is still considerable diversity among the states in the role state governments play (Stonecash 1983; Brizius 1989). States differ in how much they mandate and in how much they raise revenue and provide state aid to local governments. Figure 5.8 presents the distribution of state positions in 1991 for the percent of tax rev-

FIGURE 5.8   Diversity of State Fiscal Centralization Patterns, Local Reliance and Revenue Raising, 1991

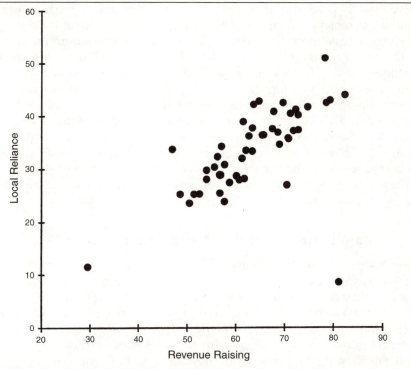

SOURCE: Data is from Advisory Commission on Intergovernmental Relations, *Significant Features of Fiscal Federalism* (Washington, D.C.: U.S. Government Printing Office), various years; and U.S. Bureau of the Census, *Government Finances*, GF-5 Series (Washington, D.C.: U.S. Government Printing Office), various years.

enue raised by the state and the percent of local revenue provided by the state government.

There is considerable variation in the role of state government in state-local fiscal responsibilities and in the degree of interdependency between the two levels. At one extreme, the state of New Hampshire raises less than 30 percent of tax revenue and local governments receive only 10 percent of their revenue from the state. The political process has made it difficult for advocates of greater state taxes to have much success in the state (Winters 1980). The state has even considered abolishing uniform state education requirements so that there will be less of a basis for any school finance lawsuits contending the state is not fulfilling its obligations to implement those standards (Celis 1992b).

At the other extreme are states such as Delaware and Arizona where the state raises 75 percent of all tax revenues, and local governments receive over 40 percent of their revenues from state aid. In these cases the state has extensive interaction with local governments about fiscal issues. In some states almost 50 percent of local revenue comes from the state.

There is no certainty that all states will become similar. Each state has a unique political history and a different political alignment of opponents who object to a greater state role. In states such as Texas and New Hampshire, change will require overcoming the strong opposition to the income tax. That will not be easy. In New York many efforts to expand the role of state government are blocked because residents outside New York City do not want to pick up the obligations of the city. That is unlikely to change. Although there has been movement toward states playing a greater role, the steps in that direction involve difficult political battles within each state.

State Politics and the Distribution of Local Aid

Over time, state and local finances have become more intertwined. States have always had control over local finances, but now there is the additional connection of extensive state aid to localities. This fiscal interdependency has drawn state and local governments together and created considerable political interdependency. Much of state politics is now devoted to questions of whether state mandates should be eased, whether state aid should be increased, and how aid should be increased.

The distribution of aid has become the focus of a particularly significant debate. Local governments have become more dependent at a time when questions about inequities among local tax bases and inequities of school expenditures have become major issues. There has been a gradual rise in the belief that socioeconomic environments have a significant effect on individuals, and inequalities among schools have become the most visible reflection of inequalities in backgrounds (Kozol 1991). These shifts affect political debates about the distribution of state aid to schools. Those in poorer districts are adamant about the need for more state aid. At the same time, continuing "white flight" has increased class and racial segregation, making equity issues more prominent. The interventions of the courts have pushed this along in ways not expected thirty years ago (Fulton and Long 1993). Groups have challenged state aid on the grounds that aid levels are inadequate and on the basis that the distribution of aid is inequitable. The courts have accepted many of these challenges and rejected existing finance arrangements (Suro 1990; Celis 1992b). In some states, such as Michigan, politicians, anticipating a battle over school finance because of serious inequities, eliminated most financing through the property tax and presented the electorate with alternative state financing systems using the sales or income tax (Vergari 1994).

These battles over state aid will continue as a fundamental feature of state-local interactions. Access to state aid has become very important to local governments. As the federal government has reduced its commitment to local governments, many states have increased their support. Unequal tax bases, changing beliefs about the need for equity in school opportunities, and the use of the courts to pursue such issues mean that state politicians cannot avoid dealing with aid issues. States and their local governments will remain intertwined.

6

Partners for Growth: State and Local Relations in Economic Development

Peter Eisinger

State government intervention in the market economy can be traced back to the beginning of the Republic, when in the first few post-Revolutionary decades Massachusetts and several other young states provided public subsidies to encourage the growth of glass-making, barrel production, and other infant industries. But this sort of active government economic role quickly fell out of fashion. For much of the nineteenth century until the Great Depression of the 1930s, state governments left decisions about how and where to invest capital almost entirely to private entrepreneurs. That the state and its localities should have a major and continuing responsibility for fostering and shaping their economies is really a late-twentieth-century notion. It is true that states in the depressed South began in the 1930s to use state money to lure industrial firms from more prosperous states, but it was not until the 1970s and 1980s that the state and local role in economic development became universal, complex, and intense.

Explaining State Economic Intervention

The convergence of several different factors in these years impelled subnational governments to take a more active role in this policy domain. Economic development, understood as government efforts designed to encourage private business investment and the creation of jobs, became a major state and local function as a result of postwar interregional population and capital shifts, sharp changes in the system of federal assistance to state and local governments, and the emergence of the international market system.

A great internal migration from east to west and north to south began in earnest after World War II, as workers flocked to the new defense, energy, and space plants located in the Sun Belt. With the spread of air conditioning and the construction of the interstate highway system, the South and Southwest became attractive to northern industrial firms seeking cheaper labor markets and to workers and retirees in search of warmer climates. Whereas in 1950 more than half (57 percent) the population of the United States lived in the Northeast and the Midwest, by 1995 the proportion in those regions had fallen to 43 percent.

This domestic migration was both a stimulus and response to regional economic growth patterns. Workers tend to migrate to areas where employment is expanding, and firms tend to move to be nearer to growing markets. In the early 1960s four of the five top states that attracted the most new manufacturing plants and corporate headquarters were in the North. By 1993 the pattern was reversed: With the exception of Ohio, the top states were all in the South or West (Venable 1994: 13).

These locational shifts of capital and population meant that as some states gained, others lost or grew more slowly. As the interstate competition for firms and workers heated up, both the gainers and the losers came to believe that policy initiatives could either maintain their high growth rates or reverse their losses.[1] Low state taxes, local tax abatements (relief from property taxes), low-interest capital, cheap land in state-subsidized industrial parks, and other incentives were seen as keys to a state's economic fortunes. Economic development policy became, then, both the means to attract and to retain the industrial and commercial activity that made for a vibrant state economy.

State efforts to foster their economies received additional impetus when federal intergovernmental aid began to decline at the end of the Carter presidency. The contraction of the system of support for subnational governments that had grown steadily since the Great Depression meant that states and their localities were suddenly faced with the need to develop unaccustomed habits of fiscal self-reliance. Between 1978, the peak year of federal intergovernmental fiscal assistance, and 1984, the end of the first Reagan term in the White House, the real value of federal aid to state and local government declined by more than 17 percent. The cuts were especially sharp for aid targeted at cities. In the dozen years after 1981, cities lost entirely Urban Development Action Grants and General Revenue Sharing. They saw Economic Development Administration Grants decline by 200 percent, mass transit aid by 100 percent, and Community Development Block Grants by more than 50 percent.[2]

Faced with declining revenues from Washington, state and local officials concluded that one way to survive in the new fiscal climate was to expand their own local tax bases. Economic development initiatives seemed to offer the possibility of doing just that: As new firms relocated to the state or formed there in response to state business incentives, the property tax base would grow, and existing property in areas undergoing economic expansion would increase in value. Officials could also expect new corporate income tax revenues to flow into the state coffers (if the state had a corporate income tax), as well as new personal income and sales tax revenue from the new workers. Thus, the surge of state and local economic development activity in the 1980s in particular can be seen as an effort to offset losses of federal aid.

Even as the federal system began to contract, state officials became conscious of a third set of forces that seemed to make active government intervention in the market a necessity: American firms and workers were increasingly becoming part of a world economic system and thus subject to its competitive strains. As traditional American industries declined in the face of imported goods or moved overseas to take advantage of cheaper labor, it became apparent that both American firms and workers faced the unaccustomed challenge of foreign competition. The only way to prosper in this contest was to develop an American comparative advantage: Businesses had to produce a steady stream of new and sophisticated products and services, and workers had to acquire the most advanced skills.

State and local officials became convinced that firms and workers could not succeed in this competitiveness-innovation-training nexus alone. The required investment of resources is not only high but the outcomes are uncertain. Government could help by encouraging basic research and development in private firms, subsidizing product innovation, prodding businesses to take advantage of new markets opening up abroad, and helping workers gain the new job skills needed in the new competitive economic order through training and education.

To summarize, state and local governments came to see themselves as stewards of their economies in a world where other states and cities—and indeed, other countries—were their competitors. Only by attracting, retaining, and strengthening business firms and upgrading workers could the vitality of the state's economy be ensured. It was in this context that economic development emerged as a major state and local government function.

The State Role in Economic Development

The economic development function at the subnational level begins as a partnership between state and local governments in which the state is clearly the dominant partner. State government's role is to make basic strategic choices to guide state and local efforts to encourage investment, to establish elements of the business climate such as the tax and regulatory system, and to provide specific development assistance and incentives. Within this framework, state and local governments, sometimes acting independently but often acting together, strike deals with business firms and entrepreneurs, creating public-private partnerships. Such partnerships are the principal vehicles for actually carrying out economic development projects. Their presumed virtue is that they unite the authority and resources of government with the managerial skills, efficiency, risk taking, and innovation thought to characterize the business world. In each case the objective is to elicit private investment that presumably would not have taken place in the state without government assistance. The expectation is that such investment—in a plant, an office complex, a new product—will ultimately lead to the creation or retention of jobs and a general increase in the economic well-being of the people of the state.

The idea that states could make a conscious strategic choice about how to pursue economic development dates only to the advent of state strategic planning in the early 1980s. Prior to the emergence of planning most states simply assumed that the way to grow economically was to recruit any footloose business concern. Today, nearly every state has a strategic economic development plan, and state officials understand that the choices they must make are complex.

Typically the product of a gubernatorial commission or development agency task force,[3] strategic plans assess the state's economic strengths and weaknesses, set goals, and offer a plan for using public and private resources to exploit the advantages. It was in the early period of strategic planning that economic development officials began to understand that they face a basic choice between seeking to attract existing industry from other states or nurturing homegrown firms and entrepreneurs. Yet even as most states embraced the latter "entrepreneurial" strategy (Eisinger 1988), there were other important but less fundamental strategic choices to consider.

Strategic planning reports tend in many respects to resemble one another these days. Most of them pledge to improve the quality of the workforce, help state firms compete in world markets, assist new small businesses, promote advanced technologies as industries of the future, and modernize aging manufacturing operations. But the evolution of strategic planning illustrates how states have confronted some key issues. In the first generation of strategic plans, for example, much attention was devoted to restructuring the tax system, a strategy designed to minimize the costs of doing business in the state.[4] In contrast, the present generation of strategic plans tends to worry less about taxes than about identifying and assisting key industrial sectors. Illinois, for example, seeks to target twelve industries, including coal mining, food processing, and biomedical services, for special state attention (Illinois Dept. of Commerce and Community Affairs 1992). To help firms in these targeted industries, the plan rejects cost minimization and proposes instead expanding vocational training for occupations needed in these industries and providing funds for technology development. Other examples of industry targeting strategies are contained in the plans of states as diverse as Arizona, New York, and Iowa.

If cost minimization through low taxes is no longer a primary element of most state economic development strategies, the tax structure is still one of several important aspects of the state's general business climate. At the very least, state officials seek to bring tax rates into line with those of neighboring states. But there is a continuing temptation in some states to lower taxes: Recent research has shown that a 10 percent state tax reduction may in the long run increase business activity in the state by as much as 2.5 percent, as long as the quality of basic services is maintained (Bartik 1991: 205). Other aspects of the business climate are important, too. States seek to create fertile ground for business growth by providing modern transportation infrastructure and a reasonable regulatory climate. Also crucial to a state's economic prospects is its system of vocational and university education. Paul Brace (1993: 39–40) recounts how Arizona learned the importance of education investment the hard way when it lost out in the competition for a major national microelectronics consortium because it had not developed top-quality engineering programs in its universities. Of course, providing good services and high-quality amenities is rarely possible if the state also aims to keep taxes at their lowest levels. States thus face a basic dilemma in crafting tax and expenditure policy.

A third element of the basic economic development framework within which state and local government intervention in the economy takes place is the direct financial expenditures the state makes to fund economic development incentives and the array of specific incentives that the state permits local governments to offer. Some state funds are granted to localities for various development purposes. A survey of municipalities over 2,500 found that about 40 percent of these communities, both big and small, relied to some degree on state grants-in-aid for economic development purposes. State assistance was the second most frequently cited source of money for development after locally raised general revenue. More communities received state aid for economic development than got federal grants or resorted to various forms of borrowing for that purpose (Prager et al. 1995).

Other state expenditures for economic development go directly to business firms and entrepreneurs. This is spent in the form of inexpensive debt financing, export assistance, venture funding, incubator grants, customized job training grants, land acquisition and clearance subsidies, manufacturing modernization assistance, and grants for research and product development in various high-tech industries. Sometimes, however, the state provides no funds for these incentives but simply enables local governments to offer them using their own funds. Two common examples are property tax abatements and tax increment financing.[5]

Development incentives have proliferated steadily (Venable and Coffee 1993). Data compiled by the Council of State Governments track the number of states offering some 31 different tax and financial incentives. If each of the fifty states offered all 31 incentives, the total possible number would be 1,550. In 1984 the fifty states in fact offered a total of 842 incentives, producing a ratio of the number of actual programs to the number of possible programs of 0.54; by 1993 the fifty states were offering 1,131 incentives, producing a ratio of 0.73 (Chi 1994).

The Role of Local Partners
in Economic Development

Local governments fit into this state economic development framework, composed of strategic guidance, tax and regulatory climate, and incentives, in several different ways.

1. *Passive beneficiary.* Many state economic development programs do not involve local governments at all. Economic activity subsidized by state programs may benefit the economy of those localities where the firm or entrepreneur happens to be located, but the local government has no role in providing support. Examples include state programs to provide export assistance to in-state firms, product development grants to emerging high-technology companies, and manufacturing modernization assistance to aging industrial concerns.

2. *Pass-through conduit.* Many states maintain business financing programs in which applications are initiated by the local government on behalf of a business firm. Funds are then released to the local government, which in turn passes the money through to the business. If the financial assistance comes in the form of a loan, it is typically repaid by the firm to the state. Some programs—say, for main street renewal in small towns—provide small grants that do not have to be repaid. The idea behind such programs is to decentralize to the local level the decisions about which firms to help.

3. *Junior partner.* State development agencies spend a good deal of time and effort competing with other states for large industrial investments. Often, the state will identify a local site to offer the target firm. The local government in whose jurisdiction the site lies will generally provide local resources to sweeten the incentive package offered to the target firm. In this case the local government is a junior partner with the state in the

sense that the competitive bid is initiated and largely funded by the state development agency.

Almost any large incentive package provides a good example of how local governments serve as junior partners with the state. Take Ohio's successful courtship of Honda in a series of deals from 1977 to 1990 (Marvel and Shkurti 1993). Over this period the state put up approximately $23 million in Industrial Inducement Grants for site improvements for four different Honda facilities and Ohio Industrial Training Program grants for job training assistance. The city of Marysville, the site of three of the plants, put up $4 million as its share of federal matching grants to upgrade sewer and water facilities to serve Honda. In addition, the city abated the property taxes (worth $8.5 million) on the increased value of the land for fifteen years, an incentive made possible by the passage in 1977 of special enabling legislation in the state legislature.

4. *Independent economic developer.* Finally, local governments seek to make deals with businesses and entrepreneurs without direct involvement by the state. The direct provision of incentives by local governments is most often accomplished by using tools that state law has specifically permitted: Offering abatements of local property taxes is an example. So is the common practice of issuing industrial revenue bonds under the city or county name to provide low-interest loans to private firms. States also pass enabling legislation to permit tax increment financing. In all of these cases, the public costs, which range from minimal in the case of industrial revenue bonds to quite high in the case of foregone property tax revenues, are borne by local taxpayers, not by the state.

Local governments also have some flexibility in establishing their own "micro" business climate. Although state law establishes the basic elements and parameters of the local tax system, localities still have some freedom to tailor their taxes to permit them to compete for business firms with neighboring communities (Schneider 1989). Thus, it is not unusual for property tax rates of the various communities in any given metropolitan area to range quite widely, as localities jockey to establish the most competitive mix of low taxes and good services.

The ability of local governments to operate as independent agents in the economic development arena is also bolstered by local control over certain federal dollars. Many cities use some portion of their annual Community Development Block Grant, an entitlement grant from Washington, to establish revolving loan funds to provide business financing or to build infrastructure in support of private development projects. State permission to receive and disburse federal grant money in this way is usually not required.

Finally, local governments act independently of the state when they spend their own locally raised revenue for development purposes. Municipally funded development offices, for example, may compile an inventory of available industrial sites, develop glossy marketing brochures, and finance visits by the mayor to trade shows. The city may acquire vacant land or abandoned housing that can later be sold to private developers or turned into a municipally owned industrial park. Some municipalities finance small business incubators to support fledgling firms, and others finance infrastructure—access roads, pedestrian malls, sidewalks, parking garages, sewer and water facilities, even landscaping—in support of development projects. Recent research has documented an increase by cities in the use of their own-source funds for development purposes in response to declines in the mid-1980s in federal aid (Clarke and Gaile 1992).

Economic Development at the Century's End: A Snapshot

It was common in the early 1980s, when states and cities were inventing new ways of supporting and encouraging private investment almost every week, to say that economic development was a "keystone" policy: By nurturing and growing the economy, the state would presumably ensure itself the necessary revenue by which it could accomplish all its other responsibilities. This was a period of enormous excitement and optimism about this relatively young field of public policy. As the states and their localities approach the year 2000, however, some of the ardor with which officials embraced economic development has diminished. One reason is that economic development initiatives in many cases do not appear to have produced dramatic benefits. In any event, evaluation turns out to be extremely difficult, making it hard to tell whether a program is worth keeping or not. The field of economic development thus finds itself in a state of some ferment and uncertainty.

Several trends seem to be occurring simultaneously. First of all, states are winnowing out economic development programs that they perceive to be too costly, too difficult to evaluate, or too slow in producing results. Second, there appears to be some regression to the old strategy of industrial recruitment, a trend that runs counter to the prevailing wisdom that entrepreneurial efforts to grow the indigenous economy are more effective. Third, states are hedging their bets by maintaining a basic set of entrepreneurial programs. Finally, a number of states are trying to shift to what is called a "Third Wave" strategy in which the state uses its resources not to provide subsidies for business formation or expansion but rather to help build the long-term capacity of workers, firms, and local governments.

To complicate matters, state funding of economic development has fluctuated from state to state and from year to year. In 1993, 25 percent of the states reported increasing their economic development agency budgets over the previous year, while 50 percent said they decreased them (Eisinger 1995; see also Venable and Coffee 1993). Sorting out these various trends is a challenge, but doing so provides a realistic, if complex, status report on subnational economic development at the century's end. When states began in the late 1970s to question the efficacy of industrial recruitment (which they began contemptuously to call "smokestack chasing") and to focus instead on their own local firms and entrepreneurs, the pace of program innovation and diffusion increased sharply. When one state invented a new program—say, a state-financed venture capital fund or a technology partnership—other states moved quickly to emulate it, generally without attempting to evaluate whether the program produced the desired results or not. What seemed more important at the time was being able to match a competitor state's program rather than putting into place a program whose efficacy had been proven.

After a decade or so of white-hot program invention and diffusion, states have begun a winnowing process. What seems to have encouraged states to scrutinize more closely their array of development programs was a combination of the recession during the Bush presidency, which had the effect of reducing state revenue that might otherwise have gone to innovative economic development programs, and the fact that economic development programs did not seem to have prevented states from suffering in bad economic times. Many programs came to be seen under the circumstances as too small or too risky or too hindered by long gestation periods to survive in a political environment keyed to the electoral cycle.

Public venture capital programs, in which the state provides long-term equity funding to new small businesses, are a good example. In the private venture capital world not only must investors exercise extraordinary patience while the new firm develops and then markets its product, but the risk of failure is extremely high. Furthermore, most venture firms that do survive do not produce enough jobs to make much difference in the state's economic profile. Thus, it was not surprising that there was a shakeout in state venture capital programs at the beginning of the 1990s (Eisinger 1993). A number of states have also eliminated or reduced funding for their science and technology partnership programs: According to one analyst, "Governors and legislators are demanding more evidence that university research designed to develop new technologies and products has a demonstrable impact on their states' economies" (Blumenstyk 1992: 1). Other programs, including foreign trade offices, marketing initiatives, and debt financing programs, have also been eliminated in recent years (Eisinger 1995).

Programs like these had been hastily put in place as part of an entrepreneurial strategy to replace industrial recruitment. States began to deemphasize industrial recruitment (though they never abandoned it entirely) because officials were taught that the key to growing a state economy lay with the homegrown small business sector. According to several influential studies, new, small businesses were by far the most important job generators.[6] Many of the new programs failed to produce dramatic results, however. Building an economic base on new and small businesses is a slow and incremental process at best. For the purposes of the political payoffs involved, as well perhaps even of the localized economic effects, attracting a large, well-known industrial concern to the state was far more satisfying than encouraging an obscure start-up company with a dozen employees. It was against this backdrop that state development agencies aggressively reentered the industrial recruitment sweepstakes. As Robert Guskind reported, "The practice of actively recruiting firms from other states has intensified" (Guskind 1993: 818).

It is difficult to demonstrate definitively that there has been a resurgence of industrial recruitment activity, but there are signs that suggest that this might be the case. It is significant, for example, that the size of incentive packages offered by states in the bidding wars for large companies has risen sharply in recent years. Commenting on Alabama's successful bid in 1993 for a Mercedes-Benz plant, *The Wall Street Journal* notes the state's $300 million worth of subsidies was a record package for a foreign company (*Wall Street Journal*, Nov. 24, 1993). The competition for foreign automobile plants escalated to this level from the comparatively modest $33 million incentive package offered to Nissan by the state of Tennessee in the early 1980s. Domestic companies, such as United Airlines and Sears, Roebuck, have been the beneficiaries of state and local assistance on a scale nearly as generous as the Mercedes-Benz deal (Chi 1994). The Walt Disney Company sought but finally did not take an even more munificent package of subsidies, asking communities in southern California, as well as the state, to help underwrite the expansion of Disneyland at a cost in public funds of nearly $800 million.

Data collected by the National Association of State Development Agencies bolster the impression that states are devoting more effort and resources to industrial recruitment: They show that a significant number of states not only report that they spend more development dollars on attracting existing firms than on retaining those already in the state, but that the amount spent for attraction has increased (NASDA 1988, 1990). In another national survey of state development agencies, officials were asked whether their state focused more on industrial recruitment or new style development, such as fostering small business growth, high-tech industries, and export. Although only one state said industrial recruitment was its main strategy, twenty-five of the forty-eight states that participated in the survey said they emphasized both approaches equally (Eisinger 1995).

In the same survey, however, an analysis of the sorts of new economic development programs that states had recently implemented indicated that just over half of all new programs (54 percent) fell in the new-style or entrepreneurial category. In contrast to industrial recruitment, entrepreneurial programs involve efforts to develop market opportunities for existing firms (for example, through export assistance), foster home-grown small businesses, and help local entrepreneurs start companies or develop innovative products. Only about 20 percent of the recently implemented new programs were designed to assist industrial recruitment. These figures suggest that the states have hardly abandoned the entrepreneurial strategies they developed in the strategic planning years of the 1980s. They may have winnowed out some of these programs, and they may have committed more resources than before to industrial recruitment, but they continue at the same time on an entrepreneurial course.

Industrial recruitment and entrepreneurial programs account, however, for only about three-quarters of all new programs implemented by the states in the early 1990s. The remainder are Third Wave approaches. The Third Wave is the term used in economic development policy for what in other policy arenas is called "empowerment" or "capacity building" or more simply, "investment." Government's role in Third Wave approaches is not to provide grants, but to leverage other resources by providing seed investment. Thus, whereas an entrepreneurial program might provide government subsidies to a firm to develop a new product, a Third Wave program might provide seed money for a community development corporation that would in turn find new businesses and new products in which to invest. Whereas an entrepreneurial strategy involves government in efforts to discover new markets for local firms (for example, by exploring export opportunities or by targeting technologies of the future in which innovative firms can establish a market niche), a Third Wave strategy seeks rather to underwrite the capacity of the firm to compete in its chosen markets more efficiently through the modernization of its processes and workforce.

Analytically, it is not always easy in practice to distinguish between entrepreneurial programs and Third Wave programs, but the proponents of the latter approach cite such initiatives as job training and worker education (building worker capacity), enhancing local planning capabilities (building local government capacity), industrial modernization programs (building firm capacity), and community development corporations (building community or neighborhood capacity) (Pilcher 1991; Ross and Friedman 1990).

In summary, a snapshot of state and local economic development in the mid-1990s looks more like a multimedia collage than a clear line drawing. At the same time that states are weeding out some programs, they are implementing others. Many of these new programs are squarely in the entrepreneurial tradition: They foster high-tech research, they provide equity and low-cost debt capital to small business ventures, they promote partnerships between academic researchers and business firms for the development of new products, and they help firms to break into export markets abroad. At the same time, however, most states appear to have taken up industrial recruitment again with a vengeance, despite widespread evidence that moving a firm from one state to another produces no net new job growth for the national economy. Furthermore, the increasing cost of incentives offered in such competition diverts scarce state resources from other uses, most notably education and training programs that foster human resource development. Some states posing for our late-century photographic portrait, however, have begun to craft an economic development strategy that focuses less on helping particular businesses than on investing in institutional and individual capacity.

Strains in the State-Local Partnership

As states seek to find their way in the economic development policy domain, they sometimes discover themselves at odds with their local government partners. This is not to suggest that there are chronic strains in the relationship between states and their localities in this area. For the most part, states and their local governments share a stake in a healthy state economy and work in concert to encourage private investment and growth. But the interests of local governments are by nature more insular. From a community's perspective every other municipality in the state is a competitor for investment. In a recent national survey of municipalities the most commonly cited source of competition for business investment was not other states but rather communities within the same state (Prager et al. 1995). From the state's point of view, however, intrastate competition is counterproductive, potentially driving tax rates down so low that communities cannot offer the basic services for which they are responsible or siphoning jobs out of central cities into the suburbs.[7]

Communities may also have a growth agenda that differs from the state's vision of development. Nashville officials, for example, believed that the state of Tennessee's focus on attracting manufacturing branch plants was at odds with the city's efforts to develop a service export economy (Bartik 1993). In New Orleans, local officials wanted to put their resources into tourist promotion, but Louisiana state officials thought that the route to prosperity lay in expanding the port and encouraging shipping (Meyer 1993). Sometimes, communities—or strong local interests— resist growth and development altogether, even when the state has pushed it. A broad coalition of preservationists and environmentalists successfully fought the Disney Company's plans for a historical theme park in Virginia, even though the governor and legislature had promised the company generous subsidies for the project.

Another important source of state-local tension is that some local economic development initiatives may be very costly to the state. Take the complex issue of tax increment financing (TIF). This device allows cities for a certain period of time to capture all of the additional property tax revenue generated by the increase in real estate values within a tax increment district. Overlying jurisdictions that share the property tax, principally school districts and the county, are denied their share of the tax increment. Their revenue is based on the "frozen" or predevelopment value of the property within the district. In at least nine states the state has had to make up the difference for school districts between the revenue derived from the frozen base and what the school share of the property tax would have been if it had received its proper share of the new tax increment.

In Minnesota the cost to the state of holding school districts harmless was approaching $50 million a year, yet the state had no say in the formation of TIF districts and thus no way to control the costs of school aid (Lemov 1994). In 1990 the state legislature amended the TIF law to require the community creating the TIF district to pay for the difference. Other states are imposing limitations on the creation of TIF districts, restricting their use, regulating the process by which they are established, and limiting the length of time a city can capture the entire tax increment.

In general, state-local tensions in the economic development partnership are far less common than cooperation. States believe that they stand to benefit in the long run from private investment and job creation within their borders, no matter what particular community ends up as the eventual location. Communities, with limited resources to devote to economic development, are grateful for what they can get from the state.

The Twenty-First Century

As the century comes to a close, it is evident that there is presently no single path to development on which all states and their local governments agree. Yet it is hardly far-fetched to predict that an eventual consensus will emerge among the states on the central importance of certain Third Wave notions. Within this often inchoate framework, the ideas of capacity building and investment nevertheless stand out. These are key ideas in many policy domains and at all levels of government. The injunction to help people and communities do for themselves, rather than doing for them, is attractive at the national level in both political parties.

Building the capacity of workers, businesses, and communities through education, training, modernization, and planning is a strategy well suited to a time of fiscal austerity and smaller government. It is also a strategy compatible with ideas about people taking responsibility for their lives. What better way to relieve government of some of its social welfare burdens and at the same time build a competitive economy for the future than by encouraging members of the labor force to gain the skills that will enable them and the firms they work for to carve out a place in the international marketplace? Besides, the idea of boosting the institutional capacity of local government and private actors is appealing at a time when demands on state resources for health care, law enforcement, prisons, environmental protection, higher education, and property tax relief preclude heavy investment of discretionary revenues in economic development.

If Third Wave ideas do indeed attract consensus, then the intense involvement of states and localities that marked the 1980s will give way to a certain detachment. In the realm of economic development, states and their local governments will come increasingly to serve not as funders or grantors or micromanagers or even deal makers, but as catalysts and facilitators. This is how the Third Wave policy theorists see the future: Government, they suggest, will look more like a wholesaler in the economic development domain and less like a retailer of grants and programs.

NOTES

1. There is considerable debate over the validity of this proposition, but the most plausible research finding is that state economic development efforts may slow, but not reverse, economic decline. See Lowery and Gray 1992; Brace 1993.

2. Raw data were furnished to the author by the U.S. Conference of Mayors covering the period from 1981 to 1993.

3. Occasionally, a state will contract out the development of its strategic plan to a consulting firm.

4. Tax reduction was a major theme (though not the only one) of a number of early strategic plans, including those generated in Wisconsin and Iowa in the mid-1980s. But contrast this emphasis with the following passage from Oklahoma's strategic plan of 1988: "While everyone desires low taxes, many experts believe that increased taxes in Oklahoma would help rather than impede economic development, if wisely invested in appropriate public services" (Oklahoma Department of Commerce 1994: 87).

5. Tax abatements provide temporary relief from property taxes for certain qualifying real estate projects. Tax increment financing uses the anticipated increment in value from a development project to back bonds that in turn raise capital to help finance certain aspects of the project, such as infrastructure and land clearance.

6. The belief that small firms were the primary job generators was the product mainly of work done by David Birch (1979). Subsequent research, however, has called into question the role of small business. Harrison (1994), for example,

points out that only a tiny fraction of small firms account for the employment gains made in the small business sector. The small firm share of employment has increased only modestly when the unit of analysis is individual plants but not when it is firms.

7. When businesses in communities in southeastern Wisconsin were ordered to comply with stringent federal air quality regulations, other communities in the state invited those firms to move to cities where regulations were more lenient. This led the state's governor, Tommy Thompson, to chide the would-be raiders. "Let's push to expand economically all over the state," he said, rather than pitting one region against another. *Milwaukee Sentinel,* July 12, 1994, A5.

7

The State-Local Partnership in Education

Daniel DiLeo

The terms of the partnership that governs American public education are currently undergoing their most rapid and profound transformation in over seventy years. The beginning of this century saw the emergence of a system administered by professional educators accountable in varying degrees to predominantly upper-middle-class community representatives composing school boards. The express purpose of the reformers who created the school boards was to cut them off from powerful political constituencies. As the school districts grew dramatically in size and the American population became increasingly mobile, the links between the school boards and their power bases became still more tenuous. When dissatisfaction with the schools brought the federal government, the states, education professionals, and a variety of interest groups and policy networks into the education policymaking arena, the school boards proved ill-equipped to assert their traditional authority.

With the growing inability of school boards to translate public preferences into public policy, we are seeing more and more programs initiated by the states that bypass and weaken school boards. The continuing need to provide parents with some form of leverage, both to protect their rights and to enlist them in the enterprise of education, suggests that if school boards cannot provide an adequate channel of local, and particularly parental, input, it will be necessary to develop other means of doing so. Whatever that means is, be it school-based management, parental choice, or some other mechanism, it will require a renegotiation of the terms of the state-local partnership that evolved during this century. Because it is likely to be a time of transition, the current period is an excellent time to take stock of the history of the state-local partnership, describe its present functioning, and identify a number of developments in education governance that are shaping the contours of a new partnership.

History

Shortly after the Revolution, the state of Massachusetts created school committees like one already established in Boston to exercise authority over the schools. These were separate governing bodies, distinct from general-purpose government. They were directly accountable to the state (Callahan 1975: 19). Other states followed Massachusetts's lead, creating school boards as agents of the state government, a legal status they retain to this day (Miron and Wimpelberg 1992: 158). This assertion of state control over local schools met strong resistance from defenders of parental rights and community control. Anticipating their position in today's battles over curricular standards and "academic bankruptcy," advocates of state control claimed that they were ensuring educational quality.[1] The states carried the day because of their superior constitutional status and because they provided funds that communities depended on (Miron and Wimpelberg 1992: 157, 158–159).

After creating the school boards, charging them with providing free education and giving them taxing authority, the states tended to leave the school boards alone. From time to time, one or more of the actors in the school districts would place new demands on the districts, but it was generally believed that the districts did not have the authority to take on new tasks without the express permission of the state. However, in 1874, the Supreme Court of the State of Michigan ruled that school districts possessed implied powers that could authorize them to take on new tasks, such as operating a secondary school, without the express permission of the state (Russo 1992: 6). This decision had an impact beyond Michigan's borders. It constituted a significant victory for school boards and strengthened them in relation to the states.

The end of the nineteenth century saw the rise of the Progressive movement, a development that had profound consequences for the governance of public education, especially in the cities. During this period, middle- and upper-class reformers took control of local school boards (Wirt and Kirst 1992: 112). As a result schools became standardized, dominated by professionals, insulated from publicly conducted politics, and less responsive to their communities. Although these developments were accompanied by a greater level of state involvement (Wirt and Kirst 1992: 256), they were primarily changes that occurred at the local level, not changes in state-local relations.

The trend toward greater professional control and less grassroots and parent control continued after the close of the Progressive Era. The consolidation of small school districts into larger ones proceeded steadily throughout the twentieth century. The number of school boards decreased from 127,520 in 1932 to 15,173 in 1991 (Iannaccone and Lutz 1995: 45), and the number of citizens per school board member increased from 200 in 1932 to 3,000 in 1970 (Guthrie 1974: 2), thus continuing the trend of diminishing participation of citizens, particularly nonelites, in school governance.

The rationale for these consolidations has been the achievement of economies of scale, enabling school systems to provide a greater range of services, educational programs, and facilities. Among the effects of consolidation have been decreased access for individual parents and citizens to school board members and the swallowing up of small, distinctive communities that formerly had their own school boards into larger, more heterogeneous districts. The management of these large, multiservice districts was a full-time job, requiring the attention of professional administrators, who increasingly displaced school board members as the day-to-day administrators of public education (Boyd 1992: 754; Iannaccone and Lutz 1995: 45). School boards took action only when controversial issues arose. Their principal function became the legitimation of the authority of professional administrators and educators (Wirt and Kirst 1992: 149).

The states played a significant role in the increasing domination of public schools by education professionals. In 1900, none of the states required elementary school teachers to have university degrees. By 1965, forty-five states had such a requirement (Goerty, cited in Wirt and Kirst 1992: 256). The result was that curricular content and pedagogical methods became less a function of personnel choices of local districts and more a function of increasingly nationalized professional standards.

The civil rights movement, in which demands for an end to segregated schooling played a prominent part, unraveled the myth that public education was above politics. By the mid-1960s, many groups, including teachers' unions, parents of students with special needs, and citizens demanding funding equalization, began to press their demands on the school systems (Iannaccone 1967; Wirt and Kirst 1992: 251–252). When groups did not gain satisfaction at the local level, they frequently took their demands to state and federal government. As a general pattern, state and federal governments implemented decisions they made in response to these demands by limiting the discretion of local school districts through laws, judicial decisions, and administrative regulations.

One of the new demands that had a particularly significant impact on state-local relations was the demand for educational equity. In the early part of this century, these demands led to state funding for public education (Wirt and Kirst 1992: 223). The pursuit of equal access was also central to the movement against segregation in public education that resulted in *Brown v. Board* (1954). After the Supreme Court ruled in *Milliken v. Bradley* (1974) that interdistrict busing could not be used to achieve equity in the absence of a history of de jure segregation, advocates of educational equity focused on the issue of resource inequality. Since the Supreme Court ruled in *San Antonio Independent School District v. Rodriguez* (1973) that the U.S. Constitution did not provide a right to a free education, advocates of funding equity took their cases to the state courts, where they have had mixed results (Rosmiller 1992: 513).[2] Advocates of educational equity who support state funding as a means of reducing the effects of unequal levels of district wealth have been assisted by opponents of local property taxes (Rosmiller 1992: 515). The demand for educational equity continues to play an important role in state-local relations.

In the 1970s, the American economy experienced its first prolonged period of stagnation in the postwar period. The early 1980s saw a deep recession, followed by a deteriorating balance of trade. During this time, many business leaders came to believe that a key element in improving the nation's economic outlook was to improve the productivity of the workforce. Informal networks composed of business leaders, policy academics, activists, and state government staffers coalesced around various perspectives on the problems of public education and proposals for improving it. The Reagan administration, although unwilling to take action, was more than willing to call attention to the perceived shortcomings of public education, most notably through the publication of *A Nation at Risk* by the National Commission on Excellence in Education in 1983.

In the meantime, governors and state legislators became increasingly interested in education policy because it was the largest single item in their budgets, because they saw educational improvement as a key to economic development, and because they also believed that the schools were not doing a good job. By the mid-1980s, educational improvement was the main priority of a newly strengthened National Governors' Association (Gray and Eisinger 1991: 315). Since the 1970s, governors and legislative leaders had developed the capacity to formulate and enact comprehensive legislation. The means and the motive converged. The states embarked on a dramatic and unprecedented course of education reform that continues to the present (Mazzoni 1995).

The policies that the states adopted during this period gave school district administrators control over more resources and authority to direct a broader range of activity than they ever had before. They became more powerful in relation to faculty, staff, and students as well as the larger community. However, school boards became less able to make their own choices. The states along with a variety of interest groups became increasingly capable of getting the school boards to do what they wanted. The major developments in education governance in the 1990s dramatize and contribute to a continuing power shift from the school boards to the states.

Education Governance Today

School District Governance

Due to its omission from the U.S. Constitution, education is formally a state function. Every state except Hawaii has created local agencies, called school districts, to administer that function. There are situations in which local control is an obstacle to equity, no matter how one defines it. The most egregious current examples are the grossly unequal resources expended on children living in different districts in almost every state. On the other hand, American courts and the majority of the American people hold that local control protects parental rights, community choice, and participatory democracy (Briffault 1992: 773).

There is no dispute that the states are superior to the school districts as guarantors of equity. Yet school districts can make a strong case that they are superior to the states as protectors of parental rights and community choice. To the extent that the school districts really do provide putative advantages of local control, the relationship between the states and the school districts is a truly intergovernmental relationship. To the extent that the school districts are essentially administrative rather than republican political institutions, the relationship is merely an intragovernmental one, in which political exchanges are strictly of the bureaucratic variety. If the school districts are administrative agencies rather than institutions for political representation, those who value parental rights and community control must reform the school districts or create new institutions.

The states specify the responsibilities, powers, and procedures of the school districts through constitutional provisions, legislative enactments, administrative rules, regulations, and decisions, as well as judicial verdicts and opinions (Russo 1992: 7). In New York, Maryland, Virginia, and Massachusetts, the state's control of the school systems is indirect because the municipal governments, themselves agents of the states, are in charge of the school systems (Gray and Eisinger 1991: 310).

Of the roughly 15,000 school boards in the United States today, approximately 85 percent are elective. Almost all of the elections are nonpartisan. Most school boards have five to seven members (Wirt and Kirst 1992: 110). Officially, school boards have only expressed, implied, and necessary powers, some of which the states require them to exercise, and some of which they may exercise at their discretion. In most states, these powers include the power to select textbooks, set teacher salaries, decide what extracurricular activities to offer, and make decisions about the curriculum, such as how much math or foreign language instruction to offer

(Russo 1992: 10; Gray and Eisinger 1991: 310). Other than ruling that the powers of school boards belong only to the board as a whole and can only be exercised at formal meetings, the courts have not interfered with the operations of school boards (Russo 1992).

Although the responsibilities and structures of school boards have not changed since the beginning of the century, changes in the social and political environment have undermined their capacity to fulfill their most basic task—balancing the state's pursuit of public purposes with the rights of parents and the values of local communities. The rapid rate at which Americans move from one locality to another has diminished the capacity of school boards to represent communities because many communities suffer from deep, irreconcilable cleavages between longtime residents and newcomers (Iannaccone and Lutz: 1995). Even when deep cleavages do not emerge, mobility diminishes the social cohesion of localities, making support and consensus harder to sustain. The consolidation of school districts has had similar effects. As school districts became larger and more heterogeneous over the course of this century, they became increasingly disconnected from the grassroots (Iannaccone and Lutz 1995: 45).

This has had both direct and indirect political consequences. One direct political consequence is that school boards lack the popular support, political clout, or often even the will to withstand encroachments on their powers by the state and other actors. In fact, local communities and parents are likely to appeal to other institutions, most prominently state government, to compel the school districts to comply with their preferences. An indirect political consequence is that schools find it extremely difficult to mobilize the support of communities and parents. The lack of community support is manifested in increasing local resistance to taxes and bonds for financing schools. As a result, schools have become more dependent on the states for their funding, which has tended to further undermine their autonomy.

The methods by which school districts are governed exacerbate these problems. Seeking to take politics and corruption out of school politics, the Progressives made the governance of education distinct from the governance of all other public functions. In addition, they made school board elections nonpartisan and scheduled them at times when other elections were not being held. As a result, turnout in school board elections has been very low, typically around 10 percent. Candidates and campaigns have generally not been very visible or competitive, and elections usually have not revolved around alternative policies. One study reported that only about half of school board candidates faced electoral opposition, and only half of those with opposition reported philosophical differences with their opponents (Ziegler et al. 1974).

Citizen involvement tends to be scant outside small, demographically stable, and homogeneous rural communities. Participation is episodic and is often stimulated by perceived crises such as desegregation or tax hikes (Wirt and Kirst 1992: 99–100). The low turnout and low visibility of school board elections enable the election of individuals whose primary loyalty is to narrow interests or points of view. Instead of taking the politics out of education, the Progressive reforms have muffled the voice of the larger community and amplified the voices of particular groups, including teachers, tax opponents, ideologues, and people who want to do business with the district. State and federal categorical programs contribute to this hyperpluralism by creating new groups of clients and providers who are more oriented toward discrete programs than to the community as a whole (Wirt and Kirst 1992: 22, 88).

A process that amplifies the voices of small interest groups while muffling the voice of the wider community no doubt contributes to the sizable distance between public opinion on education issues and the preferences of school board presidents. A survey conducted from November 1988 to February 1989 by the National Center for Educational Information reported the following responses: Seventy-one percent of the public and 76 percent of parents believe that they "should have the right to choose which local school their children should attend," but only 36 percent of school board presidents agreed with that statement; 45 percent of the general public believe that "parents should have more say in the curriculum," but only 16 percent of superintendents agreed; 74 percent of school board presidents, but only 39 percent of parents, believed that schools had improved in recent years. The opinions of school board presidents are substantially closer to those of school principals than they are to those of the public. This is not surprising—3 percent of the school board presidents are former principals and 20 percent are former schoolteachers (Feistritzer 1992).

In large part because other institutions are willing to encroach on the formal responsibilities of school boards, teachers and other groups often bring their demands to Congress, the courts, the state legislatures, and the schools. When those institutions accede to their demands, the real power of school boards is diminished even further (Wirt and Kirst 1992: 19, 89). On curricular issues, school boards are also constrained by textbook publishers, companies providing standardized testing services, and the norms and standards of educators and other professionals (Boyd 1992: 754).

The school districts remain important, in fact more important than ever, as administrative units. They have considerable discretion over the implementation of an increasing volume of policy originating in the state capitals and Washington D.C. As political institutions, however, capable of autonomous translation of demands and supports generated outside the political system into policies, school boards are becoming less significant (Wirt and Kirst 1992: 126). The combination of growing administrative capacity and diminishing capacity as institutions of representative governance explains the growing domination of school boards by their superintendents.

State Governance of Education

The institution charged with overseeing the supervision of public education in an entire state on behalf of the legislature is the state board of education (Russo 1992: 8).[3] Thirty-four states also have a state department of education, which is called the Department of Public Instruction in some states. It carries out responsibilities assigned to it by the state board of education, the legislature, and the chief state school officer, usually the secretary of education or the superintendent of public instruction.

The chief state school officer and the state board of education are selected in a variety of ways across the states (Russo 1992). The states with elected chief state school officers tend to have school systems that are more centralized and tend to allocate a greater proportion of their education resources to teacher compensation (DiLeo 1991). Typically, the state departments of education are involved in planning, implementing, and evaluating instructional programs, establishing high school graduation requirements, defining teacher certification requirements, and compiling and analyzing a broad range of data related to education (Russo 1992: 8). School district administrators usually have stronger working relationships with state boards of education, state departments of education, and chief state school officers than they do with governors and legislatures (Fuhrman and Elmore 1994: 61).

In general, state law, if not administrative regulation, requires a minimum number of annual school days, the teaching of certain courses, and a certain minimum amount of local expenditure. Many of these requirements are unfunded mandates (Pipho 1995: 511). In addition to mandates of this type, states influence the activity of school districts by providing incentives to exceed certain minimums of service, establishing requirements to organize their administration in particular fashions, and encouraging the use of certain preferred methods of administration and instruction (Wirt and Kirst 1992: 257).

In recent years, as state legislatures and governors' staffs have become more specialized and professional, they have developed some expertise, or at least intense interest, in education policy. The rising concern with education policy has been stimulated by the growing financial stake of the states in the schools (Fuhrman and Elmore 1990: 84), as well as the widespread impression that quality and equity require state intervention. As they have become more concerned with education, state officials have involved themselves in the details of finances, testing, and other matters previously left to the school boards and education professionals (Wirt and Kirst 1992: 284). They have gone well beyond their previous concerns with the welfare of targeted groups, such as disabled students, and limited functions, such as civics education. Now state officials concern themselves with the central activities of education that affect all students, issues such as what to teach, how to teach, and who should teach (Wirt and Kirst 1992: 22).

The areas in which state influence has grown the most have been in education finance, accountability, meeting the needs of students with special needs, establishing and measuring attainment of academic standards, and the administration of federal categorical grant programs (Wirt and Kirst 1992: 299). States also have their own categorical programs. Some state and federal categorical programs deal directly with school officials, avoiding direct participation by the school board and district level administrators (Wirt and Kirst 1992: 187). When this happens, the state is effectively bypassing the local institutions of representative governance, the school boards.

This is not to say that local interests have no policy input. Local interests influence the implementation and sometimes the content of state and federal policies by way of their influence on the professional educators and administrators in the schools and the district offices. For example, school-based management was a policy that originated with professionals at the school and district level before gaining popularity in the states (Fuhrman and Elmore 1990: 93). In addition, statewide associations of local school boards occasionally have a significant direct influence on education policymaking at the state level (Marshall, Mitchell, and Wirt 1989: 18). Formed in the 1970s to help individual school boards confront teachers' associations on collective bargaining issues, the statewide school board associations often have highly capable research and lobbying staffs (Wirt and Kirst 1992: 278–279). A study of six states in different regions of the country found that the statewide school board association was the most influential actor in education policy in Arizona. At the time of the study, the governor of Arizona was politically weaker than the governors of the other states, so the relative strength of the local school boards in state politics may have been a consequence of a political vacuum. Arizona was also the most conservative state in the study and the state with the least influential state teachers' organization (Marshall, Mitchell, and Wirt 1989: 30). In general, however, the school board associations have less influence on state policymaking than the teachers' organizations (Marshall, Mitchell, and Wirt 1989: 18).

Oftentimes, particular school districts, especially those in urban areas, can be more effective than statewide school board associations because their priorities are more focused (Boyd 1987, cited in Wirt and Kirst 1992: 276–277). One particularly valuable political resource for school boards is their ability to form close relationships with their local state representatives (Wirt and Kirst 1992: 277). However, these channels of school board participation in the intergovernmental system are the exception. Most of the intergovernmental interaction is among bureaucrats, primarily district superintendents and other government officials. More school board presidents reported spending "too little time" on interaction with representatives of other governments than on any other activity (Feistritzer 1992: 135).

The Federal Impact on State-Local Relations

The impact of the federal government on state-local relations has been to assign states the tasks of supervising school districts and building the capacity of the states to conduct that supervision. President Clinton's Goals 2000: Educate America Act is one recent example of many federal initiatives that fit this pattern. It calls on states to develop curricular standards for all districts and allocates funds to subsidize the development of those standards (Bowman and Pagano 1994: 9). With federal encouragement, the states are also urging districts to adopt tougher teacher certification standards (Fuhrman 1994b: 92). The pattern of federal action leading to a greater state role is a well-established one. Many years before the present reform era, a significant enhancement of the state departments of education as agencies capable of monitoring local activity was accomplished through Title V of the Elementary and Secondary Education Act and Chapter 2 of the Education Consolidation and Improvement Act (Fuhrman and Elmore 1990, 84).

The Impact of Policy Networks on State-Local Relations

As in other policy areas, networks linking public officials, their staffs, interest group advocates, and academics have played an increasingly significant role in deciding how to run the schools. These networks are national and even international in scope. In the 1970s they played an important role in promoting equity and categorical programs for students with special needs (Kirst and Meister 1983). More recently, they have promoted school choice, curricular standards, school-based management, and charter schools. In general, they are motivated by the pursuit of educational quality (Plank and Boyd 1994). Along with state and federal officials, these policy networks are now taking part in decisions about the purposes and strategies of education, decisions that once were left to local school boards.

As the states, the federal government, and policy networks have become increasingly active in making policy, the volume of policy has increased. The number of programs that the school districts have to administer, the complexity and extensiveness of the records they have to keep, the number of demands they must accommodate, and the quantity of resources they must manage have all grown dramatically. Consequently, district administrators have more responsibility and more opportunities to exercise discretion than ever (Fuhrman and Elmore 1990). On the other hand, school boards are becoming irrelevant. They are less capable than ever of providing fora for public deliberations that culminate in authoritative decisions because those decisions are made by professionals or by citizens participating in other political institutions.

Because school boards are experiencing substantial difficulties in acting as institutions of representative governance, many people doubt that they can protect parental rights and community choice. Various strategies for school improvement are being developed and implemented. So far, most of these strategies have fallen into two categories. One category consists of strategies that seek to enhance parental rights or community control, generally by defining them in ways that obviate the need for politically effective school boards. Another category consists of reforms that seek to improve the quality of education without enhancing parental rights or community control, except by recognizing parents' right to quality education for their children and by redefining community control as control by locally based professionals. So far, very few strategies for education reform have called for strengthened school boards (Danzberger 1992).

Education Reform and Its Impact on State-Local Relations

The First Wave

Over the past fifteen years, the states have launched two successive "waves" of education reform (Firestone, Fuhrman, and Kirst 1991, but see Wirt and Kirst 1992: 307–308). The first wave of state-led education reform began in the South, where state government has traditionally played the most prominent role in education (Mazzoni 1995: 56). These reforms were essentially bureaucratic in nature (Boyd 1992: 755). Forty-five states increased courses required for graduation, twenty increased instructional time, and thirty-four initiated state-supported academic enrichment programs (Doyle and Hartle 1985, cited in Wirt and Gove 1990: 466; Fuhrman 1994a: 31). Proposals such as merit pay and career ladders met with such strong resistance from teachers' unions that they were generally not enacted, not implemented, or did not survive (Boyd 1992: 757; Wirt and Kirst

1992: 308–309). For the most part, the reforms constituted an "intensification" of state educational effort: more time, more money, more planning, more supervision (Firestone, Fuhrman, and Kirst 1991). These reforms tended to require the augmentation of state and local bureaucracies. During this period, the legislatures created new categorical programs for children with special needs (Fuhrman 1994a: 32), which also had the effect of enhancing state and local bureaucracies (Fuhrman and Elmore 1994: 62).

Although most states were swept up in this wave, states with traditions of large-scale, state-directed reform, such as Florida, led the way. States that lacked such a tradition, such as Pennsylvania, were less active (Wirt and Kirst 1992: 304). As noted above, the South, with its tradition of predominance of state over local control, led the country in this first wave of education reform. The relative poverty and historic underfunding of school systems of the South and the relatively rapid economic growth of that region over the past generation probably contributed to that region's leadership role during this phase of education reform.

School boards were essentially ignored during this phase. The unmistakable implication was that, if anything, school boards were contributing to the perceived failures of American education. Reformers felt that state mandates were necessary to force the school boards to support education reform (Wirt and Kirst 1992: 160). For the most part the school boards implemented the reforms willingly, possibly because the governors and others worked at selling the reforms to the public, and possibly because these reforms were so clear that they were easy to implement and hard to avoid (Boyd 1992: 757; Fuhrman 1994a: 38). In any event, the cooperation of the school districts was often due to the support of administrators, not elected school board members, perhaps because some of the state-initiated reforms of the 1980s, such as new teacher salary schedules, encroached on turf previously controlled by school districts (Fuhrman and Elmore 1994: 63).

The trends do not look favorable for the political future of school districts. Evidence is accumulating that the "top-down" reforms of the first wave accomplished their goals (Smith 1994; Boyd 1992). This indicates that to some extent it is possible to improve learning outcomes measured in ways determined by the state without much input from local communities or parents. If that is the case, we can expect continuing pressure on the states to assert their authority, with or without the support of local school boards.

The Second Wave

The states initiated a second wave of education reforms in the mid-1980s. As was the case with the first wave, widely circulated reports played a significant role in setting the stage. This time, it was *A Nation Prepared*

(1986) by the Carnegie Commission and *Time for Results* (1986) by the National Governors' Association. The reforms of the second wave differed from those of the first in that they emphasized the autonomy of local education professionals. They were consistent with the philosophy of "reinventing government" articulated by David Osborne and Theodore Gaebler (1992), which emphasized responsive, entrepreneurial government, flat organizations, and changing incentive structures. In fact, most of the proposals that governors have made for reinventing government have been made in the area of education policy (Durning 1995). The reduction of regulations for schools in exchange for more extensive reporting on measures of outcomes and accountability for achieving explicit goals was an important part of the National Governors' Association report (Wirt and Kirst 1992: 315). The commitment of the National Governors' Association to explicit goals eventually resulted in George Bush's adoption of six education goals in 1989 (Mazzoni 1995: 66). Bill Clinton's acceptance of Bush's education goals and his adoption of two more was not surprising in view of the significant role he played in formulating them as a leader of the National Governors' Association. Like the reforms of the first wave, several of the second wave reforms, most notably public school choice, school-based management, and outcomes-based education, received crucial support from policy-issue networks (Mazzoni 1995: 67).

As these quality-oriented waves of reforms washed over the states, the struggle for equity continued. Although it has other meanings (Rosmiller 1992: 513), the two primary senses of educational equity are an equal level of funding devoted to each child's education and equal satisfaction of students' basic needs. The latter interpretation can mean spending more resources on students whose basic needs are greater, such as disabled children and at-risk children (Wirt and Kirst 1992: 336). "At-risk" children are usually defined as children with limited English proficiency, African-American or Hispanic or Native American children, and children with one-parent or low-income households. Funding for special needs populations is usually provided through categorical programs. Funding equality is the basic goal of what is known as finance reform.

Finance Reform

A movement to reform school finances so as to make funding more equal for all students came to the fore in the 1970s, but it got a second wind in the 1990s (Wirt and Kirst 1992: 337). Against a backdrop of steadily and dramatically increasing outlays on public education (Odden 1992: 457), dozens of lawsuits on behalf of children in poor school districts have played a significant role in reducing the local share of education spending and increasing the state share.[4] Plaintiffs in these lawsuits generally claim that the equal protection clause of the 14th Amendment and clauses in their state constitutions mandating a system of free education are violated by funding systems that tie per pupil expenditures to district wealth rather than state wealth (Odden 1992: 456). The decisions in these cases usually hinge on how the court interprets the relevant education clause in the state's constitution and whether it decides that education is a constitutionally protected "fundamental interest" (Rosmiller 1992: 514). So far, the courts have not clearly established whether the violations lie in the variations in the tax bases of the respective districts, in which case the state would allow localities to decide to spend less by taxing less, or in the variation in per pupil spending, which could well require the state to take over all funding (Odden 1992: 456).

The first funding equalization case brought to a state supreme court was *Serrano v. Priest,* which was heard by the California Supreme Court in 1971 (Briffault 1992: 810). Other states in which courts have decided in favor of funding equalization include New Jersey, Kansas, Connecticut, West Virginia, Arkansas, Wyoming, Washington, Montana, Kentucky, and Texas. States in which the courts upheld their states' funding systems include New York, Maryland, Oklahoma, Pennsylvania, North Carolina, Louisiana, South Carolina, Ohio, Wisconsin, Arizona, Michigan, Idaho, Georgia, Colorado, and Oregon (Rosmiller 1992: 513).

Court decisions did not necessarily result in immediate equalization of funding. In Texas, for example, the court found that funding system reforms made by the legislature in response to an earlier ruling were insufficient. New Jersey's supreme court went far beyond requiring funding equalization. By requiring that the state provide "equal opportunity" rather than equal funding for its students, the state suggested that funding for at-risk students should be more than, not equal to, funding for other students. The New Jersey court also required that the state go beyond merely providing an education. It required the state to motivate inner-city children and provide for their social and health needs as well as their educational needs (Miron and Wimpelberg 1992: 162–163).

Kentucky's supreme court has the distinction of handing down the most dramatic and far-reaching decision in a funding equalization suit. The court decided that the state's entire system of public education violated Kentucky's constitution's requirement to provide an efficient state system of common schools. It set performance requirements for the schools and required equal funding and equal property tax efforts (Miron and Wimpelberg 1992).

Court decisions are not the only factor influencing the state's share of education spending. Other factors include the wealth of the state, traditions of overall centralization of government functions in the state (Gray and Eisinger 1991: 314), and the extent to which the state has enacted legislation designed to limit local expenditures and taxes (Powell 1995). Legislatures enacted tax and expenditure limitation laws in response to the unpopularity and perceived unfairness of local taxes, particularly the local property tax, a primary source of school funds.

The relative shares of state and local funding vary tremendously across the states. Due to its royal and quasi-colonial traditions, Hawaii has virtually no history of local government, and thus the state share is 92 percent. At the other extreme is New Hampshire, which has a history of very strong local governments. There the state share of educational funding is only 7 percent (Wirt and Kirst 1992: 253–254).

The degree to which disparities in school district wealth bring about disparities in spending on behalf of pupils does not depend entirely on the proportion of expenditures provided by the state. It also depends on the type of formula that the state uses to determine how much aid it will provide for each district (Rosmiller 1992: 515–516). There are four basic types of state aid formulas. The oldest type is the flat grant. States allocate flat grants on a per pupil basis. They can be noncategorical, similar to block grants, or categorical, which is to say, earmarked for specified populations or specified purposes. Categorical flat grants tend to create constituencies of recipients and providers, who take an active interest in the continuation and growth of the grant (Rosmiller 1992: 515–516). These grants are most frequently delivered by state legislatures to urban constituencies in exchange for political support (Timar 1992).

The second type of state aid is the foundation program. Such programs are designed for the express purpose of reducing funding inequality. They guarantee minimum levels of resources per pupil or classroom unit and minimum allowable local tax efforts. These programs create a floor for expenditures per pupil, but they do not compensate for the ability of wealthy districts to raise and spend a great deal more than other districts, so states with this type of program frequently have considerable funding inequality from district to district.

Another type of state aid program is percentage equalizing. In this type of program, the state matches district spending with an amount that is inversely proportional to the wealth of the district. This type of program has a greater capacity to reduce funding inequality, while retaining an incentive for districts to raise their own funds.

Other than a complete state takeover of school financing, the type of program with the greatest impact on funding inequality is district power equalizing. Under this type of program, if a district raises more than some allowable maximum of revenue, the excess is remitted to the state. Wisconsin's supreme court ruled that this type of program was an unconstitutional violation of local control in the case of *Buse v. Smith* (1976) (Rosmiller 1992: 515–516).[5]

Other state supreme courts have ruled that their constitutions do not require a substantial component of local funding. Those that have decided against a greater state role in school funding have based their decisions instead on their state's long-standing and deeply held commitment to local control. One can make a strong case that if these commitments were really so deeply held, they would constrain the legislature and governor, thus obviating the need for protection by the state's judiciary (see Briffault 1992).

Over the past twenty years, the trend has been toward a greater recognition of the importance of funding equalization. As a result there has been a moderate increase in public school resources provided by the states and a pronounced assertion of state authority in deciding the level of resources to be allocated for the education of each student (Miron and Wimpelberg 1992: 159). During this period, voters defeated increasing proportions of local initiatives to increase borrowing or spending for the schools (Wirt and Kirst 1992: 221). This may be a consequence of increasing popular skepticism about the effectiveness or goals of public education, a resistance to property taxes, or general antigovernment sentiment. It is likely that the steady consolidation of small districts into larger ones throughout the twentieth century contributed to declining support for local school taxes. Whatever its causes, the decline in support for local taxation contributed to an increased state role in school finance, which has shifted power away from the school districts and toward the states.

Management Reforms

School-Based Management

Even as efforts to reduce resource inequities have led state governments to assume greater responsibility for finance decisions, many reformers have advocated school-based management. School-based management, also called site-based management, is a broad term that includes a wide variety of reforms that grant authority, sometimes very little and sometimes quite a bit, to one or more groups with institutional ties to individual schools. This usually means principals. It can also mean teachers, parents, elected or nonelected members of the community, and representatives of students. There is often a "school council," composed of some combination of these groups (Boyd and Claycomb 1994: 3491).

The motivations for instituting school-based management are varied. In some cases, pedagogical theory plays an important role. The "effective schools" research growing out of the work of James Coleman, suggests that autonomous schools provide better education than schools that are under the close supervision of external authorities (Boyd and Claycomb 1994: 3493). This research dovetails closely with the neoconservative rejection of bureaucracy and the welfare state (Boyd and Claycomb 1994: 3492), as well as with the doctrines of "reinventing government" that were popular in the early 1990s (Durning 1995). Therefore, it is not surprising that school-based management is more appealing to conservative school board presidents than to liberal ones (Feistritzer 1992: 142). However, the approach has some appeal across the political spectrum because it is consistent with the widely held belief that those who are most affected by decisions should have the strongest voice in making them.

Two important school-based management experiments are taking place in the City of Chicago and the state of Kentucky. The Kentucky plan was the result of a sweeping court order in a funding equalization suit (Jennings 1991: 21). Following the decision, the state legislature forced school districts to hand over budget-making authority to school councils (David 1994: 706). Each school council has three teachers selected by the teachers in the school, two parents selected by parents with children attending the school, and the principal. The school councils have power over curriculum, staff time, student assignments, schedules, school space, instructional issues, discipline, extracurricular activities, and some staffing decisions, including the selection of the principal (David 1994: 707–708). Along with the councils, Kentucky created new instruments for school assessment that could have positive or negative financial consequences for schools, depending on their performance (David 1994: 707).

The creation of school councils in Kentucky has profoundly diminished the role of school boards. The Kentucky Court of Appeals ruled that school councils, not school boards, are the bodies with authority for governing the schools. The court limited the role of school boards to one of oversight (David 1994: 707, 712; Boyd and Claycomb 1994: 3494). Kentucky's school-based management has clearly redefined local control as parental and teacher control, with teachers holding a three to two majority. Members of the community other than parents and teachers have no formal representation. Although there has been some resistance to the new system from local school boards (Luck 1992: B1), the lack of outcry from localities suggests that they were not strongly committed to the old system, either. On the other hand, parents have not shown strong commitment to the new system. Only 4 percent of the eligible parents voted in the 1992 school council elections. It is too soon to tell whether the reforms will bring about an improvement in learning outcomes, but there has been no dramatic change so far.

Like Kentucky, Illinois initiated its program for school-based management because of poor educational quality. Unlike Kentucky, Illinois limited its program to one part of the state, Chicago, where the problem with quality seemed most acute. The pivotal event was a speech by the U.S. Secretary of Education, in which he called the Chicago public school system "the worst in the nation." At the time, only 3 percent of the city's high schools scored above the national average in reading, and only 7 percent scored above the national average in mathematics (Walberg and Niemiec 1994: 713).

In response, the Illinois legislature enacted the Chicago School Reform Act of 1988, which disbanded the existing Chicago Board of Education and allowed the mayor to appoint a new one with the advice of a commission (Cronin 1992: 49). The act transferred authority from the Board of Education to local school councils. Unlike Kentucky, Illinois gave each school council a parent majority and some formal representation to community residents who were not parents. Each council has eleven members: the principal, two teachers, six parents, and two community members. The parents, teachers, and community members are elected by their peers.

The council selects the principal (Walberg and Niemiec 1994: 714). The principal receives a four-year, performance-based contract. The principal has the power to hire and fire school staff (Cronin 1992: 49). In addition to their representation on the councils, the teachers also have the responsibility to offer advice on the school curriculum through a "professional personnel advisory committee." The council has the power to approve or reject the budgeting of a lump sum that it receives from the city's Board of Education. School councils with high percentages of disadvantaged students receive larger sums of money and more discretion over its use. School councils also develop school improvement plans and advise the principal on discipline and attendance policies (Gray and Eisinger 1991: 311; Bryk et al. 1994: 75).

Some school councils appear to be functioning better than others. In the more successful councils, parents, community representatives, teachers, and principals engage in sustained, substantive debates. They see a need for fundamental change in the operation of schools and they collaborate to achieve it. These practices are most common in councils that govern small, predominantly Hispanic schools (Bryk et al. 1994: 75–76). This suggests that effective school governance, like effective district governance, requires a cohesive, homogeneous community.

The goals of the Illinois legislation were to raise achievement, attendance, and graduation rates in the Chicago school system within five years. After three years, there was a slight gain in high school attendance. Elementary school attendance, measures of achievement, and high school graduation rates declined, however (Walberg and Niemiec 1994: 714).

Legislative support for the reforms may start to erode unless these trends turn around. Parental and community support for the program is not as strong as it could be. The number of candidates for the 5,000 school council positions in Chicago's 540 schools has declined from 17,000 at the start of the program to only 1,000. On the other hand, parents, community members, and teachers currently serving on the councils believe they have been successful (Walberg and Niemiec 1994: 715). They comprise a well-informed, highly motivated group that could become a powerful defender of Chicago's council system if it comes under attack.

So far the program continues to receive support from the state and the mayor (*Education Week* 1995c: 17). Power struggles between the reconstituted Chicago Board of Education and the school councils continue to be resolved in favor of the school councils (Harrington-Lueker 1993: 32). If Chicago's school-based management system survives, it will constitute a major redefinition of state-local relations in education policy because local governance will be redefined as governance of individual schools. By constituting the councils in a way that gives added weight to parents, Illinois appears to have overcome a major shortcoming of many school boards—the failure to recognize the special rights of parents. However, the finding that small, predominantly Hispanic schools had the most effective councils indicates that even when the special claims of parents are recognized, effective local governance of schools, like effective local governance of school districts, requires some minimum level of social cohesion and homogeneity.

School Choice

Neoconservative opposition to government regulation and James Coleman's effective schools research have contributed to other strategies for shifting authority away from school districts. School choice, which in practice almost always means public school choice, has become increasingly common. Minnesota, which initiated the recent trend toward interdistrict public school choice, has seen a steadily growing number of students take advantage of its interdistrict public school choice program. A full 5 percent of Minnesota's students were participating as of 1993–1994 (Nathan and Ysseldyke 1994: 683–684). Other states with broad interdistrict public school choice plans include Arkansas, Colorado, Idaho, Iowa, Massachusetts, Nebraska, Ohio, Oregon, Utah, and Washington (Pipho 1991: 102–103; Schultz 1993). California, Missouri, and New York have voluntary interdistrict choice programs. States adopting the choice policies tend to have small school districts that might not be able to offer all of the educational services that some parents want. The states with interdistrict public school choice plans also tend to have a political culture of the moralist type. This cultural type appears to be turning against all forms of bureaucracy and government control, including government determination of the school that students attend (DiLeo 1994).

The plans vary somewhat from state to state. They generally include some provision for subsidizing transportation to the receiving district, some measures to discourage racial separation, and some shift of state funding from the abandoned district to the receiving district (Nathan and Ysseldyke 1994: 683–684). School choice plans within school districts, many of them created to promote voluntary desegregation, have also become increasingly common.

School boards have initiated or supported many of the within-district public school choice plans. On the other hand, they have almost unanimously opposed the interdistrict public school choice plans that states have adopted or proposed. These plans make it harder for districts to know how many pupils will enroll in their schools from one year to the next. They threaten to deprive districts of some of their funding. This is especially threatening to school boards governing small, poor districts that are close to larger or wealthier districts that offer more attractive programs. Most importantly, school board members and many others perceive these plans as an indictment of the school boards, an assertion that they are unable or unwilling to improve the schools significantly unless competition compels them to do so. The plans shift authority and legitimacy away from elected school boards and toward parents and state governments, which define the terms of the plans. This does not mean that the plans do not offer new responsibilities and opportunities to exercise discretion for district administrators. Interdistrict public school choice plans often rely on extensive participation from school district administrators for transportation arrangements, the dissemination of information about options to parents, and a wide variety of information-collecting activities.

The experience of Milwaukee indicates that if states create private school choice plans, they will also undercut the authority of elected school boards, while at the same time creating new responsibilities and power for district administrators.

Charter Schools

In the late 1980s, the most influential advocate of public school choice, Joe Nathan, began to argue that choice by itself might not create enough options for parents or provide sufficient competition between schools to bring about improvement. He argued that the supply of schools had to become more diverse before the demand for distinctive schools could result in higher quality or parent satisfaction. He claimed that the best way to create a more diverse supply of schools was to create publicly funded schools that were free to create innovative educational programs, bound only by agreements to meet certain standards. He called such loosely regulated schools "charter schools" (see Nathan and Ysseldyke 1994: 689).

More generally, the move to eliminate education regulations has begun to catch on in some states, notably South Dakota and Arizona (Miller 1995: 13; *Education Week* 1995b: 13). About forty states have made some moves to deregulate teacher certification by allowing certain classes of accomplished individuals to receive "alternative certification" to teach in public schools without going through the usual procedure (*Education Week* 1995a: 4). This deregulatory environment provides fertile ground for proposals to create schools that are freed from most state and local regulations.

As of August 1995, there were more than 700 charter schools operating in twenty-nine states, with dozens more scheduled to open soon (Baldauf 1997; Walsh 1995: 15). They serve a small percentage of America's public school students, but the number is growing rapidly (Harrington-Lueker 1994b: 23). Groups of parents or teachers, institutions of higher education, firms, and foundations have received charters from a variety of government bodies, including school districts, state departments of education, and state boards of education. These charters commit their recipients to certain goals of educational success in exchange for public funding and a suspension of education codes and regulations (Walsh 1995: 16). Regulations protecting the civil rights and physical safety of students and staff and requirements of financial disclosure are usually not waived (Harrington-Lueker 1994b: 22).

In some cases, the charter schools purchase certain services from the school districts where they are located. School security, school nursing, and maintenance are three services that some charter schools purchase from their school districts (Harrington-Lueker 1994b: 24). In some cases, existing schools have become charter schools. Usually, the staff remains in place (Pipho 1993: 102). The most notable exception has been the Turner School in Wilkinsburg, Pennsylvania, which is not formally a charter school. Nevertheless, the school board contracted with a private firm to operate the school, and the firm replaced the teachers. The Pennsylvania Supreme Court upheld the school board's action (Ponessa 1995).

Some of the charter schools are highly distinctive. The Noah Webster Academy in Michigan is a school that emphasizes cyberspace and teaches creationism (Harrington-Lueker 1994b: 22). About two-thirds of the charter schools offer interdisciplinary curricula. About half of them emphasize technology. Most of the schools are small and popular with the parents (Walsh 1995: 16; Harrington-Lueker 1994b: 24).

So far, twenty states have followed Minnesota in adopting charter school legislation (Baldauf 1997; Walsh 1995), but not all charter school laws are the same (Harrington-Lueker 1994b: 25). Some states have strong charter school laws. These states allow a high or unlimited number of charter schools to be established. They eliminate the vast majority of state and local regulations for charter schools. They vest the authority to grant charters in some institution other than the local school board. California, Arizona, Colorado, Minnesota, Michigan, and Massachusetts have strong charter school laws (Walsh 1995: 15). According to Daniel Elazar (1984: 135), the moralist cultural type, which has recently turned strongly against bureaucracy, is predominant in three of these states and present in all six.

States with weak charter school laws only allow existing public schools to be chartered, and they only allow the local school boards to grant charters. They have regulations to limit the discretion of the school administrator in order to protect the interests of particular groups, usually unionized teachers. States with weak charter school laws include Wyoming, New Mexico, Kansas, Wisconsin, and Georgia (Walsh 1995: 15). Charter school advocate Ted Kolderie holds that opponents of charter schools, most notably the teachers' unions, are responsible for the adoption of weak charter school laws. He maintains that when it appeared inevitable that legislature would enact charter school legislation, its opponents often switched from attempting to block the legislation to attempting to weaken it (Walsh 1995: 15).

School boards have been strongly opposed to charter school legislation, especially if it allows government bodies other than school boards to grant charters. Eighty-four percent of school board members responding to an American School Board Journal survey reported that they were "philosophically opposed to the very idea of charter schools." Many respondents expressed concern that charter schools would divert funding from schools that the school districts operated (*American School Board Journal* 1995b: 56). It is important not to underestimate the message that charter schools send. Even more than interdistrict choice, charter schools send the message that the legislature has decided that in the absense of competitive alternatives the school districts are incapable of making sufficient improvements.

School-based management, school choice, and charter schools undermine the ability of elected school boards to define educational programs by granting significant authority or leverage to teachers, parents, or others. Statewide curricular standards, full-service schools, and academic bankruptcy laws shift authority from elected school boards to the states, to other local governments, or to private individuals acting on behalf of the states.

Curricular Standards

Reformers interested in educational quality, with support from reformers concerned that all students receive educations of equivalent value or acquire particular skills or knowledge deemed especially crucial, have come together to support statewide curricular standards. The hope is that such standards can make a difference in classrooms by enabling states to launch what reformers call "systemic reform." These reformers argue that states can use clear definitions of the knowledge and skills that students should acquire to guide the education of teachers and to measure student progress. In general, conservatives suggest that when students fail to achieve the standards, schools, districts, and the people who work in them should face some negative sanctions. Liberals generally suggest that when students fail to achieve the standards, schools, districts, and the people who work in them should receive more assistance.

In the past, the academic disciplines, the textbook publishers, and the test-making companies defined what students had to know. In the late 1980s, however, many people decided that these de facto standards were unsatisfactory for two reasons. The first reason was that they allegedly ignored high-level skills (Fuhrman 1994b: 90). The second reason was that a lack of governmental endorsement limited their effectiveness because they could not be used to guide the education of teachers or affect the allocation of resources.

Over the past ten years, support for new, high-level standards has steadily gathered strength. The earliest support came from business groups concerned about workforce productivity. Before long, governors, concerned with making their states appealing to employers, also began to advocate standards. Conservative policy analysts such as Chester Finn and Diane Ravitch advocated national standards as a way of making the schools more academically rigorous (Harrington-Lueker 1994a: 41). Liberal policy analysts such as Richard Elmore and Susan Fuhrman (1994) advocated national standards as a way of ensuring that all children received a quality education. In the early 1990s, one-fourth of school board members reported that they were adopting more rigorous academic standards even before their states required them to (Harrington-Lueker 1994a: 41).

The federal government's support for national standards dates back to the Charlottesville Education Summit of 1989. With encouragement from the governors, led by then-governor Bill Clinton of Arkansas, President Bush announced six national education goals (Fuhrman 1994b: 91; Harrington-Lueker 1994a: 41). The third goal, demonstrating competence in core academic subjects at grades 4, 8, and 12, clearly implied explicit definitions of competence for those grades and ways to determine whether competence had been achieved, in short, national academic standards.

When he became president, Clinton took up the six goals of the Bush administration and added two of his own: professional development for teachers and parental involvement (U.S. Department of Education 1994: 4).

His support for standards was considerably more active than that of his predecessor. Inducements to the states to adopt and implement statewide curricular standards were a central feature of Clinton's Goals 2000: Educate America Act. Within two years, all of the states except Virginia, New Hampshire, and Montana had signed on. Since then, Virginia has developed standards that have been hailed by some as a national model (Baldauf 1997).

In the fall of 1997 the Republican congressional majority opposed national standards, but the movement's national scope is not entirely due to the sponsorship of the federal government. Private national organizations and networks such as the Committee for Economic Development are playing an important role in generating political support for national standards (see Committee for Economic Development 1994). Networks of public officials, the College Board, and the Educational Testing Service popularize the idea of having standards and play an important role in integrating the standards developed in the various states (Harrington-Lueker 1994a: 42). This is to be expected, given the lucrative market for standardized tests that would be created by national legislation.

Associations of teachers of particular subjects have played a central role in the development of standards. Mathematics teachers in particular have taken the initiative in defining the levels of knowledge and skill that students should exhibit at various points in their educational progress (Fuhrman 1994b: 91; Harrington-Lueker 1994a: 41). In the political realm state governments have been extremely active in developing and implementing standards (Harrington-Lueker 1994a: 42). Forty-five states reported in 1994 that they were involved in developing curricular frameworks by identifying content standards, desired student outcomes, performance standards, or new assessments (Massell 1994: 84).

California, under former chief state school officer Bill Honig, is a leader in adopting curricular standards (Massell 1994: 89–90). California has a highly professional, assertive state department of education and a centralized school system. These characteristics probably contributed to the early adoption of curricular standards. They certainly affected the way that California developed standards, relying on a highly centralized process led by professional academics and educators (Massell 1994: 87). However, other states with much less centralized or professionalized school systems such as New Jersey, Vermont, Kentucky, Massachusetts, and Minnesota have also made a serious commitment to developing and implementing curricular standards (Fuhrman 1994b: 93).

The degree of localism and professionalism also affects the way that states develop standards and the nature of those standards. Kentucky does not have a professionally-dominated state education department and developed curricular standards that were much more utilitarian than California's, which were largely rooted in the academic disciplines (Massell 1994: 98). Vermont, a small state with a strong tradition of popular local government, developed its standards through a much more populist, decentralized process than California did (Massell 1994: 93–94). There are some indications that California's standards are so sophisticated and extensive that teachers in the state are not using them in the classrooms (Massell 1994: 101).

The push for statewide and national standards has run into considerable opposition from religious and cultural conservatives. They complain that "critical thinking" entails skepticism of many widely held articles of religious faith and tradition, and acceptance of beliefs that are antithetical to scripture and dogma. Consequently, many religious and cultural conservatives have launched campaigns, often successful, to win seats on local school boards and press the state and federal governments to abandon their campaigns for curricular standards. The resistance in Congress to President Clinton's Goals 2000: Educate American Act is largely a product of this type of activity (Sharpe 1995: A1, A6). To the extent that conservative opponents of standards are more successful at the local level than at the state and national levels, the conflict over standards colors state-local relations in education.

Most school board members responding to an *American School Board Journal* survey reported that they supported national standards, but 35 percent are opposed, and 28 percent report that they plan to actively oppose them (*American School Board Journal* 1994a: 56). For the majority of school board members, national standards, formulated and put into effect by the states, provide an opportunity for state-local cooperation. However, a significant minority perceives any kind of standards, national or statewide, to be a significant usurpation of school district autonomy.

Full-Service Schools

Many children do not achieve the academic standards set by adults because they have serious physical, emotional, or social problems. If they are receiving assistance for these problems, the assistance often comes from several providers and agencies that do not always coordinate their work with each other or with the schools. In many cases, these agencies intervene only when a child is experiencing some kind of crisis. Laws designed to protect the privacy of children and their families contribute to the lack of coordination between agencies. The governance of schools by local officials who are independent of general-purpose government also makes coordination of education with other services especially difficult. In states with elected chief state school officers, the same problem is also present in state government.

The main reason for the lack of coordination is the specialization and mutual isolation of the helping professions from one another, which leads to battles for authority, prestige, and funding among agencies dominated by different professions. The legislative committees that create and fund the agencies operate in similar mutual isolation (Kirst 1991).

The "full-service school" is an attempt to overcome this fragmentation and provide coordinated health and social services that are supposed to enable troubled children to perform more effectively in school. However, no state has yet taken a close look at the most basic cause of the fragmentation of services, the states' own professional practice acts, which have created a score of specialized professions, each with its own members, expertise, interests, and language (see Crowson and Boyd 1993).

Like most of the reforms discussed above, strategies for coordinating education and other services may involve education professionals working in schools or, less commonly, in district offices, but they tend to bypass school boards. In Philadelphia, the mayor's office has created "family service districts" in an attempt to oversee and coordinate all of the services that children and families receive (Crowson and Boyd 1993: 148). The California legislature, with the encouragement of Governor Pete Wilson, has decided to award grants to schools, social service agencies, and counties to promote service coordination. The New York legislature provides grants to schools through its "Community Schools Programs," which supports plans to coordinate health, nutrition, and social services (Crowson and Boyd 1993: 148–149). The Minnesota Youth Coordinating Board is a joint powers agreement between the city of Minneapolis, the Minneapolis school district, and Hennepin County (Kirst 1991: 618). It has the power to levy its own property tax to fund the coordination of services for children and families. All of these projects, and many others like them, share three common features. First, they reduce the isolation of education from general-purpose government, an isolation that dates back to the creation of the Boston school district in colonial Massachusetts. Second, none of them involve school boards. Third, none of the new institutions created to coordinate services are governed by elected officials. With the possible exception of Philadelphia, which is creating districts to coordinate education with other services that are accountable to municipal government, these efforts at coordination seem to be distancing the governance of education from local voters.

To the extent that elected officials are involved in efforts to coordinate education and other children's and family services, they have been state officials or officers in general-purpose local government. The school boards have been passive in this area, probably because, according to a recent survey, most school board members believe that the schools should stick to educating (*American School Board Journal* 1995c: 48).

State Takeovers for Academic Bankruptcy

The most dramatic indication of the deteriorating political position of the school boards in their relations with the states is the advent of the state takeover. A state takeover occurs when a state department of education, with the approval of the state board of education and the authorization of the legislature, takes over the operation of a school district for a specified period of time. At first the grounds were limited to financial bankruptcy. More recently, poor academic performance of students, called "academic bankruptcy," has also provided grounds for state takeovers (Pancrazio 1992: 72). The first takeover of a school district occurred in 1989 (Berman 1995: 56). Prior to that, it was inconceivable that a state would depose a school board that was able to pay its bills. To some extent, improvement in the capacity of states to monitor student achievement may be responsible for this new development in state-local relations.

A state takeover follows a progressively intrusive review of district operations that finds serious problems and no improvement over a period of several years. Illinois's statute calls for a sequence of "technical assistance, academic watch list, [and] administrative oversight" preceding the takeover (Pancrazio 1992: 78). The statutes specify the indicators that the state department will watch and use to decide whether a takeover is appropriate. New Jersey's statute specifies "curriculum and instruction, staff, student attendance, basic skills, mandated programs (such as special education), planning and financial management, community relations, and policies regarding equal opportunity" (Pancrazio 1992, 78–79). It is safe to say that takeovers are more politically feasible when the school board lacks community support or when the state government is dominated by groups whose goals for the district differ from the goals of the targeted school board. Like other sanctions, such as consolidation with other districts or withholding of certain funds, threats of takeover can be used to get school districts to comply with state officials' policy preferences (Pancrazio 1992: 73, 75).

States with statutes allowing takeovers for academic failure include Arkansas, Georgia, Illinois, Iowa, Kentucky, New Jersey, New Mexico, Maryland, Massachusetts, Mississippi, Missouri, Ohio, Oklahoma, New York, North Carolina, South Carolina, Tennessee, Texas, and West Virginia (Pipho 1991, cited in Pancrazio 1992: 71). Few of these are moralist states, which tend to have strong traditions of local control, fairly homogeneous populations, and a growing antagonism to big bureaucracies. Key supporters of the statutes have been networks of major national businesses, such as the Committee for Economic Development. Many of the districts that have been taken over include high percentages of low-income people or minorities. So far, dozens of school districts have been taken over across the country. They include Jersey City, Paterson, and Newark in New Jersey; Cleveland; Baltimore; Hartford; Alluwe in Oklahoma; East St. Louis, Harlan County, Floyd City, Whitley City, and Pike City in Kentucky; Community District 17 in New York; Dallas; Logan County in West Virginia; and Orangeburg and eight others in

South Carolina (Education Commission of the States, cited in Berman
1995: 55–56; Education Commission of the States 1997). The results have
been mixed. Jersey City and Paterson showed evidence of more efficient
administration, but no improvement in student achievement (Berman
1995: 66).

Conclusion

Although they continue to be vital administrative units, exercising more
discretion than ever in the implementation of increasingly complex and
ambitious programs, school districts are becoming less and less significant as republican institutions. Strategies for school improvement ranging from full-service schools, school choice, and new curricular standards
to school-based management all have one thing in common. They all bypass the school boards. Nothing brings home the current political impo-
tence of the school boards as much as the recent state takeovers of districts on the grounds of academic bankruptcy. The increasing number of
school boards that are turning the operation of schools over to private
companies suggests that the boards' own assessment of their capacity to
run the schools is not much higher than that of the states.

Some of the underlying causes for the political decay of local education
governance are irreversible. The population has certainly become more
mobile, and there is less consensus in districts about how children should
be raised and educated. It is increasingly unlikely that school boards can
operate schools that are reasonably close approximations of what every
family in the district wants. This makes it virtually impossible for school
districts to avoid violating the expectation of parents to have their children educated in a manner they see fit. These violations and the frus-
trated preferences of substantial portions of communities are responsible
for many of the most paralyzing conflicts on school boards, and they motivate a great deal of the most bitter criticism of public education. In an
increasingly mobile society, with increasing religious and cultural diversity within school districts, it is difficult to imagine school districts that
are sufficiently homogeneous to find ways of running schools that do not
meet with strong objections from substantial numbers of people.

However, some of the underlying causes for the deteriorating political
position of school boards are reversible. The districts were not always as
large as they are now, and smaller districts may be better able to match
the preferences of parents and communities. The removal of education
governance from general government, nonpartisan elections, and separate election dates all depress turnout, which diminishes the legitimacy
of districts in the eyes of other governments and produces school boards
that overrepresent special interests. These problems might be less acute if

school board elections were partisan and held on the Tuesday after the first Monday in November.

The finance issue lies somewhere between a reversible problem and an irreversible problem for school board governance. As long as school boards raise funds from their own citizens, each will be relatively autonomous, but they will collectively violate society's basic notions of equity. If they are funded by grants from the states, they can be more equitable, but they come much closer to being administrative agencies rather than autonomous governments.

Recognition of the political weakness of school boards has led to a wide variety of proposals, from Chester Finn's call for their abolition (1992) to Jacqueline Danzberger's proposals for strengthening boards' policymaking capacity (1992). Calls for school choice are essentially strategies for replacing the republican governance that school boards promise with another means of protecting parental rights. School-based management implies that the school rather than the district is the appropriate unit of governance. The states are already well into the process of overseeing a variety of new ways to protect parental rights while pursuing public purposes. None of those endeavors reserve a prominent role for school boards as we know them.

NOTES

1. "Academic bankruptcy" is a term used to describe school districts that, according to the state, fail to provide students with an adequate education. After declaring a school district to be academically bankrupt, the state assumes direct control of the day-to-day administration of the district.

2. As a result of the Supreme Court's decision in Rodriguez, it has been impossible to launch court challenges to the sizable inequalities in funding across states, nor have these differences made much of an impact on the agendas of the federal government's political branches.

3. An exception is Wisconsin, which has no such body.

4. This trend seems to have reversed in the early 1990s, which has seen a slight uptick in the local share and a slight decline in the state share (Office of Educational Research and Improvement 1994: 94–115).

5. Existing school finance systems do not fit neatly into any of the four categories described above. This is because the adoption of a new system is generally accompanied by "hold harmless" provisions to ensure that no school district will actually lose state funding when the state adopts the new system (Rosmiller 1992: 516). As a result, school finance reform tends to mean a ratcheting up of the state share of school spending and a complex system that contains features of more than one finance mechanism.

8

Environmental Regulation and State-Local Relations

James P. Lester and
Emmett N. Lombard

Since the early 1980s, students of American government have noted the enhanced importance of state governments in the American governmental system. State political institutions and practices have adapted to changing conditions in the states; reforms of structures and operations within the executive and legislative branches have been accompanied by other important changes in state government (Bowman and Kearney 1986a; Dye 1984; Jewell 1982). In addition, states are adopting a more positive and facilitative posture toward their local governments in terms of funding and services, and they are demonstrating concern for local government problems, particularly as many local governments continue to struggle with financial and service provision problems (Bowman and Kearney 1986b). One area in which more cooperative state-local relations are developing is environmental protection.

Although the federal government retains overall regulatory and enforcement authority for environmental protection in the United States, the primary responsibility for policy implementation increasingly resides with state and local governments (Lester 1986, 1995; Davis and Lester 1987). This trend is likely to continue into the next century. American citizens have expressed dissatisfaction with the flow of power away from the states over the past sixty years, and the Republican Congress has signaled its intention to permit broader authority of state governments in environmental policy (as well as other areas) while at the same time requiring increased use of cost-benefit analysis and risk analysis before new federal regulations may be issued. In addition, the Congress disapproves of the "regulatory burden" that environmental legislation of the past has placed on American business, and it has pledged to grant relief during reauthorization of the Clean Water Act and future reauthorizations of other environmental legislation.

There are certain to be changes in the funding of environmental protection programs. Federal contributions to total intergovernmental environmental protection spending in the United States are projected to decline by one-third from $6.3 billion in 1981 to $4.3 billion in 2000, but state and local government spending on the environment is projected to triple by then (National Conference of State Legislatures 1991). Meeting these and other fiscal pressures presents a difficult task for many state governments, and local governments in many states are either unable or unwilling to offer much in the way of financial assistance. The federal government, on the other hand, has proven to be an important source of political, administrative, technical, and indirect financial support for meeting state goals in the area of environmental management.

In this chapter, we examine the role of local governments in environmental protection programs in the American states. We begin by presenting an analytical model that considers the roles of all three levels of government in efforts to manage problems associated with threats to human health and the environment. Next, we consider the historical development of governmental efforts to protect the environment in the United States and note important federal-level factors that have shaped state choices concerning the use of local governments in environmental policy processes. Third, we examine the role of regional, county, and city governments in state environmental policy processes.[1] Here we demonstrate that many regional governments have assumed important policy planning and formulation functions, whereas city and county governments (particularly in the area of air pollution control) have developed formidable enforcement systems in states that cultivate local environmental policy implementation. We then draw upon a case study of Michigan and note how the Southeast Michigan Council of Governments contributes to that state's environmental policy formation and enforcement efforts. Finally, we provide reasons why the role of municipal, county, and regional governments in state environmental management will continue to evolve and perhaps be expanded in the future.

An Analytical Model

In the 1970s and 1980s comparative state policy studies were primarily concerned with explaining state policy formulation. In the 1990s, however, the primary area of investigation is state implementation of federal environmental programs. Such explanations require an analytical framework that differs from the "mainstream" model used in previous comparative state policy research. Thus, a model of intergovernmental implementation is needed as a starting point for studies of state roles in carrying out federal programs (Lester and Lombard 1990).

Previous research on environmental policy in the United States has focused on either the activities of the federal or state governments.[2] Precious little attention has been paid to the interaction between the federal and state governments in this policy area, and even less to the role of local governments in these processes (Lowry 1992; Ringquist 1993). However, there are important reasons why comparative state environmental policy research must include the interaction between all three levels of the intergovernmental system in order to understand efforts to protect human health and the environment.

The model we propose conceptualizes the implementation process as resulting from choices made by the state (Lester et al. 1987; Lester and Lombard 1990; Goggin et al. 1990). State choices are in turn a function of inducements and constraints provided to or imposed on them from elsewhere in the system—above or below—as well as the state's capacity to effectuate its preferences. In addition, state choices are not those of a unitary actor, but may be the result of bargaining among parties internal or external to government who are involved in state politics. More specifically:

1. There is no unicausal explanation for differences in state implementation of environmental policies. Many factors can account for a particular program's implementation: aspects of the policy itself, features of the state or locality and its administration of the program, and characteristics of the people who make and manage state programs and whose interests are greatly affected by them.

2. The national decision that triggers an implementation process constrains by its form and content the choices and behaviors of those who have to execute instructions that are either codified by law or are implicit in the intent of the policy makers, be they lawmakers, the president, members of the judiciary, or agency representatives. Implicit in any discussion of these authoritative decisions is the degree to which they constrain choices, which varies from one environmental policy to the next.

3. State responses to federal and local inducements and constraints vary. A state's response is conceptualized as a joint decisional outcome, constrained by the nature and intensity of the preferences of state legislators and local elected officials, the local state agency—with its problematic relationship with the governor and its decentralized components (for example, county offices)—and spokespersons for interests importantly affected by what does or does not happen during implementation of an environmental program.

4. State responses are also constrained or structured by the state's capacity to act. For example, a state's ability to implement a national environ-

mental policy directive may be constrained by the availability of fiscal resources, intragovernmental fragmentation, staff resources, or the level of
public support for a program. Conversely, state implementation of environmental programs may be promoted by the skills and other resources of
state administrative personnel. Moreover, as the comparative state policy
literature suggests, many other factors are known to influence state policy
outputs, such as the severity or salience of the problem, wealth, partisanship, and organizational factors (Lester and Lombard 1990).

Future state environmental politics research needs to adopt a conceptual framework that represents the intergovernmental nature of environmental policy implementation. Such a framework demands that attention
be paid not only to the relationship between federal and state actors in
these processes, but also to the role of local governments and the interaction among all three levels of the intergovernmental system.

The Intergovernmental Context
of Environmental Protection

State government responses to problems associated with threats to the environment are not determined by state-level factors alone. What federal
and local government officials do to and/or for the environment also affects the overall capacity of state governments to protect the environment
(Lombard 1989). Environmental protection, then, is an intergovernmental
activity; it encompasses interactions between governmental officials
(elected and nonelected) of all three levels of the political system over time.
Understanding environmental protection policy formation and implementation requires us to identify the various combinations of relations among
units of government in the United States intergovernmental system. Like
other areas of intergovernmental relations, "it necessitates a focus on persons" and depicts "continuous, day-to-day patterns of contact, knowledge,
and evolution of the officials who govern" (Wright 1985).

Although pollution control efforts were first initiated at the local level
(such as air pollution control in Chicago in 1881, or Pittsburgh in 1941),
these early efforts only confirmed the scientific and technical complexities of the problems. In the case of Pittsburgh, the postwar program to
limit emissions from stationary sources of air pollution was both dramatic and impressive, but it was accomplished with little knowledge of
less visible pollutants from stationary and nonstationary sources. After
the air was cleared, local resources were inadequate to do the research
necessary for developing more sophisticated controls (Jones 1975).

By the 1950s, government officials in some states, for example,
California and Oregon, regarded air pollution as a problem deserving attention, but prior to 1963 air pollution was not considered a problem ne-

cessitating national government involvement. The federal government's first pollution control activities were limited to enhancing state and local efforts at identifying problems associated with air pollution (Jones 1976). Thus, the Air Pollution Control Act of 1955 declared that the policy of Congress was "to preserve and protect the primary responsibilities and rights of the states and local governments in controlling air pollution." Its major provisions provided research funding for five years at $5 million per year. Four years later, research grants were continued for an additional four years at the same level, and in 1960 increased federal research was concentrated on vehicle emissions. The Air Quality Act (1960), the Clean Air Act (1963), and the 1967 amendments to the Air Quality Act contained no regulatory role for the federal government; they simply encouraged states to set air pollution standards and to develop plans for attaining them. A federal regulatory role did not begin in earnest until 1970, when the Clean Air Act was passed and the Environmental Protection Agency (EPA) was established. In these early actions, the federal government was identifying and defining air pollution problems in the nation with local and state governments assisting in these efforts. However, only a few states (Oregon, California, and Pennsylvania, for example) were able and/or willing to regulate air pollution before 1963.

The first piece of national legislation dealing with water quality was the Water Pollution Control Act of 1948. As in the area of air quality, the law did little more than recognize water pollution as a potential problem and provided limited funding for studying the situation. The Water Pollution Control Act of 1956 strengthened efforts at water pollution control by creating a grant program in which the federal government funded up to 55 percent of construction costs for municipal wastewater treatment facilities. The 1956 act also authorized states to develop standards for interstate waters within their borders and implementation plans for meeting them. A limited federal regulatory role in water pollution control did not emerge until 1965 with passage of the Water Quality Act. It required state action to protect and improve water quality. However, detecting specific water quality violations and setting water quality–based permit standards (as stipulated in the act) were beyond the technical capacity of most states. In addition, most states ignored federal attempts to get them to enforce a system of water pollution permits (Ringquist 1993).

Some research indicates that despite the authority granted to states in early environmental legislation (the Clean Air Act, for example), the EPA was reluctant to devolve authority over programs to states, mainly because federal officials did not trust state officials to do what was necessary to protect the environment. Patricia Crotty (1987) suggested that state governments played a very limited role in implementation of environmental policies in the 1970s and 1980s and that policy delivery was extensively structured by federal actions and guidelines. One of the effects of national primacy in this view was that it weakened the structural components of a state's policy process, minimizing the role of the state legislature and state courts. Moreover, under "partial preemption," the most important policy contacts occurred between federal and state bureaucrats rather than among state officials.

However, case studies dispute the view that states were bystanders in the development of environmental protection policies and programs. In Colorado, for example, the state legislature was very active in approving or denying air pollution control strategies of the state and its local governments, and jealously protected its powers of intervention in virtually every aspect of air pollution control (Lombard 1988). Although states may have been equivocal in their support of environmental protection, they were much more than mere bystanders.

Despite conflicting findings about the role of states in early environmental protection efforts, the creation and growth of regional government in this and other policy areas from the 1950s to the late 1970s can be attributed to activities at the national level. The objective of federal programs that encouraged substate regionalism was to bring order to a fragmented system of local jurisdictions and greater efficiency and equity to federal programs (Wallis 1992). By the 1970s, thirty-nine federal programs ranging from coastal zone management to community economic development required coordination among local governments in planning a wide variety of activities. In the area of environmental protection alone, Congress passed and funded pollution-mitigation initiatives (with broad regional government participation) in coastal zone management resources planning (1972), noise pollution control (1972), solid waste management planning (1976), water pollution control (1977), and air pollution control with air quality control regions (1977). The growth in the number of regional governments was impressive. In the 1950s, fewer than 50 regional governments existed; by their peak in 1976, 669 regional governments existed.[3]

By the end of the 1970s, resistance to the expansion of federal authority mounted and questions about the effects of federal expenditures on the economy were raised. Much of this resistance came from state governments which found themselves saddled with new duties and responsibilities. At the same time, states were preempted by regional governments as recipients of federal aid and coordinators of activities within their own borders. Concerned observers questioned the constitutionality of such a massive intrusion into the affairs of the states.

Not only were regional governments looked upon by state governments with suspicion, they were often accused of competing with other public sector governments and private sector businesses. Some states took precautions to prohibit these activities. For example, in the early 1980s the Michigan legislature passed legislation allowing regional councils to "provide services for a reasonable fee if those services are not available through the private sector at a competitive cost" (Atkins and Wilson-Gentry 1992). In Colorado, the state government passed legislation that specified areas of regional government interest, but the regional government role was very limited (Lombard 1988).

Other circumstances worked against acceptance of regional government efforts to solve public problems. One centered on the lack of proprietorship some county and municipal governments felt toward the regional entity. Some local leaders were pulled into accepting regional governments because of the federal dollars they received; others felt that federal predominance distorted the local agenda for the regional organization, displacing it with federal policy goals and increasing the alienation of local officials from the regional government (Atkins and Wilson-Gentry 1992: 472).

Beset by criticisms from within and without, the intergovernmental pattern of broad regional government planning authority and federal funding was realigned in the 1980s. President Ronald Reagan ushered in an era in which the federal government began turning power back to the states while at the same time reducing funding for a variety of programs (Lester 1986; Davis and Lester 1987, 1989). It was also an era in which renewed emphasis was placed on market mechanisms in the provision of public services. The changes of the 1980s rested in part on a commitment to reduce the size of the federal budget deficit and on the effects of the recession. However, the basic philosophy of the Reagan reforms was to restructure government authority toward the state and local levels and the private sector, and efforts toward this end were made early on.

The 1981 Omnibus Budget Reconciliation Act eliminated fifty-nine categorical grant programs and consolidated eighty other categorical programs into nine block grants (U.S. General Accounting Office 1990). As reauthorizations for the remaining categorical programs came due, they were also recast to enlarge state authority and autonomy (Atkins and Wilson-Gentry 1992: 474). In addition, the federal government shifted the locus of regionalism to the state, permitting—through block grants and changed categorical grants—greater state discretion as to how regional governments should be used. States were made responsible for developing the procedural apparatus to accomplish intergovernmental review of federal project applications, and they were given the options of deferring on participation or participating without the regional government instrumentality.

Many of the fifty-nine grants eliminated by the 1981 Omnibus Budget Reconciliation Act were federal-local, including some that were federal-regional. All of the new block grants were state administered. The federal government rapidly moved away from substate regional organizations and established the states as the preeminent recipient of delegated authority and dollars. Some areas of regional policy emphasis lost more planning authority and federal funding than others. Particularly hard hit were federal program initiatives in community development, environmental protection, and health and human services. Left relatively intact were rural development, aging, and transportation programs (U.S. GAO 1990).

A major feature of the Reagan era was the general deemphasis on regulatory activities. The Reagan administration's efforts to decentralize the federal system included a component to curtail federal regulation of state and local governments. Federal regulatory enforcement activity itself was undercut by added program standards, the inclusion of more administrative oversight of regulatory requirements, and the loss of funds for federal oversight of regulatory activity. Two areas were especially affected: the Safe Drinking Water Act of 1986, which required monitoring of nearly one hundred new contaminants, and the Resource Conservation and Recovery Act, with its stricter regulations on solid waste and hazardous wastes (Atkins and Wilson-Gentry 1992: 476).

New federal legislation mandated additional regulation but identified states as the regulatory organs, not regional governments. At the same time, numerous programs were eliminated, areawide review was shifted to the states, the range of eligible federal grant recipients was expanded beyond regional governments, and total funding was reduced. The remaining categorical grants were more narrowly cast, reducing the discretion regional governments formerly exercised in their comprehensive planning activities. The ability to practice comprehensive planning was deemphasized, and a project-based or issue-based planning replaced comprehensive planning in many states. According to Patricia Atkins and Laura Wilson-Gentry (1992), "The situation began to replicate the nature of the private service-delivery market, even to the point of requiring payment at the point of delivery."

Although regional governments lost the support of the federal government during the 1980s, there was elevated state commitment to cooperative regional mechanisms of all types during the 1980s and 1990s, according to Atkins and Wilson-Gentry (1992). Two reasons account for this: First, state interest in regional cooperative mechanisms derives from the authority of state law to transcend the political boundaries that divide every region. Decisionmaking processes on land use, economic growth, and service delivery must be codified in state law in order for these issues to be addressed through regional mechanisms. Second, states had developed a considerable professional capacity and used that capacity to become facilitators of regional government and to make triage decisions regarding programs and agencies worth maintaining within the regional arena.

Increased professionalism and stronger fiscal positions permitted some states to undertake a more active regional policy and to provide greater funding during the 1980s. Many states supported the central purpose of regional governments as intergovernmental forums and instruments through which technical expertise could be shared, and some states gave regional governments increased authority to directly deliver areawide services, thus diversifying their activities (Atkins and Wilson-Gentry 1992: 484). Table 8.1 represents the extent of regional government development within the states in 1993 in terms of the number of regional governments in each state, their level of staffing, and the number of jurisdictions served by each regional government.[4] As can be seen, despite a decline from the level of federal support enjoyed earlier, regional governments still maintain a substantial presence in all states except Alaska, Hawaii, and Rhode Island.[5]

TABLE 8.1   Extent of Regional Government, by State

State	No. of Regional Governments	Staff	No. of Jurisdictions Served
AL	12	305	477
AK	–	–	–
AZ	6	288	112
AR	13	349	572
CA	25	495	423
CO	12	257	276
CT	15	97	167
DE	2	5	101
FL	11	272	425
GA	17	483	650
HI	–	–	–
ID	8	135	274
IL	33	361	2921
IN	13	338	934
IA	16	228	986
KS	10	124	1497
KY	17	478	625
LA	10	99	312
ME	10	69	480
MD	7	162	80
MA	13	205	353
MI	16	176	1840
MN	13	369	2150
MS	12	327	358
MO	16	247	1237

(continues)

TABLE 8.1   *(continued)*

State	No. of Regional Governments	Staff	No. of Jurisdictions Served
MT	6	32	30
NE	7	63	767
NV	2	50	6
NH	9	77	256
NJ	3	93	203
NM	8	135	105
NY	11	113	1449
NC	18	413	578
ND	9	60	1774
OH	18	345	2258
OK	12	320	663
OR	10	905	345
PA	12	461	2243
RI	–	–	–
SC	10	190	285
SD	6	54	1175
TN	9	153	459
TX	24	1214	1782
UT	8	376	223
VT	10	70	330
VA	23	334	297
WA	14	144	255
WV	12	114	284
WI	9	209	1731
WY	3	7	27

SOURCE: National Association of Regional Councils 1993.

Local Governments and
State Environmental Protection

As noted previously, local governments in most states are active participants in meeting state goals regarding environmental protection.
However, the forms of government, and their roles in carrying out environmental protection activities, vary from state to state and policy to policy. In the area of air pollution control, for example, three types of local
governments are active. Table 8.2 depicts the three types of governments
used by the fifty states to implement their air pollution control strategies:
regional governments, county or city/county governments, and city governments. Sixteen states do not use any local governments in air quality

TABLE 8.2   Local Air Pollution Control Agency Structures, by State

State	County or City/County	Regional	City
AL	X		X
AK		X	
AZ	X		
AR	–	–	–
CA	X	X	
CO	X		
CT			X
DE	–	–	–
FL	X	X	
GA	–	–	–
HI	–	–	–
ID	–	–	–
IL	X		X
IN	X		X
IA	X		
KS	X		
KY	X		
LA	–	–	–
ME	–	–	–
MD	X		X
MA		X	X
MI	X		X
MN			X
MS	–	–	–
MO	X		X
MT	X		
NE	X		X
NV	X		
NH	–	–	–
NJ	X	X	X
NM	X		
NY	X	X	X
NC	X	X	
ND	–	–	–
OH	X	X	X
OK	X		
OR	X		
PA	X		X
RI	–	–	–
SC			X
SD	–	–	–
TN	X	X	

(continues)

TABLE 8.2   *(continued)*

State	County or City/County	Regional	City
TX	X		X
UT	–	–	–
VT	–	–	–
VA	X		X
WA	X	X	
WV	–	–	–
WI	X		X
WY	–	–	–

SOURCE: National Association of Regional Councils 1993.

policy processes; a few (California, New York, Ohio) make use of regional, county, and city governments in efforts to control air pollution.

Table 8.3 tracks the growth in personnel of state and local government air pollution control agencies from 1975 to 1989. There have been some changes in the size of local structures relative to their state counterparts over time. For example, local agencies in Alabama, Arkansas, Indiana, Maryland, Massachusetts, Michigan, Minnesota, Oregon, Pennsylvania, Texas, and Wisconsin employed more personnel than their state agency in 1975, whereas the reverse was true in 1989. Arizona is the only state that saw the state agency decline relative to local agencies from 1975 to 1989 (in terms of personnel). Nine states in 1975 and 1989 had greater numbers of government air pollution control personnel (in some states much greater numbers) employed in local agencies than at the state level. They are: California, Florida, Illinois, Missouri, Nebraska, Nevada, New York, Ohio, and Washington.

Although much of the early impetus for state use of regional governments in environmental policy came from the federal government, regional governments themselves have shown a remarkable ability to survive dangerous political terrain and become important partners in state environmental management activities. Regional governments have responded to changes in state funding objectives and have reoriented their programs. Program selection for these regional governments has begun to cluster. The most frequent broad state policy vehicles for regional governments are of two types: "ecological infrastructure management" and administration (Atkins and Wilson-Gentry 1992: 481). Certain programs appear within the ecological infrastructure management cluster; most of them provide for substantial regional government participation in environmental protection policy planning activities. Environmental protection (water and air quality), growth management, solid waste disposal and management, land-use regulation, wetlands policy, and transporta-

TABLE 8.3   Change in State-Local Air Quality Personnel, 1975 to 1989

	1975		1989	
State	State Staff	Local Staff	State Staff	Local Staff
AL	29	34	44	33
AK	6	8	22	18
AZ	41	33	61	80
AR	21	0	24	0
CA	223	720	534	1440
CO	42	38	97	47
CT	104	43	105	59
DE	16	0	33	0
FL	65	129	104	200
GA	61	16	73	0
HI	20	0	34	0
ID	11	0	19	0
IL	99	202	124	194
IN	40	60	105	75
IA	30	11	17	9
KS	21	12	37	12
KY	83	33	97	42
LA	28	0	80	0
ME	12	0	44	0
MD	70	82	99	71
MA	46	75	143	92
MI	53	73	101	53
MN	27	35	68	12
MS	38	0	21	0
MO	15	72	33	58
MT	15	7	19	8
NE	5	14	10	15
NV	7	13	7	27
NH	16	0	25	0
NJ	100	28	242	41
NM	26	12	41	17
NY	221	407	228	283
NC	77	63	74	55
ND	5	0	19	0
OH	1	96	106	160
OK	26	22	29	20
OR	38	39	129	13
PA	128	172	155	132
RI	15	0	29	0
SC	51	13	77	3

(continues)

TABLE 8.3   *(continued)*

	1975		1989	
State	*State Staff*	*Local Staff*	*State Staff*	*Local Staff*
SD	16	0	10	0
TN	66	51	71	59
TX	148	169	347	170
UT	18	0	42	0
VT	11	0	17	0
VA	70	31	148	24
WA	33	67	46	83
WV	36	1	61	0
WI	34	54	99	5
WY	9	0	23	0

SOURCE: National Association of Regional Councils 1993.

tion are becoming interrelated on regional councils' agendas forming one axis of activity. John Degrove (1988: 8) has termed this the "second wave of land use." Planning activities classified under the ecological infrastructure management cluster demonstrate concern for the use of land, either through environmental programs or in programs that integrate land use and transportation policy.

The clustering of ecological infrastructure management planning is apparent in several states. According to Atkins and Wilson-Gentry (1992), states using regional governments as key actors in ecological management are all "heavy hitters" with regard to regional government funding: Connecticut, Florida, Georgia, Idaho, Maine, Minnesota, New Hampshire, Tennessee, and Vermont. Two states—Washington and Oregon—have delineated some growth-management responsibilities for their regional governments. Indiana is the only other state to assign growth-management responsibilities to all its regional governments and the only one in the "ecological group" of states to provide no state funds. Colorado has passed growth-management legislation that designates areas and activities of state interest (i.e., regional impact) but the regional government role is very limited. States with a regional government having some growth-management responsibilities include California, Idaho/Utah (an interstate), Maryland, Massachusetts, Nevada/California (interstate), and Tennessee, with general state funds provided to the Idaho/Utah regional government, the Maryland regional government, and the Tennessee regional government (Atkins and Wilson-Gentry 1992: 482).

The 1993 *Directory of Regional Councils in the United States,* an annual publication of the National Association of Regional Councils, lists

twenty-eight states in which at least one regional government partici-
pates in one or more of the following state environmental management
programs: water quality, air quality, growth management, land-use regulation, wetlands policy, energy planning, environmental health, environmental assessments, hazardous waste notification, river protection,
coastal zone management, and soil and water conservation.[6]

Another report from the National Association of Regional Councils
finds sixty-six recent examples of substantial regional government participation in water resources planning, each aiding states in meeting federal water quality and resource standards. This planning took place in
twenty states and the District of Columbia, and several instances involved regional governments encompassing portions of more than one
state (e.g., Ohio-Kentucky-Indiana Regional Council) (National Association of Regional Councils 1993a).[7]

Thus, regional governments have become important participants in
many states as vehicles for environmental management. This role may
become even more important in the future, especially in the area of water
resources management. As Congress considers reauthorization of the
Clean Water Act, many regional governments across the nation have a
vested interest in preserving and strengthening provisions for the set-
aside of water quality planning funds to regional governments. Regional
governments also have an interest in any attempts to lower water quality
standards.

Unlike regional governments, city and county governments suffer few
legitimacy problems. They are not recent creations, they were not established to further federal goals, and states gave them authority to involve
themselves in environmental protection activities early on. In fact, county
medical officers in places such as Allegheny County, Pennsylvania, were
among the first government officials to identify air pollution as a serious
problem warranting a government response. In addition, city and county
government environmental protection organizations in many states carry
out enforcement, rather than planning or policy formulation. In a few
cases (California's air pollution control regions, for example), regional
governments carry out policy formulation *and* enforcement functions.

As in the case of regional governments, the role of county governments
in environmental protection policies varies from state to state, and within
each state, from policy to policy. In the area of air quality, for example,
twenty-nine states invest their county governments with some air pollution control authority. According to the *Journal of the Air and Hazardous
Waste Management Association*, county governments especially have taken
on important enforcement responsibilities. A typical county air pollution
control agency employs many of the same types of professional personnel as do their state counterparts (engineers, technicians, meteorologists,

TABLE 8.4   Full-Time Air Pollution Control Employees, Michigan and Wayne County, 1988–1994

	1988	1989	1990	1991	1992	1993	1994
Michigan							
Administrators	1	2	3	3	3	3	3
Chemists	1	1	3	3	3	3	3
Engineers	41	41	44	45	45	47	64
Meteorologists	–	4	4	4	4	2	3
Office Staff	17	9	10	10	10	9	12
Technicians	6	7	6	7	7	8	7
EQ Analysts	25	33	30	34	34	34	48
EQ Managers	–	–	5	6	6	8	9
Data Processing	–	–	12	–	–	–	2
Enforcement Spec.	–	–	3	3	3	–	–
Toxicologists	1	2	3	4	4	–	6
Total	92	99	123	119	119	114	157
Wayne County							
Administrators	1	1	1	2	2	2	–
Technicians	5	5	5	5	5	5	4
Attorneys	2	2	2	1	1	1	1
EQ Specialists	–	–	–	–	–	–	1
Chemists	6	6	6	5	5	5	5
Meteorologists	1	1	1	1	–	–	–
Engineers	12	12	12	11	12	12	17
Inspectors	14	13	13	12	14	14	9
Office Staff	9	7	8	6	8	8	6
Tech. Svcs. Director	1	1	1	1	–	–	–
Total	51	48	49	44	47	47	43

SOURCE: Compiled by authors from *Journal of the Air and Hazardous Waste Management Association,* various years.

chemists, and so forth) and these may enhance a state's capacity to protect the environment. Table 8.4 presents the number of full-time employees in the air pollution control agencies of the state of Michigan and in Wayne County from 1988 to 1994. In 1988, Wayne County's agency was more than half the size of the state's; however, by 1994, the county's air pollution control agency had declined by almost 16 percent whereas the state's had expanded by over 75 percent. Nevertheless, county pollution control agencies complement state structures to a considerable degree. In the following section, we describe recent environmental protection enforcement efforts of the state of Michigan and provide specific examples of how local government activities assist in meeting state environmental policy goals.

Environmental Protection in Michigan

Although Michigan has assumed primary implementation responsibilities from the federal government in the area of environmental management, it has recently demonstrated a willingness to provide "regulatory relief" without waiting for the Congress to act. For example, with approval from the state legislature the administration of Governor John Engler initiated a broad range of economic development initiatives that could have long-term consequences for the environment in that state. In addition, during his first term Engler pared the Department of Natural Resources (DNR) staff and limited their discretion. Due to staff cuts, the state DNR has not been able to review 280–300 hazardous waste sites (Williams 1994). The governor also dismantled nineteen state advisory committees that provided citizen input in various areas of environmental policymaking. The nineteen boards and commissions were replaced with working groups and a biweekly calendar that provides only seven days' notice of major DNR decisions. Critics say these are no substitute for face-to-face contact with pollution decisionmakers such as members of the former Air Pollution Control Commission and Water Resources Commission (Moltine 1994).

In terms of state enforcement vigor, the story is mixed. Table 8.5 represents state inspection activity in the Air Quality Division for the period 1987–1994. Michigan's office of air quality shows an increase in the number of full-time equivalent (FTE) employees over the period, but the number of FTEs devoted to inspections and the number of major sources inspected have declined.[8] In addition, while the number of major sources of air pollution has increased considerably, the number of letters of violation sent has decreased since 1991.

The same mixed picture is evidenced in the area of hazardous waste inspections. State inspections of fully regulated generators (FRGs) declined from 1990–1991 to 1993–1994; inspections of treatment, storage, disposal facilities (TDSF) and transporters (TRAN) remained relatively stable, while inspections of small quantity generators (SQG) increased dramatically. "Non-notify" was an initiative mandated by the EPA for the states to concentrate on facilities that have the potential to generate hazardous waste but have not yet notified the proper authorities (for example, car body shops or printers).[9]

As can be seen in the state of Michigan, with states becoming increasingly concerned with attracting new and maintaining existing industries and jobs, local governments may become even more important to a state's

TABLE 8.5   Michigan Air Quality Enforcement, 1987–1994

FY	No. of Field FTEs	No. of FTEs Devoted to Major Source Inspections	No. of Major Sources	No. of Major Sources Inspected	No. of Major Sources Committed to Inspect	No. of Letters Sent to All Violating Sources
87	NA	NA	676	615	530	NA
88	38	NA	669	486	474	200[a]
89	36.5	13.5	693	603	525	348
90	36	12	753	641	565	457
91	36	8	781	619	590	920
92	38	6	856	503	514	638
93	34	5	870	322	315	474
94	48	5	896	433	398	376

[a]Approximately
SOURCE: Michigan Department of Natural Resources, Air Quality Division.

capacity to protect the environment. One regional entity in Michigan with an important role in the area of environmental management is the Southeast Michigan Council of Governments (SEMCOG).

Michigan is not considered one of the "ecological group" of states that places a high priority on regional governments' participation in environmental policy decisionmaking; at least it is not identified as such by Atkins and Wilson-Gentry (1992). However, a brief description of SEMCOG's activities and services demonstrates a substantial role in carrying out the planning of the state's environmental protection activities for that region.[10] For example, members of SEMCOG acting through the Environmental Policy Advisory Council and the Areawide Water Quality Board have addressed concerns of air quality, water quality, solid waste management, and hazardous waste management.[11] Addressing air quality specifically, a special committee, advisory to SEMCOG and the Michigan Department of Natural Resources has successfully developed strategies to reduce ozone-causing pollution in order to meet mandates of the Clean Air Act. SEMCOG plays a vital role in developing air quality data analysis and helping draft needed state legislation, and it has contracted with Radion, Inc., a Los Angeles environmental consulting firm, to model ozone pollution in the area covered by SEMCOG. In addition, SEMCOG received an $8 million grant (80 percent from the federal government) in 1993 to develop air toxics reduction strategies for the region.[12] This represents a substantial source of indirect financial assistance in meeting the state's obligations under the Clean Air Act.

SEMCOG continues to play a key role in the restoration of the Rouge River as a natural resource: The agency provides planning and public outreach services for the Rouge River Watershed Council, and public information and education services for the Rouge River Wet Weather Demonstration Project. The Areawide Water Quality Board addresses legislation dealing with pesticides and wetlands at the state level, monitors proposed amendments to the federal Clean Water Act, and conducts forums on water quality standards being developed pursuant to the Federal Great Lakes Critical Programs Act.[13] Moreover, under the Remedial Action Plan for the Detroit River SEMCOG ensures that there is "adequate" public participation and that planning activities meet the needs of the citizens and local governments of southeast Michigan. SEMCOG staffs the seven-county solid waste management task force. Concerns of this body have centered on waste-to-energy facilities, landfills, recycling, and compost issues.

SEMCOG's DataCenter is a primary source for demographic information about southeast Michigan. The DataCenter Advisory Council works with staff to monitor regional development trends and changes in regional demographic characteristics. It produces a yearly Profile of the Region containing population, employment, development activity, transportation, and environmental data. Work continues on implementing a regional-scale geographic information system to enable more efficient management, analysis, and graphic display of planning information such as land use, census data, and transportation data.

SEMCOG's library is the most comprehensive regional planning collection in southeast Michigan. Local elected officials, community planning staffs, and citizens frequently consult the library's 20,000-volume collection. Of special interest to municipalities is a unique collection of more than 2,000 ordinances on 400 topics. Searches of this collection are currently the most popular request. Information services has an aerial photograph collection dating back twenty years that provides a historical record of regional growth and development. Demographic data, housing development activity, forecasts, traffic volume, and other data resources are also available and are used extensively by both public and private sectors. Information services and the library annually respond to more than 10,000 information requests, including more than 100 searches of LOGIN (Local Government Information Network), a computerized database that helps provide solutions to governmental problems by accessing a national network.

Based on these activities, SEMCOG has made a place for itself in several areas of environmental concern. However, there are intergovernmental factors that tend to undermine the viability of this regional government in environmental policy processes. One is the tendency of some local governments to pursue their own preferences at the expense of the regional government. This is precisely the problem SEMCOG faces in the area of toxic cleanup. In February 1994 three bills were introduced in the state legislature that would have given responsibility for toxic cleanup in Wayne County to county officials. Wayne County officials said they needed the authority to speed up cleanups and to ensure that the county gets its fair share of state funds.

The proposal has been attacked as wasteful by manufacturing and business groups, environmental organizations, and the state attorney's office. In addition, the EPA has raised concerns about setting up an independent county agency to run environmental cleanups because of the effects it would have on EPA's ability to work with the state in managing various programs (Williams 1994). The EPA would have to spend more money to deal with the proposed county authority and might have to reevaluate federal funding for other programs. The state's attorney general said that it would set a bad precedent nationally because it raises the possibility of the federal agency having to deal with a multitude of local agencies instead of directly with state governments. Some business people have said they fear the prospect of having many different sets of standards. In addition, the proposal would set aside $20 million for cleanups in Wayne County and just over $2 million for administering the program (Williams 1994).

Future of Local Governments in Environmental Management

There are several important reasons why the role of local and regional governments may become more important to state environmental management in the future. First, these governments have become an important point of access for groups and individuals who see state governments responding more and more to pressures to provide regulatory relief to business interests. When Michigan Governor Engler reorganized the Department of Natural Resources, he promised ample opportunities for public participation in its policy processes. However, critics say this has not happened; they say that the ability of people to know what decisions are pending at the DNR, and to offer comments on them, has suffered under the Engler reorganization. In an ever-changing political environment, and in order to respond to the concerns of citizens for environmental protection, regional governments may become more important as channels of access to environmental decisionmaking.[14] Furthermore, as more and more states shift their pollution control strategies from sanctions-based or enforcement-based regulation to industry self-monitoring and pollution prevention strategies, regional governments, especially those that span portions of two or more states, may become the logical instruments for monitoring the activities of polluting industries within their jurisdictions and ensuring that the public has access to, and some influence upon, environmental decisionmaking. Finally, local and regional governments in the United States are not only adapting to changes in the wider policy environment, they are also becoming involved in areas of public policy in which the states and the federal government have had great difficulty in formulating solutions to public policy problems.

In the preceding discussion we have examined the role of substate governments in environmental management and identified some of the states in which they are most active in the area of environmental regulation. We have also identified some of the more important intergovernmental factors that influence state choices concerning the use of local and regional governments in the area of environmental regulation. The most important inducements have been federal legislation that encouraged local government participation in states' efforts to meet federal goals, and the political, administrative, and technical support that entities such as SEMCOG bring to bear in assisting states in solving environmental problems. Finally, we have given reasons why regional, county, and municipal governments will become even more important to state environmental management in the future. These reasons include the ability to adapt to the changing political environment; to become an important avenue of citizen access to government in policies affecting environmental quality; to coordinate a variety of policies and programs involving local service delivery; and to balance the tendency of state governments toward regulatory relief against the demands of citizens for effective environmental protection. Clearly, our understanding of environmental regulation is enhanced by the realization that this area of concern occurs within an intergovernmental context involving federal, state, regional, county, and municipal governments.

NOTES

1. In this study, "regional government" and "regional council" refer to the same broad category of substate government organizations that provide planning services for state governments in the area of environmental protection. These regional government organizations also include the Metropolitan Planning Organization, Area Agency on Aging, Economic Development District, Local Development District, Service Delivery Area for Job Training Partnership Act programs, and Certified Development Company (see National Association of Regional Councils 1993).

2. Haskell and Price 1973; Lester 1980; Lester et al. 1983; Duerksen 1983; Ridley 1987, 1988; Crotty 1987, 1988; and Lombard 1993.

3. Advisory Commission on Intergovernmental Relations 1982. In 1991, 529 remained (Atkins and Wilson-Gentry 1992).

4. These figures from the NARC's *Directory of Regional Councils in the United States, 1993* cannot include all personnel employed in California's air quality regions (please see Table 8.3).

5. These states have never used regional governments to carry out state initiatives.

6. These states are Arkansas, Colorado, Connecticut, Florida, Georgia, Idaho, Illinois, Indiana, Maine, Massachusetts, Michigan, Minnesota, Missouri, New Hampshire, New Mexico, New York, North Carolina, North Dakota, Ohio, Oklahoma, Oregon, Tennessee, Texas, Vermont, Virginia, Washington, West Virginia, Wisconsin. Also, California's air quality regions, although not designated as such in the NARC Directory, are heavily involved in air pollution control.

7. National Association of Regional Councils 1984. The states are California, Colorado, Connecticut, Florida, Georgia, Illinois, Indiana, Iowa, Kentucky, Maryland, Massachusetts, Michigan, New Mexico, Ohio, Oklahoma, Oregon, Tennessee, Texas, Virginia, and Washington. Note that these are the very same states identified by Atkins and Wilson-Gentry (1992).

8. A large number of the Air Quality Division's enforcement staff have been reassigned to permit-processing activities. Interview with Barb Rosenbaum, DNR Air Quality Division, March 28, 1995.

9. Interview with Elizabeth Bols, DNR Hazardous Waste Management Division, March 29, 1995.

10. In 1993, the SEMCOG served a total of 244 jurisdictions with a full-time staff of 81 (NARC 1993).

11. SEMCOG undertook the most comprehensive water quality planning effort in southeast Michigan—the Water Quality Management Plan for Southeast Michigan (or 208 Plan). This plan was developed pursuant to the requirements of Section 208 of the Federal Clean Water Act and adopted by SEMCOG. The plan created the Areawide Water Quality Board (AWQB), which is responsible for oversight, monitoring, and coordination of the plan's implementation and serves as an advocate of local water quality concerns at the federal and state levels. The AWQB is a 27-member board composed of representatives from local units of government, business, citizen interest groups, government agencies, and the educational community. SEMCOG serves as staff to the AWQB.

12. Interview with Professor Paul Tomboulian, Air Quality Technical Advisory Committee of SEMCOG, September 22, 1993.

13. SEMCOG has worked with the Michigan DNR on water quality issues since the 1970s. In 1985 the DNR contracted with SEMCOG to prepare a Remedial Action Plan (RAP) for the restoration of the Rouge River. SEMCOG worked with the DNR, basin municipalities, local and federal agencies, industry, and interest groups to develop the RAP (SEMCOG Annual Report, 1992–1993).

14. For example, regional governments are an appropriate arena in which to deal with emerging concerns over "environmental racism." Although there is mixed evidence in support of the view that "communities of color" bear a heavier burden in the disposal of hazardous waste, regional governments offer a possible "first line of defense" in dealing with perceived threats because they can transcend the borders of communities where minorities and poverty are concentrated. For a discussion of environmental racism, see, e.g., Allen, Lester, and Hill (1995).

9

Untidy Business: Disaggregating State-Local Relations

Timothy Tilton

The language of political science abounds with metaphor; indeed, upon careful examination theories often dissolve into metaphors writ large. Governmental institutions are portrayed as systems (cybernetic, mechanical, hierarchical, or otherwise), games, ships, partners, raging beasts, rational actors, irrational actors, cesspools—the list is virtually endless. The study of intergovernmental relations offers some colorful figures as well; layer cakes, marble cakes, picket fences, and bamboo fences adorn the literature of American federalism.

With few exceptions, these images mislead by their simplicity. Most local government officials would rejoice if their work were as simple as playing a game or even a series of games if they participated only in clear and explicit partnerships, if governing could be reduced to the logical calculation of strategic decisionmaking or rational choice theory. The multiplication of metaphors should alert observers to the messiness of the reality they try to depict. In general, the reigning images err by characterizing governments as relatively self-contained spheres with a relatively clear ("sovereign") source of authority. To describe state-local relations adequately one must instead disaggregate them into all their complicated particularity.

At the risk of injecting still another metaphor into the discussion, I contend that students of governmental relations might do well to reflect on the changes in modern biology's view of the cell. In place of the nucleus embedded within a relatively rigid membrane, modern biology envisions the cell as internally complex with complicated information and command systems, its exterior permeated by various molecules, its boundaries porous and open to penetration and exchange. This cell is capable of connecting in numerous ways with other cells, loosely, compactly, singly or compound. This image comes much closer to capturing the character of state or local government as it connects in myriad ways with another "cell."

In this essay I want to draw on my experience as a local government official and political scientist to illustrate the complexities of local government and its relations with the state of Indiana. As a county commissioner I served on three bodies, the county commission, the solid waste district, and the plan commission, each of which has a different style of relations with the state. The plan commission's relations proceed almost exclusively through constitutional and judicial channels and are mentioned here only in passing to indicate one distinct kind of politics. A closer examination of the county commission's place in local government, of the creation of solid waste districts as special districts in 1990, and of both entities' relations with the state of Indiana afford compelling evidence for the variety and complexity of state-local relations.

Ties That Bind

Monroe County lies in the rolling hills of south central Indiana. It is the seat of Indiana University's main campus at Bloomington; the university's 36,000 students give the county's population of 110,000 a profile quite distinct from its neighbors. Local limestone quarries provided building stone for the Empire State Building and the Washington Monument. The RCA/Thomson plant produces more color televisions than any other facility in the world; the General Electric plant produces the largest number of side-by-side refrigerators. The community's industrial base developed relatively late, beginning in the 1940s and 1950s. Bloomington, arguably the most liberal city in the state, sits in the midst of a deeply conservative rural and small town political culture.

Local government in Monroe County is, of course, a creature of state government. The fundamental fact about Monroe County government is that it is highly fragmented. In addition to county and city government, local government consists of two town governments, eleven township governments, two school districts, one solid waste district, five sewer districts, eight water companies, one rural fire district, one conservancy district, a county library board, and a host of not-for-profit social service agencies with financial links to the public sector. Need one add that coherent coordination of policy is virtually nonexistent?

County government, the oldest of local government institutions, is marked by internal fragmentation as well. The citizens of Monroe County elect three commissioners, seven county council members, an auditor, treasurer, clerk of courts, six (soon to be seven) judges, a prosecutor, sheriff, surveyor, coroner, recorder, and assessor. In addition the parks board, plan commission, board of zoning appeals, health board, convention and visitors commission, and airport board all enjoy independent authority. Traditional separations between legislative, executive, and judicial branches blur; the commissioners, for example, exercise a part of the executive power, legislate local ordinances (the council, the county "fiscal body," retains the power of the purse), and adjudicates poor relief appeals brought against township trustees. Even the geographical domain of county government resists clear description. For public health and bridges "the county" is all of its territory; for roads and parks, it is the unincorporated area of the county; for land-use planning, it is the unincorporated area less a "two-mile fringe" around Bloomington. The total configuration resembles a ramshackle collection of medieval fiefdoms and depends on a high level of cooperation among officials to produce good results. Efforts to reform this structure have been few and faltering; a state effort to eliminate township trustees foundered on the obdurate opposition of the more than 1000 locally elected trustees.

Intrusive state regulation heightens the ungainliness of county institutions. The state oversees the processes of county government in excruciating detail, from prescribing the form for payments toward veterans' funerals, to requiring public notice of county claims, to extensive audits. Although Indiana counties ostensibly enjoy the benefits of home rule, the limits of their authority are carefully bounded. For example, the state recently prohibited local restrictions on firearms. Most importantly, Indiana freezes the local property tax levy and has done so since 1973. It customarily limits the increase in local tax revenue—not rates—to 5 percent per year.

The state's organization and regulation of county government structures much of state-county relations. The term "state-county relations," however, may obscure the fact that these relations involve *parts* of the county dealing with *parts* of the state. This circumstance opens the obvious possibility that different county officials or different state officials (or both!) may be in disagreement with one another. Politics then becomes the art of playing one set of officials against another. A number of recent cases illustrate this point.

Indiana law has for some years prescribed that electoral precincts contain no more than eight hundred voters. Thus when the number of registrants in a precinct exceeds eight hundred, the precinct needs to be subdivided or otherwise reorganized to come into conformity with the law. As a result of this legislation and modest population growth, the number of precincts in Monroe County has increased from fifty-two to eighty-

four. At a cost of approximately $8,000 for each new precinct (voting ma-
chines, election officials, food, and incidentals), the cost of complying
with this mandate approximates $250,000. In addition, the clerk must find
suitable polling places with rest rooms, handicap accessibility, and sufficient parking, and must locate additional election workers to staff the
new precincts. What makes this situation particularly galling is the low
turnout (often in the teens or even single digits) in some student
precincts. Given that the voting rolls are purged only every four years,
and given the high mobility of the student population, the number of officially registered voters greatly overstates the number of eligible voters,
not to mention the number of likely voters.

The county obviously had strong financial and convenience incentives
to alter this regulation. It pursued both an administrative and a legislative strategy. First, the clerk and commissioners approached the State
Board of Elections seeking a reinterpretation of the rule so that precincts
would be limited to eight hundred *actual* voters rather than eight hundred *registered* voters—to no avail. It then concentrated on changing the
law to allow more than eight hundred registered voters in student
precincts. Through vigorous lobbying of its state legislators and useful assistance from the Association of Indiana Counties, the statewide county
lobby, the county was able to obtain modest changes in the statute,
though not full local control. In 1995 Indiana counties obtained a temporary suspension of this law.

A second set of cases concerns exemptions to the property tax freeze.
Traditionally, the law has allowed supernormal increases in the levy only
under exceptional circumstances. In order to be successful with the State
Board of Tax Officials a county must be united; in particular, the board
weighs the auditor's views heavily. When Monroe County has had the
auditor's support, as in a special increase for a proposed juvenile deten-
tion project, it has obtained the exemption; when it has not, appeals have
failed. Thus, the politics of tax appeals dictate unity among local officials
and allow the state to divide and conquer—or simply reject county en-
treaties.

The third case, a proposal for a hazardous waste incinerator, generated
the most intense and complicated intergovernmental lobbying. In 1984
the Environmental Protection Agency (EPA), the state of Indiana, the city
of Bloomington, Monroe County, and the Westinghouse Corporation
signed a consent decree requiring Westinghouse to clean up roughly
650,000 tons of PCB-laden hazardous waste. The decree specified the
building of a hazardous waste incinerator southwest of Bloomington,
using trash as a fuel, unless Westinghouse chose an alternative technology that met EPA stipulations. The proposal provoked enormous local
opposition, but the federal judge in charge of the case rejected appeals.

This judicial roadblock eventually produced a complicated politics of legislative and administrative persuasion, in which the local community sought an alternative from the state legislature, the state Department of Environmental Management, their congressional representatives, and the EPA itself. The twists and turns of this process defy summary in this space, but the strategy has produced a modest achievement, a thoroughgoing review of the cleanup with an eye to avoiding incineration.

A fourth case illustrates the failure of local government lobbying. In accordance with state enabling legislation, Monroe County instituted first a 3 percent and later a 5 percent hotel-motel tax. A five-member Convention and Visitors Commission manages the proceeds from this tax, subject to approval of their general budget by the county council. The precise makeup of the commission has varied over time reflecting the debate over the purpose of the tax: Is it first and foremost to promote the interests of the lodging industry or is it to promote tourism and public interests more generally? Those who see the commission as a corporatist extension of the lodging industry favor domination of the board by representatives of that industry and want money spent primarily on marketing. Those who see the commission as a broader public institution desire broader public representation (most recently a county commissioner and a county councilman) and interpret the commission's mandate as a wider promotion of tourism: supporting the development of a convention center and such potential tourist attractions as a rail trail, for example. In the 1995 legislative session, one of the county's state representatives, piqued by the presence of "politicians" on the board and by the failure of the county commissioners and county council to appoint three representatives sought by the lodging industry, succeeded in rewriting the statute so as to ensure control by the hoteliers. Given that the county council must approve the commission's budget, the practical impact of this amendment remains unclear. What is clear is that both sides in the debate felt real issues were at stake and that the division within the local community afforded the state representatives greater freedom of maneuver.

Politics between state and local representatives do not always produce clear winners and losers as in the previous cases. More typical are the results in a fifth case, the county's effort to free itself from what it regards as excessive state regulation. Following the private sector's lead in reducing rules and trusting the judgment of employees, Monroe County officials decided in 1990-1991 that to operate more efficiently they had to reduce the overhead imposed by state requirements. In August 1992 the county attorney and one of the county commissioners testified before the Local Government Finance Subcommittee of the state legislature, seeking redress on a number of procedural mandates. (By "procedural mandate" I mean stipulations as to how something is to be done as distinguished from "substantive mandates" directing what is to be done. Obviously this distinction grows fuzzy at the margin, but it has general utility, not least because much of the aggravation and waste that mandates engender come from their imposition of inefficacious procedures.) County officials worked with the Association of Indiana Counties to adopt and bring to fruition a legislative program embodying modest reforms. Some valuable changes have occurred. The state legislature has loosened, though not abolished, county purchasing regulations. The legislature has made public notice laws somewhat more consistent. It has made welfare departments rather than county commissioners responsible for the tuition payments of children placed outside of counties; previously the commissioners were obligated to pay the school bills even though they had no notice or authority in placement decisions.

The state also legislated an intriguing compromise between newspapers and counties on the publication of county claims. The law had formerly required counties to publish all claims, including payroll claims, in two newspapers before the county acted on them. This procedural mandate, which applied only to counties and no other unit of government in Indiana, resulted in the ludicrous spectacle of every county employee's salary being printed in two newspapers every two weeks! The legal notices cost Monroe County thousands of dollars each year. The 1995 legislature, in its wisdom, decided to eliminate the requirement to publish salaries biweekly, but allowed newspapers to raise rates substantially for the remaining advertising. The counties thus scored a partial success on the publication of claims, but fell well short of their original money-saving goal.

Another matter, the payment of veterans' funeral benefits, illustrates the difficulty of reforming processes. State law requires the county commissioners to pay $100 toward the burial of veterans. The state prescribes a detailed form for each claim and each must be processed separately. Monroe County currently handles hundreds of such claims each year—first in the commissioners' office, then in the auditor's office, and again in the treasurer's office. When the county explored the possibility of amalgamating claims into larger batches and simplifying the form, the State Board of Accounts categorically rejected the proposal.

These cases produce no monumental results for political science, but they reinforce two commonsense maxims. First, they confirm the thesis of this paper—that state-local relations proceed not between two large unified entities, but in myriad ways between various parts of both organizations. Second, they verify the wisdom of the old political saw that in unity there is strength. The more components of local government that support a particular change (and the fewer interests they offend), the greater the chances of success. It is vital to note one unstated assumption of this analysis—that local officials are, in Gaetano Mosca's (1939) term, "politically available";

that is, they have the time and resources to lobby state offices. This point is far from trivial; in Monroe County the commissioners remain part-time officials, earning their livings primarily from other employment.

State Mandates

Thus far this study has touched only marginally on issues of finance. The central issues of fiscal politics, who pays and who benefits, obviously operate between governments as well as in political life more generally. For some years local officials, living at the end of the political food chain, have complained about "unfunded mandates." The Association of Indiana Counties estimates that about thirteen cents of each Indiana county government dollar is spent on compliance with federal and state mandates. Local governments now appear on the verge of some success in their campaign to stop such mandates, at least from the federal government, only to face the prospect of what I shall call "mandates by dereliction," the need to cope with problems of housing, health care, and gainful employment for which higher levels of government have abdicated responsibility.

The first question in a local official's consideration of mandates is "Do they really mean it?" The statute books abound with prescriptions, some current and critical, others outdated and mercifully ignored; some intended very strictly, some as appropriate guidelines, some as hopeful advice without much expectation of performance. (In general, one may say that mandates limiting breaks for businesses are the most lax and easily avoided.) Once the local official ascertains the existence of a mandate—and this step is far from certain despite the availability of newsletters and conferences—he or she must decide whether or not to observe the mandate. Here several additional considerations arise: The first is whether the official wants to observe the mandate. The properly opportunistic official may seize on a mandate to implement a long-desired policy that had insufficient local support. The ideologically opposed official may dig in and ignore or resist the mandated change. Next, the official must consider the legal and political costs of noncompliance. Who will sue? Who will get mad and withdraw support? The higher these potential costs, the greater the likelihood of compliance. Finally, the official must consider whether the necessary human, financial, and other resources are available to allow compliance. Hard-strapped local governments, however well-inclined, may simply not be able to comply. Mandate compliance may then turn into bargaining between the enforcers and the mandated party with the degree and timing of compliance the central issue. (This presumes that the enforcers are sufficiently vigilant to notice, sufficiently disposed to seek compliance, and committed to a compliance rather than a punishment strategy of enforcement.)

The local response to the Americans with Disabilities Act (ADA) illustrates that mandates in practice may not be as rigid as they sound in theory. In general, Monroe County officials responded positively to the prospect of taking measures to improve the situation of the disabled. In recent years the county had taken independent initiatives to improve access to its buildings. Upon passage of the ADA the commissioners convened a committee to recommend appropriate measures without waiting for clarification of the regulations. They undertook some modest initiatives to alleviate problems for people with hearing problems in the courts and the main meeting room; the fact that one county attorney and one county councilman had difficulty hearing encouraged these steps. The commissioners hired a local architect to recommend and prioritize additional measures. Two factors have combined to delay further improvements—uncertainty about the final federal requirements and competition for available funds. Local disability advocates have been patient and no federal enforcement efforts have been mounted. Thus, despite the good intentions of local officials, the mandate remains unfilled, largely because of uncertainty about precisely what would constitute compliance.

The most expensive sphere for mandates in recent years has been corrections. These mandates can be highly specific as in the stipulation of salaries for judges, prosecutors, and probation officials. They can be as general as the prohibition of cruel and inhumane treatment of prisoners, which led to the closure of the previous jail and launched the construction of a $30 million Justice Building. Mandates have pushed staffing of the new jail steadily upward as local officials strive to comply with state inspectors' guidelines. They have forced law enforcement personnel to detain juveniles in separate youth facilities, although county officials had been assured that the new jail could provide adequate adult-juvenile separation. One temporary solution was to house the more serious juvenile offenders in a state facility located in Bloomington. Twice local judges thought they had a working agreement, first for twenty-five and then for four beds. Both times state corrections officials effectively scuttled the agreements. Driven by their need to incarcerate rapidly growing numbers of prisoners at the lowest cost, states have shifted more of the burden to local governments.

In general, local officials have closely adhered to corrections mandates, not because of any great enthusiasm for them, but because of a range of state inducements and threats. The state Department of Corrections provides major funding for the local community corrections program and offers a $35 per diem for the local housing of state prisoners. If local officials resist state mandates too strenuously, they risk the loss of funding or the imposition of additional mandates by the state or by the local judiciary. Local officials have yet to organize to resist the state's "cost-shifting" in the area of corrections and consequently are consistently steamrollered.

In dealing with mandates, local governments have tended to neglect grants from higher levels of government, save possibly to deplore their decline from the palmy days of federal revenue sharing. Nonetheless, grants constitute an important part of local government finance and should be considered together with mandates in a comprehensive balance sheet. In Monroe County they account for roughly one-sixth of all expenditures, about seventeen cents on the dollar or more than the purported cost of unfunded mandates. The fit between mandates and grant monies is, of course, far from exact.

Local governments vary greatly in their capacity to obtain grants. To obtain grants above and beyond certain basic distributions requires substantial capacity—the ability to obtain knowledge about existing grant programs, the legal authorization to access a particular program (by state participation in a federal initiative, for example), the time to compile an application, the writing skills to present a compelling case, the financial resources to provide any required local match, the expertise to administer a grant, and the political support to pursue such funding. Smaller counties operating at the margins often cannot afford the human and financial resources needed to be successful; they may not even appreciate the potential resources available to them.

Local government officials also customarily neglect to cite the additional funding sources the state legislature has made available to them. In recent years the Indiana legislature has permitted a local option income tax (now capped at 1 percent in most cases), a "wheel tax" for highway expenditures, tax-increment financing for infrastructure, a very cumbersome system of impact fees, and taxes on lodging, food, and beverages. Many, but by no means all, counties have availed themselves of these opportunities. Monroe County has imposed the local option income tax, wheel tax, and lodging tax (earmarked for the Convention and Visitors Commission) and has one tax increment financing district. The income tax generates roughly one-third of the county's general fund revenue, nearly as much as the property tax. Thus to say that the state has imposed obligations without the resources to fund them is not completely accurate; the state has allowed local politicians to assume the risk of raising taxes for the programs state and federal politicians have imposed. State officials have also withdrawn previous sources of funding; in 1995 the state legislature claimed 70 percent of local court revenue rather than the previous 50 percent and reduced excise tax revenue going to counties. From the perspective of local officials, Indiana state politicians have cynically mouthed the platitude of "no new taxes" while shifting the burden to local governments and school boards. State legislators have transferred the political costs of raising taxes while retaining the political benefits of disbursing benefits to local communities.

Monroe County has done well in acquiring grants. The city of Bloomington and the county have channeled millions of dollars in economic development funds to local industries. The Parks Department has a commitment of $950,000 in state funds for a rails-to-trails project. The state Commerce Department granted $500,000 from its Community Focus Fund to an affordable housing project. The Indiana Department of Corrections offered $500,000 for a juvenile detention center, but the project was still too expensive for the county to complete (not least because of the regulations governing the construction and staffing of such facilities). The county has also received federal funds. Its modest airport has received millions of dollars from the Federal Aeronautics Administration (FAA); now having extended and repaved its runways, it learns that the FAA is withdrawing funding for its control tower staff! The Rural Development Administration has extended $720,000 in grants and loans for a sewer project. The county has received little in the way of housing funds, largely because of its failure to mount an effective effort.

"Seek and ye shall find; ask and it shall be given unto you" has been the operative principle of county grantsmanship, at least until the present. For a lengthy period the county lacked a full-time grants person; a part-timer administered the flow of economic development monies, but lacked the time to seek additional grants. The county's airport administrator, a former Air Force colonel, with an excellent civilian board successfully found time to conduct lucrative assaults on FAA coffers. Once a full-time grants person was employed and a conscientious effort begun, the county became much more successful. The fact that a new state administration recruited several previous Bloomington officials into key positions did not hurt the cause.

The 1995 state budget illustrates the need to ask. Although the county had done well extracting funds from various state departments, its state legislators had brought little bacon home directly through the state budget. A prospective opponent of the sitting state senator suggested that this fact stemmed from the senator's lack of interest or capacity. The senator replied that she had not been asked; local officials had not informed her of their needs. Suitably prompted, local officials produced a list of requests. The senator, the leading minority member of the budget committee, promptly delivered $300,000 for an industrial park project.

The Politics of Solid Waste

Indiana local officials assumed new responsibilities in 1990 with the passage of House Bill 1240 on solid waste and recycling. Based on earlier legislation in Ohio, the new legislation called for the formation of local solid waste districts, either single-county or multicounty. Single-county districts would be governed by the three county commissioners, a county council representative, the mayor of the largest city, a city council representative, and a representative of the largest town. Multicounty districts would be governed by larger composite memberships. The legislature enjoined districts to form a plan for solid waste management and to reduce the amount of waste going to landfills by 50 percent by 2001. The state delegated broad authority to raise taxes, collect fees, pass ordinances, and receive grants, but withheld "flow control."

Special districts like Indiana's solid waste districts often arise as local units of government seek to escape the impact of property tax freezes, but in Indiana the impulse was overwhelmingly environmental. Under siege by rising demands from local and East Coast trash haulers and by improved environmental regulations, Indiana's landfills appeared to be rapidly approaching capacity. State officials sought to slow the decrease in landfill capacity and to improve Indiana's dismal environmental record. Nonetheless, in counties such as Monroe, the creation of the solid waste district produced a large financial windfall for the county. The county had owned a landfill since the early 1970s and subsidized it heavily through taxes. When the solid waste district took over the landfill, the county was able to divert roughly a million dollars to other purposes. In an ironic twist, the state's mandating solid waste districts allowed the county much greater leeway under the mandated property tax freeze.

The coming of solid waste districts also allowed the county to escape a likely state closure of its landfill and hundreds of thousands of dollars in fines. Never properly permitted, the county landfill lacked many features required by current environmental regulations, most notably a liner. For years the county had virtually no restrictions on what citizens could unload. County officials pursued the avoidance of expense as their dominant objective, even though they failed to establish a separate budget for the landfill. When the operation of the landfill failed to meet state regulations, the county commissioners of the early 1980s replaced their informal arrangements with local citizen operators by formal bidding for a contract open to solid waste management companies. At first this initiative worked well enough that state authorities entered a consent decree with the county that allowed for continued use of the landfill.

These efforts to privatize solid waste management soon showed their limitations. Under Indiana's reigning public purchase statutes the contract for the operation of the landfill and dumpster sites had to go to the low bidder. In their eagerness to obtain the contract, companies submitted bids so low that they could not comply with environmental regulations and still make a profit. Indiana's tardy acceptance of its environmental responsibilities allowed contractors to evade compliance for a period—particularly since the county as legal owner bore the final responsibility. By the mid-to-late 1980s, however, the state increasingly found the county in violation. The county sought to compel its operators to fulfill their contractual obligations to comply with the law, but with minimal success. Trusting almost entirely the good will of its contractors, the county failed to provide itself with any means of regular supervision. It belatedly added this responsibility to the portfolio of the county attorney (who held a second degree in engineering) and then in the late 1980s hired a "landfill director" to monitor the contractor.

These efforts to obtain satisfactory performance from the private contractor failed as well. The County Council, consistent with its frugal impulses, refused to authorize a salary that would have allowed the commissioners to hire a landfill director with strong professional credentials. The appointee struggled mightily and the county enlisted some skilled volunteer help, but it faced an unpleasant dilemma: If the county forced the contractor into compliance, the contractor would face financial ruin, withdraw services, and leave the county with the option of hiring a much more expensive new operator or assuming operation itself (an option the commissioners rejected). If county officials allowed the contractor to continue operating the landfill below acceptable standards, they faced massive fines and the closure of their facility. In fact, the Indiana Department of Environmental Management (IDEM) was slowly moving toward such penalties. To make matters worse, the contractor's undisciplined operation of the landfill was rapidly leading to the exhaustion of remaining space, opening the prospect that the landfill would have to close in any case.

At this point the state legislature passed a bill on solid waste districts. This mandate fell on fertile soil in Monroe County. Disappointed with an earlier abortive effort to establish a recycling program, the city and county had formed ad hoc solid waste management committees to consider the imminent closure of the landfill and opportunities for recycling. In succession these two committees deliberated for several years during the late 1980s and produced reports replete with suggestions for improvements. Their membership was drawn heavily from the urban and university-educated sections of the community. The League of Women Voters and environmental activists played leading roles. Of all their recommendations, perhaps the most significant was the endorsement of higher landfill tipping fees. This recommendation, accepted by county officials, simultaneously increased the potential resources available to solve the landfill's problems and created an incentive to reduce and recycle waste.

County government, however, lacked both the overall political resolve and the good will of IDEM necessary to solve its landfill problems. Leading officials decided to establish a single-county district and transfer the landfill to it. They favored a single-county district for two basic reasons. First, Monroe County alone would likely be a more progressive district, and second, it could act more expeditiously if it did not have to dicker with other counties. The new district's board consisted of five Democrats and two progressive Republicans. After extended negotiations the county agreed to transfer the minimal assets and substantial liabilities of the landfill to the new solid waste district. The state's institutional mandate effectively shifted solid waste management away from conservative county officials to highly progressive forces.

The new district not only had to solve the landfill's daunting operational difficulties, but had to persuade IDEM that it could and would do so. Both tasks demanded solid new professional management. The district had the good luck to be able to hire two retiring public works officials from the nearby Crane Naval Weapons Ordinance Center. Mike Frey, the new district director, and Jim Conley, the landfill director, came with extensive landfill experience, superior leadership skills, enthusiasm for the task, bureaucratic savvy, and a willingness to accept modest salaries because of their navy pensions. As past managers of Crane's landfill, one of the state's model facilities, they brought not only expertise, but instant credibility with IDEM to offset the county's tarnished image.

Frey and Conley recommended that the district dismiss its landfill contractor, buy its own equipment, and take over daily operation of the landfill. The district would issue bonds to finance the new equipment. Although the district board had reservations about a decision of this magnitude, the absence of an attractive alternative left them with little choice. To close the landfill meant facing state fines with no source of revenue other than taxes. It would leave county citizens dependent upon a virtual private monopoly for final waste disposal—an expensive and unpalatable option.

The district began to improve operations immediately, but still had to persuade IDEM that they could act responsibly. Since IDEM was moving to condemn the landfill and three of seven district officials were the same county officials who had been responsible for its operation, a major persuasive effort was required. From 1991 to 1994 district officials made regular pilgrimages to the state capital in Indianapolis. The credibility Frey and Conley had established at Crane, the obvious commitment of the elected politicians, and the intercession of the county's state legislators, two of whom were critical supporters of the Indiana Department of Environmental Management, bought time for the county and gradually Frey, Conley, and a new crew of district employees transformed the landfill into an exemplary facility. Where inspectors once found multiple violations, they now found cause to praise. Eventually IDEM accepted the results, modified its position, negotiated a new consent decree, permitted the landfill for the first time in years, and approved an expansion. The new consent decree nominally established "fines," but it accepted needed and planned landfill improvements as "payment in kind."

Much of the district's persuasive effort involved urging IDEM to adopt a compliance rather than a punishment approach to regulation. As a relatively new, underfinanced, understaffed state agency charged with unpopular tasks, IDEM officials often adopted a combative posture. Missing the technical expertise that a more experienced staff might have possessed and constantly in need of funds, IDEM lacked both capacity and incentive to work with the district and help it comply with regulations. Frey, Conley, and district officials had to gently prod the state regulators toward a different view of their task. Given the high turnover of IDEM personnel, this persuasive effort had to be repeated with new officials. Fines and closure, the district's representatives argued, would accomplish no constructive purpose. They wanted to correct previous failings; thus, there was no point in punishing simply to break the will of local officials. Eventually, through a combination of persuasion, greatly improved landfill management, and pressure from area legislators, the district convinced IDEM of the merits of the compliance view of regulation—at least in this instance. IDEM agreed to investments for improving the landfill in lieu of fines.

Simultaneously the solid waste district embarked on ambitious recycling projects. The district hired the city's former recycling director and gave her responsibility for promoting recycling and waste prevention. The district rented property, hired staff, constructed a processing center and drop-off site, and began operations. The city and the general public served as its chief clients. In addition, the district added recycling facilities at its rural dumpster sites (now duly renamed "Recycling and Solid Waste Stations"). To encourage recycling the district instituted a pay-for-use program at these sites. Fees for trash but not for recyclables created an effective market incentive. By 1995 recycling had become so successful that the existing site was bursting at the seams and the district decided to accept a private contract for processing recyclables.

The city and the county had cooperated for several years in sponsoring an annual Tox-Away Day to capture hazardous household wastes before they entered the waste stream. Although successful, this program proved costly in relation to the wastes gathered. The district found that for a modest additional investment it could run its own household hazardous waste program on a continuous basis—and do it less expensively. The political district board members expressed fears about liability issues but voted to proceed with Indiana's first public program of this sort. Soon they added a program for recycling household batteries that has now expanded to include more than thirty counties. As the program succeeded and fears about liability subsided, the district expanded its collection to small business. This "small quantity generator" program is just beginning but is off to an auspicious start.

The Monroe County Solid Waste Management District has earned a reputation as one of the state's top districts, if not the best. It has won three Governor's Awards for recycling, more than any other recipient. It has received hundreds of thousands of dollars in state grants to help fund its programs. These successes reinforced the state's willingness to reject the punishment option at the landfill.

The contrasting fate of solid waste management in county hands and in district hands refutes any notion that state-local relations comprise a single distinctive pattern. The state's mandate to create solid waste districts allowed Monroe County to create a new and different relation with the state of Indiana. Where the county's traditional conservative methods alienated the new and more aggressive state Department of Environmental Management and pushed it toward regulation through punishment, the solid waste district substituted progressive policies and allowed the state to practice regulation through incentives for compliance. As relatively new institutions, IDEM and the solid waste district also enjoyed slightly more freedom of maneuver and capacity to invent or alter procedures than did older county and state institutions.

As the cases in this essay demonstrate, relations between the state of Indiana and local government vary greatly, even within the same county, depending upon the issue, the parts of each government involved, and the degree of common interests within and between the parties. The much-discussed issue of mandates turns out to be a variety of issues depending on the nature of the mandate, the kinds of sanctions and inducements available to the state, and the willingness and capacity of local governments to comply. Politics constantly reshapes the constitutional framework and the actors who operate within it. For these reasons any search for a general theory of state-local relations appears vain, condemned to failure in the messy particularity and steady evolution that even the best static metaphors fail to capture.

10

The Politics of State Health and Welfare Reforms

Charles Barrilleaux

State governments directly touch the lives of citizens through their health and welfare policy packages. State decisions determine the types of health care services that are delivered within a state, influence the type and number of facilities that are available, establish the methods by which professionals receive licensure, and for the poor, determine who has, and does not have, insurance coverage and what services that insurance covers. Welfare policy choices determine who receives how much assistance and also provide a gateway for the receipt of state-sponsored health insurance coverage. Recent demands for health and welfare reform will significantly alter the status quo in each area, and current calls for a reduced national government role in setting the rules for health and welfare coverage, along with a shift to block grants in lieu of existing methods of federal contribution, will force the states to introduce innovations to their methods of providing both health and welfare coverage in the future.

The term "health policy" is confusing since no American state, let alone the nation, has a single identifiable policy. Instead, health policies in the states are a jumble of often contradictory rules and pieces of legislation that seldom add up to a meaningful whole. Politics leads states to do seemingly illogical things. Florida invests large sums of money to improve prenatal and neonatal care for the poor in hope of improving birth outcomes, yet the state is reluctant to provide birth control information in schools due to resistance from conservatives. North Carolina seeks to strike information regarding the hazards of smoking during pregnancy from materials provided to pregnant women because tobacco interests take exception to the information. Legislators in a number of states seek to reduce the costs of trauma care yet they also support raising speed limits even though there is strong evidence that reducing them will decrease

deaths and injuries. In each of these cases, and in countless others, the political logic of the decisions is clear but the public health reckoning is
flawed. Political sense often overrules "good" policy, so it is not likely
that state health policies will be rationalized in the near future.

The situation is no different in welfare policy, which is one of the most
important indicators of "who gets what" in state politics. Despite a drift
toward national government supremacy in welfare policymaking since
the passage of the Social Security Act in 1935, state and local governments
have always been important in welfare policymaking. In this essay I focus
on two aspects of current debates surrounding welfare policy reform—
the philosophical justification for reform and the political basis for support of particular policy positions. The crux of the argument is that welfare reform is driven largely by politics, state income, and state fears
regarding Medicaid spending. The amounts of money spent on public assistance are trivial (relative to other major policy areas). "Workfare" and
other training-based strategies to get long-term recipients of public aid off
the dole may be preferable inasmuch as they reduce the welfare dependency problem, but they are not likely to save money. In addition, there
is reason to believe that state and local governments, the units most likely
to be charged with implementing welfare reform, do not have the administrative capacity to do so. Thus welfare reform, which is taking a
number of different forms in the states, may prove to be largely symbolic.
The most important change is the gradual erosion of benefits to the most
needy citizens: children and their caretakers.

Prior to the passage of the Social Security Act of 1935, social policy in
the United States was viewed primarily as a state and local responsibility. State and local governments were staggered by the enormity of problems attending the Great Depression, however, and this provided an avenue for national government expansion into the realm of social policy.
Parts of the programs established by the Social Security Act, particularly
grants to the aged, disabled, and the minor dependents of beneficiaries,
were then and are now run by the national government. Social support
for the "able-bodied" poor, usually unmarried or widowed women with
minor children who were deprived of male financial support, is the
purview of the states. As a result the United States has established and
maintained dual systems of poor support. Persons whose need is generally accepted by the public, that is, those in need because of aging, disability, or other misfortune—"the deserving poor"—receive nationally
uniform benefits from the central government. Others, whose need is not
so uniformly agreed upon, receive services and cash transfers through a
system administered largely by the states but funded jointly by the states
and the national government. Consequently, the level of support varies
considerably among units of government.

The lack of consensus regarding the appropriate government role in providing cash transfers and other forms of social support does not end at state borders. There are intrastate disagreements about welfare as well. Local governments are involved in the management of programs and sometimes they help finance "state" programs. Thus the intergovernmental politics of welfare are volatile, and the issue often figures prominently in political campaigns and rhetoric. Self-sufficiency and individual responsibility are central tenets of American political belief systems. Welfare is an especially attractive target in times of prolonged economic stagnation, erosion of work-related benefits, and fear of a reduced standard of living.

In this chapter I discuss the current politics of welfare reform and link welfare reform to current efforts to reform health care. Given that states are seeking to gain increased control of their spending, health and welfare are significant issues, and it is important to treat them in tandem. Until 1996, Aid to Families with Dependent Children (AFDC) was the gateway to Medicaid eligibility for large numbers of the recipient population. Since states are faced with mounting difficulties in their efforts to fund Medicaid, it was only natural that they sought to control health spending by regulating AFDC spending. Here, I focus on state efforts in AFDC spending, describing changes between 1980 and 1990 and estimating ordinary least squares models to explain variations in state efforts in the two time periods. The purpose of this exercise is to test three popular explanations for state efforts in AFDC spending—politics, economics, and as a reaction to runaway Medicaid spending. The results may be helpful in anticipating the effects of recent reforms that replaced AFDC, an entitlement program, with Temporary Assistance to Needy Families (TANF) in the form of block grants to states.

Health and Welfare Reform

State and local governments become intimately involved in the lives of citizens via health and welfare policies. Politics, history and custom, national government policy, and economic conditions converge to influence the character and substance of state and local health and welfare policies. Together they form an intricate and important set of policies that are largely redistributive in intent and yet distributive and regulatory in practice. As a result, health and welfare policies are surrounded by tumultuous politics in which core values and partisan politics figure prominently. Health and welfare policies provide opportunity for the revival of states' rights positions, place class politics squarely on the table, lead the parties to take divisive stands, and appropriate increasing shares of state budgets. Compounding the difficulty are widespread citizen antipathy toward taxes and legislative reluctance to eschew the large national government financial transfers that accompany state health and welfare service delivery. The result is that health and welfare reform have been and continue to be prominent items on the domestic policy agenda.

New Federalism and the Search for Spending Limits

Aside from its political appeal, elective officials have other strong incentives to "reform" state health and welfare policies. The prominence of health care as a domestic policy area is easily justified in financial terms: Health care costs are high and are increasing at rates well above those of the consumer price index (CPI). Estimates of the numbers of uninsured Americans range from as low as 31 million to almost 40 million, depending on the source of data. Many of these people qualify for Medicaid, and there is widespread belief that Medicaid is consuming too large a portion of state and local budgets, taking away from education and other areas of state concern. Welfare reform's political cachet is not so easily explained in financial terms. Spending for welfare, or at least the direct cash subsidies normally thought of as welfare, rose only modestly during the 1980s despite increases in caseloads. According to a 1992 Government Accounting Office (U.S. GAO) study, about 12.6 million family units in the United States, about 14.4 percent, were living in poverty in 1980; the percentage living in poverty declined to 14.1 percent by 1988, but the number rose to 14.2 million families (U.S. GAO 1992: 2). Spending increases were controlled by making eligibility standards more stringent and by reducing the amount of transfer payments to families.

Given that spending trends for welfare and health care differed markedly in the 1980s, one might expect their priorities on the reform agenda to differ substantially. However, they are closely linked, particularly in the area of welfare medicine, where state and county governments are especially active given their responsibilities under Medicaid, the state-federal program that provides health insurance for the poor and near-poor. One critical aspect of both health and welfare reform lies in the evolution of responsibilities in the U.S. federal system. The devolution of some federal responsibilities, particularly in social services and education, gained impetus during the Reagan administration and has had important effects on state and local spending and policy responsibility.

The first wave of effects of Ronald Reagan's New Federalism gave the states greater responsibility for both policy development and finance in the areas of health care and welfare. The second wave, which is ongoing and is bolstered by the recent popularity of the "reinventing government" movement (Osborne and Gaebler 1992), is now forcing reconsideration of county and municipal roles in developing and funding health and welfare services. Republican wins in the 1994 congressional elections and in state legislative and gubernatorial races, based in part on the notion that many responsibilities residing with national government should be returned to the states, rekindled interest in block grant funding and otherwise limiting the federal role in favor of decisionmaking at the state and local level.

On the positive side, counties and cities are proving to be strong policy innovators and are altering programs to fit their citizens' needs. On a less positive note, these new responsibilities are forcing governments to finance expensive services once funded by the national government, placing huge strains on budgets. This might be seen as radical decentralization that forces a return to the policymaking envisioned by the Founders (Dye 1990). But a skeptic might view this simply as the latest in buckpassing. States, by virtue of their constitutionally superior position to local governments, may require localities to assume responsibility for the delivery of certain public services. Unfortunately, they often fail to provide revenue for local governments to do so, giving rise to what county and city officials call the mandate problem.

This new era of fiscal crisis, linked to popular opinion and changes in national policy, has forced states and localities to seek new ways of delivering and paying for services. Given the high costs of Medicaid and the relative political weakness of the clientele receiving public assistance, it is understandable that these programs are susceptible to drastic overhaul in times of fiscal strain. Recent research (Barrilleaux, Brace, and Dangremond 1995; Brace and Barrilleaux 1995) indicates that state health and welfare policies can be expected to diverge more sharply with the withdrawal of federal involvement, as some states seek to improve services, while others try to limit both health and welfare benefits. The different responses are driven largely by ideology, state political and administrative capability, and economic circumstance. Hence the world of competitive federalism may have dire effects for some citizens, particularly those who are unable to relocate in order to find a better "mix" of benefits.

Party Politics and Health and Welfare Reform

For purposes of electoral posturing, welfare policy is the wedge that most effectively separates Democrats and Republicans in the United States. Republicans, aware of public antipathy toward government spending and people getting something for nothing, hold up the presumed failures of various Great Society programs as evidence of government's inability to improve peoples' lives (Murray 1984). Indeed, attacks on welfare have been cast as sometimes subtle and sometimes overt appeals to racial antipathies, used by Republicans as part of their successful "southern strategy" (Carmines and Stimson 1989). On the other hand, some authors point to considerable successes that are partially attributable to the antipoverty initiatives of the past thirty years; infant mortality rates have dropped, illiteracy is down, life expectancies among the poor and non-whites have increased, and so on (see Marmor et al. 1990). On balance, it seems fair to say that the War on Poverty was neither an enormous failure nor an overwhelming success. It was a massive, ambitious, and well-intended policy gamble that had both good and bad effects. Great Society programs established the grounds upon which eventual policy changes will be made, however, and its influence can not be removed from the matrix of health and welfare policies.

Democrats have a more difficult position than Republicans in the welfare debate. The party of the poor in U.S. national politics since the New Deal realignment of 1932, Democrats were long hamstrung by a seeming inability to take a firm position on welfare policy. Before the Democratic Leadership Council gained control of the national party apparatus, which resulted in the nomination and eventual election of Bill Clinton, Democratic presidential candidates proved easy targets for Republicans because of the positions they were forced to take on welfare. Democratic candidates attempted to hold the New Deal coalition together, fearing a loss of African American, labor, and other voting blocs. The desire to maintain this electoral coalition was evident in the party's failure to take a stand on welfare reform. Thus Republicans attacked the 1988 Democratic platform as beholden to special interests. Clinton's willingness to depart from traditional party positions on welfare and other economic issues helped make him electable. Despite a dramatic shift from long-held tenets regarding welfare policy, however, Democrats were outflanked by Republicans in the U.S. House of Representatives, who staked out positions far to the right of what was deemed extreme a decade ago. Democrats have been hard-pressed to win the battle of welfare constriction, and it is uncertain that doing so will provide much electoral reward.

Americans are ambivalent about welfare policy. Public opinion polls regularly unearth considerable support for the notion that Americans should have a social safety net that protects them from poverty, poor health, and other misfortunes. Likewise, large majorities of Americans support the premise that health care should be treated as a right of citizenship. Yet, when asked about taxes and their willingness to pay for such programs, support dwindles. As a result the United States is, and has long been, a laggard in social welfare policy when compared to other industrialized democracies. The lack of consensus on what constitutes an appropriate government role in providing social insurance, income support, health care coverage, and the like contributes to the volatile politics of social policy. No politician is safely "for" welfare, but most accept it, in varying degrees, as a necessity in an industrialized nation. Historically, and in contemporary debates, the accepted position has been that the government has an obligation to provide some protection from the world's vicissitudes, but that citizens have a responsibility to avoid the need for public assistance and to remove themselves from the social aid system as soon as possible.

Health politics are similar, but they are complicated by the presence of large and well-financed clientele groups representing health providers (physicians, hospitals, nursing homes, and so on), vendors of medical equipment, insurance companies, health maintenance organizations, and others. Nonetheless, the politics of health reform have been centered on a sort of class politics, with representatives of insurors taking a large role in pitting the haves, those with adequate health coverage, against the have-nots, those without adequate coverage and enrollees in Medicaid. Throughout the history of health politics in the United States, the specter of "socialized medicine" and images of huge new bureaucracies are invoked as likely consequences of changing the existing system (Poen 1979). Although none of the suggested remedies for the health spending and coverage problem approximates a system of socialized medicine, and the administrative costs of both Medicare and Medicaid are miniscule when compared to those of private insurance companies, the language is politically powerful and raises fears among many Americans.

The partisan politics of health reform are similar to those of welfare reform. Republicans, having failed to convince the public that there is no crisis, now focus on market-oriented solutions to health insurance reform. Most of these plans offer incremental changes that broaden the market for existing insurance groups and place responsibility for purchasing health insurance upon individuals. Although there is considerable variation in plans offered by Democrats, they all differ from those floated by Republicans in their willingness to use the public sector as a regulatory mechanism to monitor the system. Also, consistent with Democrats' needs to appeal to the have-nots in the population, Democratic-sponsored plans typically are more likely to offer universal coverage or at least to guarantee coverage of a larger proportion of the population than Republican-sponsored plans.

Public Assistance and Medicaid

Welfare programs are generally viewed as having a redistributive intent, that is, they take from the haves and give to the have-nots. Although that is true, a number of programs that could be viewed as "welfare" do not receive that label inasmuch as they provide benefits for large portions of the nonpoor population. Such programs include crop subsidies, public higher education (of which the author and a number of the readers are beneficiaries), tax credits for interest paid on house mortgages, and the list goes on. Although a variety of antipoverty programs have redistributive features—the earned income tax credit, food stamps, Supplemental Security Income, among others—the U.S. welfare system is based largely on two programs, public assistance and Medicaid. Until 1996, Aid to Families with Dependent Children (AFDC) was the main public assistance program. AFDC has now been replaced by Temporary Assistance to Needy Families (TANF). Public assistance and Medicaid are financed jointly by the states and the national government, with county contributions in some states, and each program gives the states tremendous latitude in determining who among their citizens will be provided services. The management of the two programs thus stands in stark contrast to Social Security, which provides cash benefits to Americans who are aged, disabled, or otherwise impaired and incapable of working, or to the minor survivors of persons eligible for benefits at the time of death, and Medicare, a health insurance program for the same clientele.

Both Social Security and Medicare are nationally administered entitlement programs, whereas public assistance and Medicaid are means-tested, which is to say that income is considered when citizens apply for benefits. Public assistance and Medicaid enrollees are mainly adults and children living in single-parent households. In the case of public assistance, states are given the responsibility of establishing eligibility criteria that define which persons or families qualify for benefits. The primary tool for establishing eligibility is the income test, which sets amounts of income and/or assets beyond which persons may not receive benefits. States also set payment levels, which is the amount to be paid the beneficiary each month. The national government required states to provide AFDC benefits to caretakers and their children, but states were allowed to cover additional categories of citizens under the AFDC umbrella without reimbursement from Washington, D.C. Thus AFDC coverage decisions were complex and varied from state to state; the implementation of TANF will almost certainly increase differences between state programs.

Health and Welfare as Reform Issues

It is a mistake to view either health care or welfare reform as new issues. Each has been a continual source of concern for all levels of government since the 1940s. For example, government's role in health care has expanded dramatically since the early 1940s. Seeing the need to develop some form of health care coverage, Congress built upon the existing system of coverage by private movers, offering significant tax advantages for the provision of both retirement and health benefits by employers. This response to emerging shortfalls in coverage dealt with the problem incrementally rather than globally. The cumulative effect of these policy band-aids was the development of coverage rife with perverse incentives that led providers of health care and enrollees in health plans to overuse services. Similarly, the incremental policymaking system for other forms of social insurance resulted in the development of policy with incentives antithetical to the idea of personal responsibility.

The seeds of the current employment-based system of insurance were sown by the Congress's imposition of wage and price freezes during World War II. The policy of freezing wages during a period of labor shortage led employers to entice new employees with benefits, notably health care insurance and pensions. Congress responded to this development by providing generous tax treatment of employer-paid benefits, thereby institutionalizing the employment-based system and encouraging the rise of a proprietary insurance industry. Basing insurance coverage on employment was a sensible but shortsighted strategy. It made sense inasmuch as private insurers—largely nonprofit state Blue Cross/Blue Shield organizations—were in place and operating successfully at the time that demand increased for health insurance. As with the GI bill, which provided veterans with vouchers to attend public and private universities, the national government sought to use private insurers as a vehicle for broadening health insurance coverage.

When unemployment was extraordinarily low in the years immediately following World War II and throughout the 1950s, the employment-based health insurance system worked fairly well. Although some people were without insurance, notably the unemployed and the elderly, some states ran small programs to provide the poor with health insurance under the auspices of Kerr-Mills legislation, the predecessor of Medicaid. The decline of the economy beginning in the 1960s and the concomitant increase in structural unemployment contributed to the development of a society in which the majority of Americans were overinsured and provided perverse incentives in the use of health services (Pauly 1986). A growing number of persons, the chronically unemployed and those employed in low-wage jobs, accepted life without insurance. The uninsurance crisis, as we now know it, was first recognized as a massive problem in the early 1980s, when the adoption of fixed-price reimbursement schemes (for diagnosis-related groups, for example) diffused among insurers, and hospitals were no longer able to charge variable rates to insured patients in order to recoup the costs of uncompensated care.

The ramifications of the employment-based health and other social insurance coverage (unemployment benefits, workers' compensation, pensions, and so forth) are great. As noted previously, large numbers of insured persons are essentially overinsured. The tax treatment afforded insurance led businesses to provide it as a perquisite of employment in lieu of higher salaries. Individuals, too, gain from insurance-based benefits inasmuch as they are not taxed as income. In the case of health insurance, individuals who are enrolled in a "traditional" health plan, either one with first dollar coverage (that is, one in which insurance picks up all expenses associated with a medical episode, a now rare form of insurance) or in a plan with a deductible (in which an individual pays for care out-of-pocket up to a given amount, say $500, after which the insurer pays all expenses), there is no strong incentive to seek less expensive treatment. Although some plans seek to control use of services via case management or through the imposition of copayments, as in most health maintenance organizations (HMOs), it is unclear whether the incentives to hold down use of services are sufficiently strong to influence individual behavior (Thorpe 1993).

The design of the health insurance system also gave perverse incentives to providers of health services—physicians, hospitals, and other institutions. They held an enviable position in the market given their control of expert information, the emotionalism surrounding the purchase of health services by consumers, and the lack of a meaningful financial constraint on the part of patients. Providers of services were able to establish demand for services and to set prices for the services delivered. In addition, they received strong government-financed support to expand facilities and services and to otherwise improve their market positions. Hospital capital improvements were folded into bills for services received, tax laws enabled hospitals to organize as charitable organizations despite their investment in a wide variety of profitable ancillary enterprises, and so on. The medical industry holds a privileged position and is able to exert significant influence on policymaking either through direct acts, such as lobbying or making campaign contributions, or indirectly, by constraining the range of options open to policy makers, since some options (a national single-payer system, for example) are viewed as so politically dangerous as to be infeasible (Lindblom 1977).

As with health care reform, the roots of welfare reform are deep. The most visible transfer program, and that with which states and counties were most directly involved, was Aid to Families with Dependent Children (AFDC), established alongside the Social Security program in 1935. Aid to Families with Dependent Children was designed to provide cash grants to needy children without fathers. In its most recent incarnation AFDC provided cash grants to poor children who were in need of assistance due to one parent's being absent from the home, deceased, unable to work, or unemployed. Each of the fifty states as well as the District of Columbia and four of the five territories voluntarily operated an AFDC program.

Although AFDC was a national program, states were given considerable latitude in establishing need and payment levels, defining eligibility criteria, and determining how and at what level of government to administer the program. The national government stimulated AFDC (and Medicaid) participation by providing matching grants, ranging from about 50 percent of total benefits spending to about 80 percent, with wealthier states receiving the lesser match and 50 percent of the cost of administration. Temporary Assistance to Needy Families (TANF), the successor to AFDC, is a version of "workfare." Although there are wide variations on the workfare notion, the gist is that transfer payments come with some obligation to move off the welfare roles in favor of self-suffi-ciency. Workfare schemes typically require that individuals enrolled in the categorically based eligibility system enter some sort of work, ideally work in the private sector, as a condition for their receipt of cash trans-fers. This is easier said than done. Job placement and child care are prob-lematic, and there are serious program-induced barriers to individuals' leaving the welfare rolls. Doing so often results in recipients losing health care benefits, food stamps, and other necessary subsidies.

This confounding feature of welfare, that loss of cash transfers typically leads to the loss of other benefits, is the point at which welfare and health care are most clearly linked. A considerable amount of research addresses the question of welfare dependency and indicates that the design of the U.S. system of social welfare creates a class of persons for whom receipt of government assistance is simply the most rational economic choice. David Ellwood (1988) argues that several features of AFDC discouraged poor women with children from marrying, obtaining jobs, or otherwise remov-ing themselves from the categorical aid system. In central cities, where a large proportion of the public assistance population is clustered, the un-employment rate among young men often exceeds 30 percent. Thus the market for marriageable men is poor; a woman faced with the decision to marry under those economic circumstances would rationally choose to re-main on public assistance; she lost Medicaid benefits for herself and for her children if she married or took a low-paying job. Current reform of welfare addresses this problem, and most states are providing avenues for gradual loss of welfare benefits as recipients leave welfare rolls for employment.

Welfare reform revolves around the theme "rights and responsibility." True to his position as a welfare reform–oriented governor, President Clinton pledged during his campaign to "end welfare as we know it." In his 1994 State of the Union Address he placed welfare reform, including workfare and a two-year limit on receipt of benefits, on the administration's agenda alongside health care reform. The items President Clinton noted are but the most visible and controversial components of welfare reform. Welfare policy is at times guided by mythical thinking. People believe that welfare has caused divorce and rewarded women for having children out of wedlock. Many believe that women have had additional children to in-crease the amount of their monthly supplement. The thinking goes that welfare recipiency spawned a class of welfare recipients who passed their lifestyle along over the course of generations. In response to this thinking, new policies are designed to deter families from having additional children by denying grant increases for children born after a family has entered welfare. Reforms also tie family benefits to children's school attendance and halt benefits to families whose children are convicted of felonies.

Less dramatic, but constituting the bulk of reforms are policy objectives falling into six broad areas. According to a report by the National Governors' Association, by early 1994 at least twenty states had proposed or enacted legislation to (1) reduce penalties in the welfare system that are linked to earnings and savings, thereby increasing the incentive for enrollees to work; (2) step up child support enforcement; (3) eliminate certain welfare rules that penalize two-parent families; (4) streamline the administrative obstacles to the receipt of welfare benefits, particularly through the use of electronic "smart cards"; (5) create jobs for welfare enrollees; and (6) provide better support for families leaving welfare for work by enhancing child care and health care (NGA 1994). Most of these reforms are preserved in the new TANF programs; indeed, national welfare reforms adopted in 1996 were inspired by these earlier experiments at the state level.

Despite the "get tough" rhetoric of much welfare policy discussion, the most frequently invoked reforms are designed to mediate the most often-cited flaws of AFDC, notably its tendency to punish those who seek to enter the workforce or those who maintain or establish intact families. Fifteen states proposed or adopted variants of policies designed to provide financial incentives for independent teens and financial penalties for families who do not ensure that their children attend school regularly. Although most members of the Clinton administration's welfare reform work group preferred training, education, and supportive child care programs, workfare became the basis for the reform enacted in 1996.

This distinction points to the new ideological rift in welfare policy, ignoring for the moment the extreme positions taken by Charles Murray and others, who would abolish income transfers almost completely and establish orphanages for the offspring of poor unwed mothers. The new orthodoxy, represented by the workfare camp, holds that it is acceptable for the poor to be placed in minimum-wage, low-skill jobs to "earn" their public assistance check, or at least a portion of it. Those who reject workfare argue that it introduces a new series of problems in that it fails to provide the poor with meaningful work skills and displaces currently working persons with low skills, thereby exacerbating the problem of poverty and maintaining and reinforcing the prevailing class system. Of course, these problems are felt directly at the local level.

But the most striking change in public assistance is the diminishing investments states are making in income transfers via the program. Data in Table 10.1 illustrate this trend: In 1980 the average state effort (defined as

TABLE 10.1   State AFDC Spending per $1,000 Personal Income, 1980 and 1990

State	1980 Effort	1990 Effort	Ratio
Alabama	0.806	0.280	0.347
Alaska	2.455	2.696	1.098
Arkansas	0.819	0.439	0.536
California	4.187	4.149	0.991
Colorado	1.228	1.064	0.867
Connecticut	2.757	1.839	0.667
Delaware	2.581	1.079	0.418
Florida	0.861	0.827	0.960
Georgia	1.002	1.139	1.138
Hawaii	4.375	1.996	0.456
Idaho	1.029	0.349	0.339
Illinois	2.902	1.866	0.643
Indiana	1.174	0.675	0.575
Iowa	2.291	1.233	0.538
Kansas	1.736	1.026	0.591
Kentucky	1.472	0.905	0.615
Louisiana	1.053	0.839	0.797
Maine	1.966	1.707	0.868
Maryland	2.341	1.445	0.617
Massachusetts	4.021	2.382	0.592
Michigan	5.654	3.287	0.581
Minnesota	2.251	2.046	0.909
Mississippi	0.787	0.521	0.662
Missouri	1.582	1.088	0.688
Montana	0.984	0.979	0.996
Nebraska	1.262	0.855	0.677
Nevada	0.585	0.581	0.993
New Hampshire	1.154	0.748	0.648
New Jersey	3.260	1.188	0.364
New Mexico	1.216	0.852	0.701
New York	4.235	2.941	0.694
N. Carolina	1.056	0.767	0.727
N. Dakota	1.234	0.812	0.658
Ohio	2.394	1.915	0.800
Oklahoma	1.182	0.897	0.759
Oregon	2.497	1.141	0.457
Pennsylvania	2.936	1.666	0.567
Rhode Island	3.338	2.374	0.711
S. Carolina	0.882	0.497	0.563
S. Dakota	1.119	0.593	0.530
Tennessee	0.704	0.689	0.978

(continues)

TABLE 10.1   *(continued)*

State	1980 Effort	1990 Effort	Ratio
Texas	0.396	0.590	1.492
Utah	1.310	0.677	0.517
Vermont	2.298	1.899	0.826
Virginia	1.314	0.740	0.563
Washington	2.820	3.283	1.164
W. Virginia	1.256	1.065	0.848
Wisconsin	3.220	2.098	0.652
Wyoming	0.833	0.920	1.104

SOURCE: Author's calculations, from various editions of the *Statistical Abstract of the United States.*

state-only spending, i.e., state spending minus the federal match) was $1.94; by 1990 that effort had dropped to $1.33. These figures are especially remarkable since they are not adjusted for inflation. The state with the lowest effort in 1980, Texas, devoted about forty cents per $1,000 personal income to AFDC. In 1990, Alabama made the least effort, contributing twenty-eight cents per $1,000 income to AFDC grants.

On average, state AFDC efforts in 1990 were about 72 percent of their efforts in 1980, in dollars not adjusted for inflation. Texas spending in 1990 was about 1.5 times its 1980 effort, but Idaho's 1990 commitment was only about 34 percent of its 1980 effort. In general, state AFDC efforts declined greatly over the decade despite increases in the numbers of persons falling into the poverty population.

In contrast to AFDC spending efforts, state efforts in Medicaid spending (Table 10.2) increased drastically over the 1980–1990 period. The states spent an average of less than $4.00 per $1,000 of personal income from its own funds to support the Medicaid program in 1980; by 1990 the average state effort rose to more than $17.00. The state with the lowest change in Medicaid effort over the era was New York, with a 1990 effort only 48 percent of its 1980 effort; Rhode Island was the only other state to reduce its effort, with the ratio of 1980 to 1990 spending of 0.90. The average increase in Medicaid effort between 1980 and 1990 was $5.77 per $1,000 personal income.

That state efforts in AFDC declined is not surprising: States assumed increased responsibilities for spending and for policy management in a number of areas and did so in an environment where increased public spending and taxation were politically anathema. As is shown in Table 10.3 the relationships between income, AFDC effort, and Medicaid effort changed markedly from 1980 to 1990. In 1980, wealthier states exerted

TABLE 10.2   State-Funded Medicaid Spending per $1,000 Personal Income, 1980 and 1990

State	1980 Effort	1990 Effort	Ratio
Alabama	2.53	27.96	11.06
Alaska	2.43	14.38	5.92
Arizona			
Arkansas	3.77	18.87	5.01
California	4.91	16.24	3.31
Colorado	2.75	19.27	7.00
Connecticut	4.61	10.31	2.23
Delaware	3.65	14.95	4.09
Florida	1.66	18.20	10.95
Georgia	3.36	16.25	4.84
Hawaii	4.63	21.06	4.55
Idaho	2.23	25.72	11.53
Illinois	4.79	17.03	3.56
Indiana	2.99	15.51	5.19
Iowa	3.66	16.30	4.45
Kansas	4.03	18.15	4.51
Kentucky	3.20	17.04	5.33
Louisiana	3.53	13.00	3.69
Maine	4.30	11.37	2.64
Maryland	3.50	16.29	4.66
Massachusetts	7.96	9.60	1.21
Michigan	5.70	14.76	2.59
Minnesota	6.42	11.12	1.73
Mississippi	2.72	21.85	8.03
Missouri	2.57	19.48	7.59
Montana	3.23	21.16	6.56
Nebraska	3.27	18.00	5.51
Nevada	2.39	27.08	11.34
New Hampshire	3.07	16.03	5.22
New Jersey	4.40	14.18	3.22
New Mexico	2.04	22.65	11.13
New York	12.00	5.79	0.48
N. Carolina	2.75	18.73	6.81
N. Dakota	3.63	13.02	3.59
Ohio	3.46	12.81	3.71
Oklahoma	3.41	18.48	5.42
Oregon	3.04	19.71	6.48
Pennsylvania	4.03	14.45	3.59
Rhode Island	7.44	6.67	0.90
S. Carolina	3.18	21.46	6.76

(continues)

TABLE 10.2   *(continued)*

State	1980 Effort	1990 Effort	Ratio
S. Dakota	3.23	18.94	5.86
Tennessee	3.14	17.21	5.48
Texas	2.90	23.48	8.11
Utah	2.17	30.88	14.22
Vermont	4.26	13.64	3.20
Virginia	2.95	20.08	6.81
Washington	3.70	12.04	3.26
W. Virginia	2.17	19.41	8.95
Wisconsin	6.26	14.29	2.28
Wyoming	1.33	24.15	18.11

SOURCE: Author's calculations from various years of *The Medicare/Medicaid Data Book* (Health Care Financing Administration).

TABLE 10.3   Correlations Among AFDC Effort, 1980 and 1990, Medicaid Effort, 1980 and 1990, and Income, 1980 and 1990

	AFDC 1980	AFDC 1990	Medicaid 1980	Medicaid 1990	Income 1980	Income 1990
AFDC 1980	1.000					
AFDC 1990	0.855	1.000				
Medicaid 1980	0.708	0.626	1.000			
Medicaid 1990	−0.569	−0.616	−0.707	1.000		
Income 1980	0.451	0.544	0.421	−0.259	1.000	
Income 1990	0.427	0.523	0.404	−0.243	0.993	1.000

SOURCE: Author's calculations.

stronger AFDC and Medicaid efforts, and AFDC and Medicaid effort were related positively. By 1990, however, less wealthy states were exerting greater AFDC and Medicaid efforts, and the relationship between AFDC and Medicaid efforts was negative. Thus it is fair to link reductions in AFDC efforts with increases in Medicaid efforts; states financed high and increasing Medicaid spending by limiting their AFDC effort. However, evidence also suggests that AFDC changes were driven at least partly by politics within the states.

Models of State AFDC Effort

Following much of the rhetoric surrounding present discussions of welfare reform, it is clear that state AFDC efforts result at least partly from state political circumstances. Consider three hypotheses regarding political influences on AFDC effort:

1. AFDC effort increased in the presence of more liberal state legislatures.
2. AFDC effort diminished in the presence of legislatures more strongly controlled by Democrats.
3. AFDC effort increased where governors are accorded more constitutional powers.

The justification for hypothesis 1 is straightforward: AFDC was a redistributive program, and redistributive programs historically receive their greatest support from the more ideological portions of the U.S. population. Since voters tend to elect representatives whose ideological stances are consistent with their own (Erikson, Wright, and McIver 1989), more liberal legislators should enact more generous redistributive policies as a reflection of voter demands. The reasoning underlying the second hypothesis is not so clear; briefly, the presence of large numbers of Democrats in a legislature, even if they are the more liberal of the two parties (Erikson, Wright, and McIver 1989), leads to less liberal policies because of the absence of interparty competition for legislative seats. Following the logic of the competing parties thesis (Key 1949), competition should spur increased spending for redistribution as parties seek to attract the votes of lower income voters, whose interests are rarely represented in the absence of competitive politics. Low levels of competition will have the opposite effect.

The final hypothesis taps state government capacity. Where state constitutional officers are accorded relatively greater powers to carry out their jobs, they are more likely to use the tools of the state to achieve particular ends. Stronger governors are not only better able to marshal portions of their platforms through the budgetary process, but are more likely to do so in states where citizens accept the legitimacy of redistributive policy. Brace (1993) shows that states with stronger governors were more successful in fomenting growth in personal income during the 1980s, citing that as evidence of the value of aggressive state action in seeking to determine their own economic fates. Following his logic, states with greater institutional capacity should make relatively larger investments in the AFDC population to augment other attempts at boosting income.

Aside from political influences on state AFDC efforts, income clearly is important. A number of studies show that income is positively associated with redistributive effort (Dye 1990). Thus AFDC effort should rise with increases in personal income. Also, there is a tradeoff between AFDC and

TABLE 10.4   Influences on State AFDC Effort, 1980

Variable	b	s.e.b	B	t
CONSTANT	−0.444	0.587	0.000	−0.757
Legislative liberalism	0.588	0.118	0.512	4.984*
Democratic legislative strength	−0.894	0.526	−0.148	−1.698*
Gubernatorial powers	0.069	0.039	0.160	1.744*
Medicaid effort, 1980	0.193	0.064	0.308	3.015*
Income, 1980	0.003	0.002	0.129	1.463**
Adjusted R^2 = .75; s.e.e. = .59; F = 26.71, prob. F = .000				

* one-tailed significance ≤ .05; ** one-tailed significance < .10.
NOTE: Effort is equal to state AFDC spending per $1000 of personal income.
SOURCE: Legislative liberalism is described in Erikson, Wright, and McIver
(1989) and provided by the author. Democratic legislative strength is described
in Erikson, Wright, and McIver (1989) and provided by the author.
Gubernatorial power is the Schlesinger index calculated by the author from
data included in *Book of the States,* various years.

Medicaid spending; state welfare generosity will be associated positively
with Medicaid efforts in the first period in which models are tested (1980)
and negatively linked to AFDC generosity in the 1990 model. That is, the
1980s were marked by heightened state concerns that Medicaid spending
was out of control, and those concerns were coupled with tremendous citizen antipathy toward taxation and successful challenges to "liberal" policymaking by conservative Republicans and Democrats in both national
and state and local elections. Thus the Medicaid hypothesis is that AFDC
effort increased with increased Medicaid effort in 1980, but higher
Medicaid efforts were associated with diminished AFDC efforts in 1990.

The hypotheses can be tested using ordinary least squares regression
analysis. Data for the analysis are drawn from a number of sources and
are described in footnotes to the tables.

Results

Matching models of AFDC effort are tested using cross-sectional data representing 1980 and 1990. Each contains measures intended to reflect elements of each of the prevailing explanations for differences in state AFDC
generosity: ideology and politics, wealth, and pressures from Medicaid.
Table 10.4 reports estimates for the 1980 model. The model explains 75 percent of the variation in the dependent variable and is statistically significant.
All predictors are statistically significant within accepted critical ranges for
one-tailed tests, and all influence AFDC effort in the expected manner.

AFDC effort increased about fifty-nine cents with each unit increase in
legislative liberalism, yet declined about eighty-nine cents with each unit

TABLE 10.5   Politics, Economics, and Medicaid Effort as Influences on State AFDC Effort, 1990

Variable	b	s.e.b	B	t
CONSTANT	0.887	0.618	0.000	1.437**
Legislative liberalism	0.313	0.106	0.368	2.943*
Democratic legislative strength	−0.598	0.449	−0.134	−1.332**
Gubernatorial powers	0.047	0.033	0.149	1.443**
Medicaid effort, 1990	−0.048	0.019	−0.285	−2.475*
Income, 1990	0.002	0.001	0.329	3.330*
Adjusted R² = .67; s.e.e. = .50; F = 18.54, prob. F = .000				

* one-tailed significance ≤ .05; ** one-tailed significance < .10.

NOTE: Effort is equal to state AFDC spending per $1000 of personal income.

SOURCE: Legislative liberalism is described in Erikson, Wright, and McIver (1989) and provided by the author. Democratic legislative strength is described in Erikson, Wright, and McIver (1989) and provided by the author. Gubernatorial power is the Schlesinger index calculated by the author from data included in *Book of the States*, various years.

increase in Democratic party dominance in the legislature. Democratic dominance in the legislature resulted in lower effort inasmuch as party dominance indicates an absence of electoral competition, a situation in which parties have little incentive to produce generous policies. A one-unit increase in the formal powers of the governor yielded about a seven-cent increase in AFDC effort, supporting the hypothesis that institutionally stronger executives are better able to use the powers of the state to redistribute income. Each dollar's increase in Medicaid spending per $1,000 personal income in 1980 resulted in a nineteen-cent increase in AFDC spending effort. Finally, each $1,000 increase in personal income yielded less than a penny's increase in AFDC effort in 1980.

The 1990 results are reported in Table 10.5. The signs of all but the Medicaid effort coefficient remain unchanged, although their magnitudes shifted. Most notably, the influence of legislative liberalism declined by almost one-half, with a unit's increase resulting in only about a thirty-one-cent increase in AFDC effort. The negative influence of Democratic legislative strength declined, too, with a unit's increase in Democratic strength in 1990 producing about a sixty-cent decline in AFDC effort in 1990, down almost one-third from the preceding decade. The influence of gubernatorial powers remained positive, with each unit increase resulting in about a five-cent increase in AFDC spending effort, and the effect of income changes remained almost constant across the two years. The most interesting result is the Medicaid spending effort coefficient, which reverses the sign over the two time periods. In 1990, a dollar's increase in

Medicaid spending effort lessened AFDC efforts by about five cents; it produced a nineteen-cent increase in 1980.

Discussion

AFDC spending efforts were functions of state politics, economics, and other spending obligations, in this case Medicaid. The implications of these results are not trivial. In much research, public assistance generosity is a benchmark for assessing states' willingness to support some of their most needy citizens—low-income families with children. Increasingly, public assistance efforts have been cast as a form of economic development policy. Some analysts argue that states limit public assistance generosity in order to avoid becoming welfare magnets (Peterson and Rom 1989). They claim that state decisions regarding public assistance generosity are tempered by the efforts of their neighbors, with states suppressing benefits so as not to attract too many welfare recipients for fear of fouling the business climate. Other analysts argue that public assistance generosity is largely driven by ideology (Wright, Erikson, and McIver 1987). In either case, choices are made on the basis of regional and intrastate considerations.

These results, particularly the demonstration that AFDC efforts are sensitive to Medicaid efforts, suggest a different possibility: Suppressing public assistance spending may be a means of offsetting increases in Medicaid spending. Because AFDC was the gateway to Medicaid for large numbers of enrollees, legislatures tried to control Medicaid spending by reducing AFDC. The shift in coefficients for the Medicaid effort measure in the two models tested here provides some evidence that state decisions on AFDC were driven in part by concerns over rises in Medicaid spending. As state efforts on Medicaid increased, AFDC efforts diminished. Since spending on AFDC was trivial, in some cases less than one dollar per $1,000 personal income, the AFDC savings were trivial. In addition, since AFDC enrollees were the least expensive group of Medicaid enrollees, with higher costs accruing to the much smaller but much more needy Supplemental Security Income population, the Medicaid savings from such a strategy are questionable. However, what is important for this analysis is that AFDC decisions were driven at least in part by the high financial demands of another program, one that is apt to expand greatly in the near future.

Welfare reform is undertaken for a number of reasons, many of which are political. One important strain, however, and one that is not trumpeted as loudly as others, is the fact that income transfers are only a part of a larger system of policymaking. The Medicaid-AFDC link is not trivial; as states engage simultaneously in welfare and health care reform it is important to keep in mind the link between these two key policy areas. Medicaid is the biggest problem area in state budgets (Grizzle and Power 1993); absent reasonable Medicaid reforms, attempts to reform AFDC are almost assured to fail. Also, attempts to rationalize and reform health care without reforms of public assistance ignore the strong link between the two programs.

Conclusion

Health and welfare reform are driven by related impulses in the states: the desire for cost control and ideology. High costs of health care and the states' seeming inability to regulate the use or price of care have led states to seek methods that limit their exposure to health spending, primarily via Medicaid programs. Reforms to AFDC programs were driven partly by ideology, but according to the quantitative analyses, they were also driven largely by experiences with Medicaid spending. As Medicaid spending increases states seek to reduce their liabilities by reducing the amount spent on public assistance. State policy makers certainly realize that the welfare population is relatively inexpensive in its consumption of health care, but the small portion of that population that requires the most health care assistance—the disabled and elderly—are more resistant to spending cuts because of their political organization and public support. This leaves the "able-bodied" poor—mostly single mothers and their children—to take the brunt of welfare and, by implication, health care spending cuts.

Reductions in public assistance pose problems for local governments. Problems of juvenile delinquency, domestic violence, and homelessness may result from states' reduction in effort. Malnutrition and poor health may affect school attendance and performance, too. These become local issues, forcing local policy makers to deal with the consequences of "mandating by dereliction." In this era of government devolution, local governments are already financially overburdened; county and municipal officials will have to either raise taxes or rely on private charities to take on responsibilities previously borne by states. In that sense, decentralization of authority may not solve poverty problems; it may only shift the burden of responding to them.

Reforming health care and welfare in the states are noble enterprises. Effecting meaningful changes, though, will be difficult and will force states to muster political will and administrative and organizational capabilities in coming to grips with the many problems that attend such large policy enterprises. The system of health and welfare policies that emerges from a more decentralized system will likely heighten the variations in state programs and will provide opportunities to observe a variety of approaches to addressing these public problems. Variations within states will increase, too. In the absence of federal regulations that require uniformity, state legislatures may allow local governments to experiment with different forms of public assistance. The political logic of devolution points in the direction of local control, and it would not be surprising if rural and urban areas demanded freedom from "one size fits all" programming. In that case, the existing patchwork of public assistance would become even patchier, as Medicaid spending continues to increase in the states.[1]

NOTES

1. Funding for this research was provided by the Florida Institute of Government under the auspices of the Florida Megatrends initiative and by the Florida State University Council on Faculty Research. Miles Hughes and Frank Schaub provided research assistance. The author assumes sole responsibility for the content of this analysis.

References

Adrian, Charles and Michael Fine. 1991. *State and Local Politics*. Chicago: Lyceum Books/Nelson-Hall.

Advisory Commission on Intergovernmental Relations. 1973. *Striking a Better Balance: Federalism in 1972*. Washington, DC: USGPO.

_____. 1977. *State Limitations on Local Taxes and Expenditures*. Washington, DC: USGPO.

_____. 1978. *State Mandating of Local Expenditures*. Washington, DC: USGPO.

_____. 1982. *State and Local Roles and the Federal System*. Washington, DC: USGPO.

_____. 1990. *Significant Features of Fiscal Federalism*. Washington, DC: USGPO.

_____. 1992. *Significant Features of Fiscal Federalism*. Washington, DC: USGPO.

_____. 1993. *State Laws Governing Local Governments Structure and Administration*. Washington, DC: USGPO.

Allen, David; James P. Lester; and Kelly M. Hill. 1995. "Prejudice, Profits and Power: Assessing the Eco-Racism Thesis at the County Level." Paper delivered at the annual meeting of the Western Political Science Association, Portland, March 16–18.

American School Board Journal. 1994a. "Ballot Box: Finding: Full Speed on National Standards." April: 56.

_____. 1994b. "Ballot Box: Finding: A Big No to Charter Schools." November: 56.

_____. 1995. "Ballot Box: Finding: Schools Should Stick to Educating." July: 48.

Ammons, David N. 1996. *Municipal Benchmarks: Assessing Local Performance and Establishing Community Standards*. Thousand Oaks, CA: Sage Publications.

Anderson, William. 1955. *The Nation and the States: Rivals or Partners?* Minneapolis: University of Minnesota.

Atkins, Patricia and Laura Wilson-Gentry. 1992. "An Etiquette for the 1990s Regional Council." *National Civic Review* (Fall/Winter): 466–487.

Baldauf, Scott. 1997. "Fifteen Years of School Reform: New Ideas, Modest Results." *Christian Science Monitor*, September 2: 1.

Barnes, William R. and Larry C. Ledebur. 1994. *The U.S. Common Market of Local Economic Regions*. Washington, DC: National League of Cities.

Barrilleaux, Charles; Paul Brace; and Bruce Dangremond. 1995. "The Sources of State Health Reform." Revised version of a paper presented at the annual meetings of the American Political Science Association, New York, September 2, 1994.

Bartik, Timothy. 1991. *Who Benefits from State and Local Economic Development Policies?* Kalamazoo, MI: Upjohn Institute.

_____ . 1993. "What Should the Federal Government Be Doing About Urban Economic Development?" A paper prepared for Regional Growth and Community Development Conference, U.S. Department of Housing and Urban Development, Nov. 18.

Bensel, Richard Franklin. 1990. *Yankee Leviathan: The Origins of Central State Authority in America, 1859–1877*. New York: Oxford.

Berman, David R. 1995. "Takeovers of Local Governments: An Overview and Evaluation of State Policies." *Publius* 25,3: 55–70.

Birch, David. 1979. *The Job Generation Process*. Cambridge, MA: MIT Program on Neighborhood Change.

Bish, Robert and Vincent Ostrom. 1973. *Understanding Urban Government*. Washington, DC: American Enterprise Institute.

Blair, George. 1986. *Government at the Grass Roots*, 4th ed. Pacific Palisades, CA.: Palisades.

Blumenstyk, Goldie. 1992. "States Reevaluate Industrial Collaborations Built Around Research Grants to Universities." *Chronicle of Higher Education*, Feb. 26: 1.

Bowman, Ann O'M. and Richard C. Kearney. 1986a. "Indexing State Government Capability." Paper presented at the annual meeting of the Southwestern Political Science Association, Dallas, March 19–22.

_____ . 1986b. *The Resurgence of the States*. Englewood Cliffs, NJ: Prentice-Hall.

Bowman, Anne O'M. and Michael A. Pagano. 1994. "State of American Federalism, 1993–1994." *Publius* 24,3: 1–21.

Boyd, William Lowe. 1992. "Local Role in Education." In Marvin C. Alkin, ed., *Encyclopedia of Educational Research*, 6th ed., pp. 753–761. New York: Macmillan.

Boyd, William Lowe and C. L. Claycomb. 1994. "Local Education Authorities, School Boards, and School Councils." In Torsten Husen and T. Neville Postlethwaite, eds. *The International Encyclopedia of Education*, 2nd ed., pp. 3491–3496. Oxford: Pergamon.

Brace, Paul. 1993. *State Government and Economic Performance*. Baltimore: Johns Hopkins University Press.

Brace, Paul and Charles Barrilleaux. 1995. "A Unified Model of State Policy Reform." A paper presented at the annual meeting of the American Political Science Association, Chicago, August 30–September 2.

Briffault, Richard. 1992. "The Role of Local Control in School Finance Reform." *Connecticut Law Review* 24,3: 773–811.

Brizius, Jack A. 1989. "An Overview of the State-Local Fiscal Landscape." In E. Blaine Liner, ed., *A Decade of Devolution: Perspectives on State-Local Relations*, pp. 51–79. Washington, DC: Urban Institute Press.

Bryk, Anthony S.; John Q. Easton; David Kerbow; Sharon G. Rollow; and Penny Sebring. 1994. "The State of Chicago School Reform." *Phi Delta Kappan* (September): 74–78.

Callahan, Raymond E. 1975. "The American Board of Education, 1789–1960." In Peter J. Cistone, ed., *Understanding School Boards*, pp. 19–46. Lexington, MA: Lexington Books.

Carmines, Edward G. and James A. Stimson. 1989. *Issue Evolution*. Princeton: Princeton University Press.

Cater, Douglas. 1964. *Power in Washington*. New York: Random House.

Caves, Roger W. 1992. *Land-Use Planning: The Ballot Box Revolution*. Newbury Park, CA: Sage Publications.

Celis, William, 3rd. 1992a. "Furor in New Hampshire on Vote to Cut Standards." *New York Times*, August 26: B7.

_____. 1992b. "23 States Face Suits on School Funds." *New York Times*, September 2: B7.

Chi, Keon. 1994. "State Business Incentives." *State Trends and Forecasts* 3: 1–29.

Chrislip, David D. and C. E. Larson. 1994. *Collaborative Leadership: How Citizens and Civic Leaders Can Make a Difference*. San Francisco: Jossey-Bass.

Cigler, Beverly A. 1989. "Trends Affecting Local Administrators." In James L. Perry, ed., *Handbook of Public Administration*, 1st ed., pp. 40–53. San Francisco: Jossey-Bass.

_____. 1990. "Public Administration and the Paradox of Professionalization." *Public Administration Review* 50, 6: 637–653.

_____. 1993a. "Challenges Facing Fiscal Federalism in the 1990s." *PS: Political Science & Politics* 26, 2: 181–186.

_____. 1993b. "State-Local Relations: A Need for Reinvention?" *Intergovernmental Perspective* 19, 1: 15–18.

_____. 1994. "The County-State Connection: A National Study of Associations of Counties." *Public Administration Review* 54, 1: 3–11.

_____. 1995a. "County Governance in the 1990s." *State and Local Government Review* 2,1: 55–70.

_____. 1995b. "Just Another Special Interest: The Intergovernmental Lobby." In Allan J. Cigler and Burdett Loomis, eds., *Interest Group Politics*, 4th ed., pp. 131–153. Washington, DC: Congressional Quarterly Press.

_____. 1996a. "Adjusting to Changing Expectations at the Local Level." In James L. Perry, ed., *Handbook of Public Administration*, 2nd ed., pp. 60–76. San Francisco: Jossey-Bass.

_____. 1996b. "Revenue Diversification Among American Counties." In Donald C. Menzel, ed., *The American County: Frontiers of Knowledge*. Tuscaloosa, AL: University of Alabama Press.

Cisneros, H. G., ed. 1993. *Interwoven Destinies: Cities and the Nation*. New York: Norton.

Clarke, Susan and Gary Gaile. 1992. "The Next Wave: Postfederal Local Economic Development Strategies." *Economic Development Quarterly* 6, 2: 187–198.

Cole, Stephanie, ed. 1976. *Partnership Within the States*. Philadelphia and Urbana: Center for the Study of Federalism and Institute of Government and Public Affairs.

Committee for Economic Development. 1994. *Putting Learning First: Governing and Managing the Schools for High Achievement*. New York: Committee for Economic Development.

Conlan, Timothy. 1988. *New Federalism*. Washington, D.C.: Brookings Institution.

Council of State Governments. 1992. *Book of the States*. Lexington, KY: Council of State Governments.

Cremin, Lawrence A. 1970. *American Education: The Colonial Experience, 1607–1783*. New York: Harper and Row.

Cronin, Joseph M. 1992. "Reallocating the Power of Urban School Boards." In Patricia F. First and Herbert J. Walberg, eds., *School Boards: Changing Local Control*, pp. 22–27. Berkeley: McCutchan.

Crotty, Patricia M. 1987. "The New Federalism Game: Primacy Implementation of Environmental Policy." *Publius* 17, 2: 53–67.

_____ . 1988. "Assessing the Role of Federal Administrative Regions: An Exploratory Analysis." *Public Administration Review* 48, 2: 642–648.

Crowson, Robert L. and William Lowe Boyd. 1993. "Coordinated Services for Children: Designing Arks for Storms and Seas Unknown." *American Journal of Education* 101, 2 (February): 140–179.

Danielson, Michael. 1976. *The Politics of Exclusion.* Princeton: Princeton University Press.

Danzberger, Jacqueline P. 1992. "School Boards: A Troubled American Institution." In *Facing the Challenge.* New York: Twentieth Century Fund Press.

David, Jane L. 1994. "School-Based Decision Making: Kentucky's Test of Decentralization." *Phi Delta Kappan* (May): 706–712.

Davis, Charles E. and James P. Lester. 1987. "Decentralizing Federal Environmental Policy: A Research Note." *Western Political Quarterly* 40, 3: 555–565.

_____ . 1989. "Federalism and Environmental Policy." In James P. Lester, ed., *Environmental Politics and Policy: Theories and Evidence*, pp. 57–84. Durham, NC: Duke University Press.

Degrove, John. 1988. "A Second Wave Emerges." *State Government News* 31, 5 (May): 8.

Derthick, Martha. 1970. *The Influence of Federal Grants.* Cambridge: Harvard University Press.

de Tocqueville, Alexis. 1945. *Democracy in America.* New York: Vintage.

DiLeo, Daniel. 1991. "Bureaucracy's Guardians or Democracy's Tribunes: Who Helps Sick Kids?" A paper presented at the annual meeting of the American Society for Public Administration, Washington, D.C., March 23–27.

_____ . 1994. "Effects of Political Culture on State Education Policy as Indicated by Content Analysis of Governors' State-of-the-State Speeches." Unpublished Ph.D. thesis, Temple University.

Dillon, John F. 1911. *A Treatise on the Law of Municipal Corporations*, 5th ed. Boston: Little, Brown.

Downs, Anthony. 1994. *New Visions for Metropolitan America.* Washington, D.C.: Brookings Institution.

_____ . 1996. "The Devolution Revolution: Why Congress Is Shifting a Lot of Power to the Wrong Levels." Brookings Policy Brief No. 3. Washington, DC: Brookings Institution.

Duerksen, Christopher. 1983. *Environmental Regulation of Industrial Plant Siting.* Washington, DC: Conservation Foundation.

Durning, Dan. 1995. "Reinvent State Government or Reorganize It? Governors' Proposals for Administrative Reform in 1995." Presented at the annual meeting of the American Political Science Association, Chicago, August 30–September 2.

Dvorin, Eugene P. and Arthur J. Misner, eds. 1966. *California Politics and Policies.* Redding, MA.: Addison-Wesley.

Dye, Thomas R. 1984. "Party and Policy in the States." *Journal of Politics* 46, 4: 1097–1116.

_____ . 1990. *American Federalism: Competition Among Governments*. Lexington, MA: D. C. Heath/Lexington Books.

_____ . 1995. *Understanding Public Policy,* 8th ed. Englewood Cliffs, NJ: Prentice Hall.

Education Week. 1995a. "News Roundup: National Survey: Most States Allow Alternative Certification." May 10: 4.

_____ . 1995b. "News in Brief: Razing Arizona Mandates." May 10: 13.

_____ . 1995c. "News in Brief: Daley Names Team in Takeover of Chicago Schools." July 12: 17.

Eisinger, Peter. 1988. *The Rise of the Entrepreneurial State*. Madison: University of Wisconsin Press.

_____ . 1993. "State Venture Capitalism, State Politics, and the World of High Risk Investment." *Economic Development Quarterly* 7, 2: 131–139.

_____ . 1995. "State Economic Development in the 1990s: Politics and Policy Learning." *Economic Development Quarterly* 9, 2: 146–158.

Elazar, Daniel J. 1962. *The American Partnership*. Chicago: University of Chicago Press.

_____ . 1984. *American Federalism: A View from the States*, 3rd ed. New York: Harper & Row.

_____ . 1994. *Federal Systems of the World*, 2nd ed. London: Longman.

Eldersveld, Samuel. 1982. *Political Parties in American Society*. New York: Basic.

Ellwood, David. 1988. *Poor Support*. New York: Basic Books.

Elmore, Richard F. and Susan H. Fuhrman. 1994. "Governors and Education Policy in the 1990s." In Susan H. Fuhrman and Richard F. Elmore, eds., *The Governance of Curriculum*, pp. 1–10. Alexandria, VA: Association for Supervision and Curriculum Press.

Erikson, Robert S.; Gerald C. Wright, Jr.; and John P. McIver. 1989. "Political Parties, Public Opinion, and State Policy in the United States." *American Political Science Review* 83, 3: 729–750.

Farber, Stephen B. 1989. "Federalism and State-Local Relations." In E. Blaine Liner, ed., *A Decade of Devolution: Perspectives on State-Local Relations*. Washington, DC: Urban Institute.

Feistritzer, Emily. 1992. "A Profile of School Board Presidents." In Patricia F. First and Herbert J. Walberg, eds., *School Boards: Changing Local Control*. pp. 132–153. Berkeley: McCutchan.

Finn, Chester. 1992. "Reinventing Local Control." In Patricia F. First and Herbert J. Walberg, eds., *School Boards: Changing Local Control*. pp. 22–43. Berkeley: McCutchan.

Firestone, William A.; Susan H. Fuhrman; and Michael W. Kirst. 1991. "State Education Reform Since 1983: Appraisal and the Future." *Educational Policy* 5, 3: 233–256.

First, Patricia F.; Joan Curcio; and Dalton L. Young. 1994. "State Full-Service School Initiatives: New Notions of Policy Development." In Louise Adler and Sid Gardner, eds., *The Politics of Linking Schools and Social Services*, pp. 66–73. Bristol, MA: Falmer.

Freeman, J. Leiper. 1965. *The Political Process*, rev. ed. New York: Random House.

Fuhrman, Susan H. 1994a. "Legislatures and Education Policy." In Susan H. Fuhrman and Richard F. Elmore, eds., *The Governance of Curriculum*, pp. 30–55. Alexandria, VA: Association for Supervision and Curricular Development Press.

_____ . 1994b. "Clinton's Education Policy and Intergovernmental Relations in the 1990s." *Publius* 24,2: 83–97.

Fuhrman, Susan H. and Richard Elmore. 1990. "Understanding Local Control in the Wake of State Education Reform." *Educational Evaluation and Policy Analysis* 12 (Spring): 82–86.

Fulton, Mary and David Long. 1993. *School Finance Litigation: A Historical Summary*. Denver: Education Commission of the States.

Gage, Robert W. and Myrna Mandell, eds. 1990. *Strategies for Managing Intergovernmental Policies and Networks*. New York: Praeger.

Galster, George C. and Edward W. Hill, eds. 1992. *The Metropolis in Black and White*. New Brunswick, NJ: Center for Urban Policy Research.

Galster, George C. and Sean P. Killen. 1995. "The Geography of Metropolitan Opportunity: A Reconnaissance and Conceptual Framework." *Housing Policy Debate* 6,1: 7–43.

Glaab, Charles and A. Theodore Brown. 1983. *A History of Urban America*, 3rd ed. New York: Macmillan.

Glendening, Parris and Mavis Reeves, 1984. *Pragmatic Federalism*, 2nd ed. Pacific Palisades, CA.: Palisades.

Goggin, Malcolm L.; Ann O'M. Bowman; James P. Lester; and Lawrence J. O'Toole. 1990. *Implementation Theory and Practice: Toward a Third Generation*. New York: Harper Collins.

Gold, Steven S. 1995. *The Fiscal Crisis of the States: Lessons for the Future*. Washington, DC: Georgetown University Press.

Grant, Daniel and H. C. Nixon. 1982. *State and Local Government in America*, 4th ed. Boston: Allyn and Bacon.

Graves, W. Brooke. 1964. *American Intergovernmental Relations*. New York: Scribners.

Gray, Virginia and Peter Eisinger. 1991. *American States and Cities*. New York: Harper Collins.

Grizzle, Gloria and Gwen Power. 1993. "Medicaid Spending Dynamics: Implications for Cost Control Strategies." *Public Budgeting and Financial Management* 13, 4: 18–28.

Grodzins, Morton. 1966. *The American System*. New Brunswick, NJ: Transaction.

_____ . 1983. *The American System: A New View of Government in the United States*, posthumous edition by Daniel J. Elazar. Chicago: Rand McNally.

Guskind, Robert. 1993. "The New Civil War." *National Journal*, April 3: 817–821.

Guthrie, James W. 1974. "Public Control of Public Schools." *Public Affairs Report* 15, 3. Berkeley: University of California Institute of Government Studies.

Hansen, Susan. 1983. *The Politics of Taxation*. New York: Praeger.

Hanson, Russell L. 1983. "The 'Content' of Public Policy: The States and Aid to Families with Dependent Children." *Journal of Politics* 45, 3: 771–785.

_____ . 1984. "Medicaid and the Politics of Redistribution." *American Journal of Political Science* 28, 2: 313–339.

Harrington-Lueker, Donna. 1993. "Updating Governance Reforms in Kentucky and Chicago." *American School Board Journal* (February): 32.

———. 1994a. "Toward a New National Yardstick: Like It or Not, Here Come the National Education Standards." *American School Board Journal* (February): 41–43.

———. 1994b. "Charter Schools: Another Ho-hum Reform of Genuine Reformation Thumping Your Schoolhouse Door?" *American School Board Journal* (September): 22–26.

Harrison, Bennett. 1994. "The Myth of Small Firms as the Predominant Job Generators." *Economic Development Quarterly* 8, 1: 3–18.

Harwood, Robert. 1991. *Citizens and Politics: The View from Main Street America*. Dayton, OH: Kettering Foundation.

Haskell, Elizabeth and Victoria Price. 1973. *State Environmental Management*. New York: Praeger.

Haynes, Monica L. and Roger Stuart. 1995. "All Is Quiet During First Day of Classes at Turner School." *Pittsburgh Post-Gazette*, September 6: C1, C6.

Heclo, Hugh. 1977. *A Government of Strangers*. Washington, DC: Brookings Institution.

Iannaccone, Laurence. 1967. *Politics in Education*. New York: Center for Applied Research in Education.

Iannaccone, Laurence and Frank W. Lutz. 1995. "The Crucible of Democracy: the Local Arena." In Jay D. Scribner and Donald H. Layton, eds., *The Study of Educational Politics*, pp. 39–52. Bristol, MA: Falmer.

Illinois Department of Commerce and Community Development. 1992. "Economic Leadership in Illinois: New Approaches for the 1990s." Center for Economic Competitiveness, SRI International and DRI/McGraw Hill.

Jennings, Edward T. 1977. "Some Policy Consequences of the Long Revolution and Bifactional Rivalry in Louisiana." *American Journal of Political Science* 21,2: 225–246.

———. 1979. "Competition, Constituencies, and Welfare Policies in the American States." *American Political Science Review* 73,2: 414–429.

Jennings, Michael. 1991. "Reform Law Adds to Power of Local School Boards, Boysen Tells Association." *Louisville Courier-Journal*, February 16: 21.

Jewell, Malcolm. 1982. "The Neglected World of State Politics." *Journal of Politics* 44, 3: 638–657.

Jones, Charles O. 1975. *Clean Air*. Pittsburgh: University of Pittsburgh Press.

———. 1976. "Regulating the Environment." In Herbert Jacobs and Virginia Gray, eds., *Politics in the American States*, 3rd ed., pp. 388–427. Boston: Little, Brown.

Judd, Dennis R. and Todd Swanstrom. 1994. *City Politics*. New York: Harper Collins.

Kelly, Eric D. 1993. *Managing Community Growth: Policies, Techniques, and Impacts*. Westport, CT: Praeger.

Kenyon, Daphne A. 1989. "Reforming State Policies That Affect Local Taxing and Borrowing." In E. Blaine Liner, ed., *A Decade of Devolution: Perspectives on State-Local Relations*, pp. 223–257. Washington, DC: Urban Institute Press.

Key, V. O., Jr. with the assistance of Alexander Heard. 1949. *Southern Politics in State and Nation*. New York: Vintage.

Kirst, Michael. 1991. "Improving Children's Services." *Phi Delta Kappan* (April): 615–618.

Kirst, Michael and Gail Meister. 1983. "The Role of Issue Networks in State Agenda-Setting." Stanford University: California Institute for Research on Educational Finance and Governance.

Kone, Susan L. and Richard F. Winters. 1993. "Taxes and Voting: Electoral Retribution in the American States." *Journal of Politics* 55,1: 22–40.

Koppich, Julia. 1994. "The Politics of Policymaking for Children." In Louise Adler and Sid Gordon, eds., *The Politics of Linking Schools and Social Services*, pp. 57–62. Bristol, MA: Falmer.

Kost, John. 1996. *New Approaches to Public Management: The Case of Michigan.* Washington, DC: Brookings Institution.

Kozol, Jonathon. 1991. *Savage Inequalities.* New York: Crown.

Leach, Richard. 1970. *American Federalism.* New York: Norton.

Lehne, Richard. 1978. *The Quest for Justice.* New York: Longman.

Lemov, Penelope. 1994. "Tough Times for TIF." *Governing* 7, 5: 18–19.

Lester, James P. 1980. "Partisanship and Environmental Policy: The Mediating Influence of State Organizational Structures." *Environment and Behavior* 12, 1: 101–131.

_____ . 1986. "New Federalism and Environmental Policy." *Publius* 16, 1: 149–165.

_____ . 1995. "Federalism and State Environmental Policy." In James P. Lester, ed., *Environmental Politics and Policy: Theories and Evidence*, 2nd ed., pp. 39–60. Durham, NC: Duke University Press.

Lester, James P.; Ann O'M. Bowman; Michael L. Goggin; and Lawrence J. O'Toole, Jr. 1987. "Public Policy Implementation: Evolution of the Field and Agenda for Future Research." *Policy Studies Review* 7,1: 200–216.

Lester, James P. and Emmett N. Lombard. 1990. "The Comparative Analysis of State Environmental Policy." *Natural Resources Journal* 30, 2: 301–319.

Lester, James P.; James L. Franke; Ann O'M. Bowman; and Kenneth W. Kramer. 1983. "Hazardous Wastes, Politics, and Public Policy: A Comparative State Analysis." *Western Political Quarterly* 36, 2: 257–285.

Lindblom, Charles. 1977. *Politics and Markets.* New York: Basic Books.

Lombard, Emmett N. 1988. "Intergovernmental Relations and Air Quality Policy Formation: The Case of Colorado." A paper presented at the annual meeting of the American Political Science Association, Washington, D.C., September 1–4.

_____ . 1989. Intergovernmental Determinants of Air Quality Policy. Unpublished Ph.D. thesis, Colorado State University.

_____ . 1993. "Determinants of State Air Quality Management: A Comparative Analysis." *American Review of Public Administration* 23, 1: 57–73.

Lowry, William R. 1992. *The Dimensions of Federalism.* Durham, NC: Duke University Press.

Lowery, David and Virginia Gray. 1992. "Holding Back the Tide of Bad Economic Times: The Compensatory Impact of State Industrial Policy." *Social Science Quarterly* 73, 3: 483–495.

Luck, Jamie. 1992. "State School Board Clears Up School Councils' Powers." *Lexington Herald-Leader*, November 6: B1-B2.

Macmahon, Arthur. 1972. *Administering Federalism in a Democracy.* New York: Oxford.

Marks, Thomas and John Cooper. 1988. *State Constitutional Law in a Nutshell.* St. Paul: West.

Marmor, Theodore J.; Jerry L. Mashaw; and Philip L. Harvey. 1990. *America's Misunderstood Welfare State: Persistent Myths, Enduring Realities.* New York: Basic Books.

Marshall, Catherine; Douglas Mitchell; and Frederick Wirt. 1989. *Culture and Education Policy in the American States.* Bristol, MA: Falmer.

Martin, Roscoe. 1965. *The Cities and the Federal System.* New York: Atherton.

Marvel, Mary and William Shkurti. 1993. "The Economic Impact of Development: Honda in Ohio." *Economic Development Quarterly* 7, 1: 50–62.

Massell, Diane. 1994. "Achieving Consensus: Setting the Agenda for State Curricular Reform." In Susan H. Fuhrman and Richard F. Elmore, eds., *The Governance of Curriculum,* pp. 84–108. Alexandria, VA: Association for Supervision and Curricular Development Press.

Maxwell, James and J. Richard Aronson. 1977. *Financing State and Local Governments,* 3rd ed. Washington, DC: Brookings Institution.

Mazzoni, Tim L. 1995. "State Policymaking and School Reform: Influences and Influentials." In Jay D. Scribner and Donald H. Layton, eds., *The Study of Educational Politics,* pp. 53–74. Bristol, MA: Falmer.

McBain, Howard Lee. 1916a. "The Doctrine of an Inherent Right of Local Self-Government." *Columbia Law Review* 16: 190–299.

_____. 1916b. *The Law and Practice of Municipal Home Rule.* New York: Columbia University Press.

_____. 1918. *American City Progress and the Law.* New York: Columbia University Press.

McCarthy, David. 1990. *Local Government Law in a Nutshell,* 3rd ed. St. Paul: West.

Mead, Lawrence. 1997. "Some Effects of Welfare Reform in Wisconsin." Paper presented at the annual meetings of the Midwest Political Science Association, Chicago, April 10–12.

Meyer, Peter, ed. 1993. *Comparative Studies in Local Economic Development: Problems in Policy Implementation.* Westport, CT: Greenwood.

Miller, Laura. 1995. "South Dakota Board Asked to Rethink State Guidelines for Schools." *Education Week,* May 10: 13.

Miron, Louis F. and Robert K. Wimpelberg. 1992. "The Role of School Boards in the Governance of Education." In Patricia F. First and Herbert J. Walberg, eds., *School Boards: Changing Local Control,* pp. 154–175. Berkeley: McCutchan.

Moltine, Curt. 1994. "The New DNR Is Much Less Accessible." *Detroit Free Press,* August 2: A6.

Mosca, Gaetano. 1939. *The Ruling Class (Elementi di scienza politica).* Translated by Hannah D. Kahn, edited and revised with an introduction by Arthur Livingston. New York: McGraw-Hill.

Mosher, Frederick and Orville Poland. 1964. *The Costs of American Governments.* New York: Dodd, Mead.

Murphy, Russell D. 1992. "Connecticut: Lowell P. Weicker, Jr., a Maverick in the 'Land of Steady Habits.'" In Thad Beyle, ed., *Governors and Hard Times,* pp. 61–76. Washington, DC: Congressional Quarterly Press.

Murray, Charles. 1984. *Losing Ground.* New York: Basic Books.

Nathan, Joe and James Ysseldyke. 1994. "What Minnesota Has Learned About School Choice." *Phi Delta Kappan* (May): 682–688.

Nathan, Richard. 1983. *The Administrative Presidency.* New York: Wiley.

National Association of Regional Councils. 1993a. *Accomplishments in Regional Water Resources Management: Success Stories of Regional Councils.* Environmental Advocacy and Services Group. Washington, DC: NARC.

_____ . 1993b. *Directory of Regional Councils in the United States.* Washington, DC: NARC.

National Association of State Development Agencies. 1988 and 1990. *State Economic Development Expenditure Survey.* Washington, DC: NASDA.

National Commission of Excellence in Education. 1983. *A Nation at Risk.* Washington, DC: USGPO.

National Conference on State Legislatures. 1991. "States Left to Pay to Protect the Environment." *State Legislatures* 17: 8.

National Governors' Association. 1994. *State Welfare Reform Proposals, February 1994.* Denver: NGA.

_____ . 1996. *Ideas That Work: Education Reform.* Washington, DC: NGA.

National Performance Review. 1993. *Creating a Government That Works Better and Costs Less.* New York: Plume.

Nice, David and Patricia Fredericksen. 1995. *The Politics of Intergovernmental Relations,* 2nd ed. Chicago: Nelson-Hall.

Nunn, Samuel and Mark S. Rosentraub. 1996. "Metropolitan Fiscal Equalization: Distilling Lessons from Four U.S. Programs." *State and Local Government Review* 28, 2: 90–102.

Odden, Allan. 1992. "School Finance in the 1990s." *Phi Delta Kappan* (February): 455–461.

Oklahoma Department of Commerce. 1994. *Oklahoma's Strategic Development Plan, 1988–1993.* Tulsa.

Orfield, Gary. 1993. "The Growth of Segregation in American Schools: Changing Patterns of Separation and Poverty Since 1968." Cambridge: Report of the Harvard Project on School Desegregation to the National School Boards Association.

O'Rourke, Timothy. 1980. *The Impact of Reapportionment.* New Brunswick, NJ: Transaction Books.

Osborne, David and Theodore Gaebler. 1992. *Reinventing Government.* Reading, MA: Addison Wesley.

Ostrom, Vincent. 1987. *The Political Theory of a Compound Republic,* 2nd ed. Lincoln: University of Nebraska Press.

Pagano, Michael. 1990. "State-Local Relations in the 1990s." *The Annals of the American Academy of Political and Social Science,* vol. 509: 94–105.

Pancrazio, Sally Bulkley. 1992. "State Takeovers and Other Last Resorts." In Patricia F. First and Herbert J. Walberg, eds., *School Boards: Changing Local Control,* pp. 88–109. Berkeley: McCutchan.

Pauly, Mark V. 1986. "Taxation, Health Insurance, and Market Failure in the Medical Economy." *Journal of Economic Literature* 24 (June): 629–676.

Peirce, Neil R. 1993. *Citistates: How Urban America Can Prosper in a Competitive World.* Washington, DC: Seven Locks Press.

Peterson, Paul E. and Mark Rom. 1989. "American Federalism, Welfare Policy, and Residential Choices." *American Political Science Review* 83, 3: 711–728.

Pilcher, Dan. 1991. "The Third Wave of Economic Development." *State Legislatures* 17, 11: 34–37.

Pipho, Chris. 1991. "Stateline: The Vouchers Are Coming." *Phi Delta Kappan* (October): 102–103.

_____ . 1993. "Stateline: Bipartisan Charter Schools." *Phi Delta Kappan* (October): 102–103.

_____ . 1995. "Stateline: Life Along the Federal, State, and Local Food Chain." *Phi Delta Kappan* (March): 510–511.

Plank, D. N. and William Lowe Boyd. 1994. "Politics and Governance of Education." In Torsten Husen and T. Neville Postlethwaite, eds., *The International Encyclopedia of Education*, pp. 4587–4595. Oxford: Pergamon.

Poen, Monte. 1979. *Harry Truman and the Health Lobby*. Columbia: University of Missouri Press.

Ponessa, Jeanne. 1995. "Pa. Court Backs Private Management of Wilkinsburg School." *Education Week*, November 8: 11.

Powell, David Clayton. 1995. "The Effects of TEL Design on Local School Districts: Restrictive by Design." A paper presented at the annual meeting of the American Political Science Association, Chicago, August 30–September 2.

Prager, Adam; Philip Benowitz; and Robert Schein. 1995. "Local Economic Development: Trends and Prospects." *Municipal Yearbook, 1995*, pp. 23–35. Washington, DC: International City/County Management Association.

Putnam, Robert D.; Robert Leonardi; and Raffaella Y. Nanetti. 1993. *Making Democracy Work: Civic Tradition in Modern Italy*. Princeton: Princeton University Press.

Rabe, Barry G. 1994. *Beyond NIMBY: Hazardous Waste Siting in Canada and the United States*. Washington, DC: Brookings Institution.

_____ . 1995. "Integrated Environmental Permitting: Experience and Innovation at the State Level." *State and Local Government Review* 27, 3: 209–220.

Reich, Robert. 1991. *Work of Nations: Preparing Ourselves for 21st-Century Capitalism*. New York: A. A. Knopf.

Ridley, Scott. 1987. *The State of the States: 1987*. Washington, DC: Fund for Renewable Resources.

_____ . 1988. *The State of the States: 1988*. Washington, DC: Fund for Renewable Resources.

Riker, William. 1964. *Federalism*. Boston: Little, Brown.

Ringquist, Evan J. 1993. *Environmental Protection at the State Level*. New York: M. E. Sharpe.

Rosmiller, Richard. 1992. "Financing Schools." In Marvin C. Alkin, ed., *Encyclopedia of Educational Research*, pp. 512–521. New York: Macmillan.

Ross, Doug and Robert Friedman. 1990. "The Emerging Third Wave." *The Entrepreneurial Economy* 9: 3–10.

Rusk, David. 1993. *Cities Without Suburbs*. Washington, DC: Woodrow Wilson Center Press.

Russo, Charles J. 1992. "The Legal Status of School Boards in the Intergovern-mental System." In Patricia F. First and Herbert J. Walberg, eds., *School Boards: Changing Local Control,* pp. 1–21. Berkeley: McCutchan.

Schattschneider, E. E. 1960. *The Semisovereign People.* New York: Holt, Rinehart, and Winston.

Schneider, Mark. 1989. *The Competitive City.* Pittsburgh: University of Pittsburgh Press.

Schultz, Kristin L. 1993. "States Experiment with School Choice." *Comparative State Politics* 14, 3: 12–24.

Schwarz, John. 1988. *America's Hidden Success,* rev. ed. New York: Norton.

Sharpe, Rochelle. 1995. "Primary Lesson: Federal Education Law Becomes Hot Target of Wary Conservatives." *Wall Street Journal,* August 30: A1, A6.

Smith, Kevin B. 1994. "Education Reforms in the 1980's: A Quasi Experiment." A paper presented at the annual meeting of the American Political Science Association, New York, August 1–September 3.

Sokolow, Alvin and Keith Snavely. 1983. "Small City Autonomy in the Federal System: A Study of Local Constraint and Opportunity in California." *Publius* 13, 1: 73–88.

Southeast Michigan Council of Governments. 1993. *Member Handbook.* April.

_____ . Undated. *SEMCOG 1992–1993 Annual Report.*

Sroufe, Gerald E. 1995. "Politics of Education at the Federal Level." In Jay D. Scribner, Donald H. Layton, eds., *The Study of Education Politics,* pp. 75–88. Bristol, MA: Falmer.

Stephens, G. Ross. 1974. "State Centralization and the Erosion of Local Autonomy." *Journal of Politics* 36, 1: 44–76.

Stonecash, Jeffrey M. 1981a. "Centralization in State-Local Fiscal Relationships." *Western Political Quarterly* 34,2: 301–309.

_____ . 1981b. "State Policies Regarding Local Resource Acquisition." *American Politics Quarterly* 9,4: 401–425.

_____ . 1983. "Fiscal Centralization in the American States: Increasing Similarity and Persisting Diversity." *Publius* 13,4: 123–137.

_____ . 1985. "Paths of Fiscal Centralization in the American States." *Policy Studies Journal* 13,3: 653–661.

_____ . 1986. "Incremental and Abrupt Changes in Fiscal Centralization in the American States, 1957–1983." In David R. Morgan and J. Edward Benton, eds., *Intergovernmental Relations and Public Policy,* pp. 189–200. New York: Green-wood Press.

_____ . 1987–88. "Inter-Party Competition, Political Dialogue, and Public Policy: A Critical Review." *Policy Studies Journal* 16,2: 243–262.

_____ . 1988. "Fiscal Centralization in the American States: Findings from Another Perspective." *Public Budgeting and Finance* 8,4: 81–89.

_____ . 1990. "State Responses to Declining National Support: Behavior in the Post-1978 Era." *Policy Studies Journal* 18,3: 214–226.

_____. 1992. "'Split' Constituencies and the Impact of Party Control." *Social Science History* 16, 3: 455–477.

_____ . 1995a. "The Legacy of the Great Depression: Taxpayer Revolts and Changes in the Role of the State." Department of Political Science, Maxwell School, Syracuse University.

_____ . 1995b. *American State and Local Politics.* New York: Harcourt and Brace.

Suro, Roberto. 1990. "Courts Ordering Financing Changes in Public Schools." *New York Times,* March 11, A1.

Svara, James. 1994. *Facilitative Leadership in Local Government: Lessons from Successful Mayors' Chairpersons.* San Francisco: Jossey-Bass.

Syed, Anwar. 1966. *The Political Theory of American Local Government.* New York: Random House.

Thomas, Clive and Ronald Hrebenar. 1990. "Interest Groups in the States." In Virginia Gray, Herbert Jacob, and Robert Albritton, eds., *Politics in the American States,* 5th ed., pp. 123–158. Glenview, IL.: Scott, Foresman/Little, Brown.

Thorpe, Kenneth E. 1993. "The American States and Canada: A Comparative Analysis of Health Care Spending." *Journal of Health Politics, Policy, and Law* 18 (Summer): 477–489.

Tiebout, Charles. 1956. "A Pure Theory of Local Expenditure." *Journal of Political Economy* 64, 5: 416–435.

Timar, Thomas B. 1992. "Urban Politics and State School Finances in the 1980s." In James G. Cibulka, Rodney J. Reed, and Kenneth K. Wong, eds., *The Politics of Urban Education in the United States,* pp. 105–121. Washington, DC: Falmer.

United States Department of Education. 1994. "National Education Goals." Goals 2000: Community Update no. 14: 4.

United States Department of Health and Human Services. 1997. *Personal Responsibility and Work Opportunity Reconciliation Act: A Compilation of Implementation Materials.* Washington, DC: U.S. Department of Health and Human Services, Assistant Secretary for Planning and Evaluation.

United States General Accounting Office. 1990. *Federal-State-Local Relations: Trends of the Past Decade and Emerging Issues.* Washington, DC: USGPO.

_____ . 1992. *Poverty Trends, 1980–1988.* Washington, DC: USGPO, report GAO/PEMD–92–34.

Venable, Tim. 1994. "Ohio Wins Landslide Victory in 1993 Facility Location Race." *Site Selection* 39, 1: 12–26.

Venable, Tim and Hoyt E. Coffee. 1993. "Incentives Boosted, Budgets Bashed in '93 Legislative Sessions." *Site Selection* 38, 5: 1086–1094.

Vergari, Sandra. 1994. "School Finance Reform in the State of Michigan." A paper presented at the annual meeting of the Midwest Political Science Association, Chicago, April 14–16.

Vidal, Avis C. 1995. "Reintegrating Disadvantaged Communities into the Fabric of Urban Life: The Role of Community Development." *Housing Policy Debate* 6,1: 169–230.

Walberg, Herbert J. and Richard P. Niemiec. 1994. "Is Chicago School Reform Working?" *Phi Delta Kappan* (May): 713–715.

Walker, David. 1981. *Toward a Functioning Federalism.* Cambridge, MA.: Winthrop.

Wallis, Allan D. 1992. "New Life for Regionalism? Maybe." *National Civic Review* (Winter-Spring): 19–26.

Walsh, Mark. 1995. "Twelve States Join Move to Pass Charter Laws: Twenty More Considering Legislation This Year." *Education Week,* May 10: 1, 15.

212

References

Walton, John. 1967. "The Vertical Axis of Community Organization and the Structure of Power." *Southwestern Social Science Quarterly* 48, 3: 353–368.

Wheare, K. C. 1964. *Federal Government,* 4th ed. New York: Galaxy.

Wildavsky, Aaron. 1974. *The Politics of the Budgetary Process,* 2nd ed. Boston: Little, Brown.

Williams, Mike. 1994a. "State Losing Chance to Sock Polluters." *Detroit Free Press,* June 18: 1B.

_____ . 1994b. "Wayne County Cleanup Plan Worries EPA." *Detroit Free Press,* June 2: 1B.

Williams, Oliver J. 1971. *Metropolitan Political Analysis: A Social Access Approach.* New York: Free Press.

Winters, Richard F. 1980. "Political Choice and Expenditure Change in New Hampshire and Vermont." *Polity* 12, 4 (Summer): 598–621.

Wirt, Frederick M. and Michael W. Kirst. 1992. *The Politics of Education: Schools in Conflict,* 3rd ed. Berkeley: McCutchan.

Wirt, Frederick M. and Samuel Gove. 1990. "Education." In Virginia Gray, Herbert Jacob, and Robert B. Albritton, eds., *Politics in the American States,* 5th ed., pp. 447–478. Glenview, IL: Scott, Foresman.

Wright, Deil. 1985. "Models of National/State/Local Relations." In Laurence O'Toole, Jr., ed., *American Intergovernmental Relations,* pp. 58–66. Washington, DC: Congressional Quarterly Press.

_____ . 1988. *Understanding Intergovernmental Relations,* 3rd ed. Pacific Grove, CA.: Brooks/Cole.

Ziegler, L. Harmon; M. Kent Jennings; and G. Wayne Peak. 1974. *Governing American Schools: Political Interaction in Local School Districts.* North Scituate, MA: Duxbury.

Zimmerman, Joseph. 1991. "Federal Preemption Under Reagan's New Federalism." *Publius* 21, 1: 7–28.

_____ . 1992. *Contemporary American Federalism.* New York: Praeger.

About the Editor

Russell L. Hanson is a political scientist at Indiana University Bloomington, where he has taught since 1980. He is interested in the history of American political ideas, including federalism. Hanson also studies the development of public assistance in the United States, which involves a complex division of labor between national, state, and local governments. The growing prominence of states in this intergovernmental partnership is the subject of his current research.

About the Contributors

David Nice is a political scientist at Washington State University in Pullman and the coauthor of *The Politics of Intergovernmental Relations*.

Daniel Elazar holds appointments at Bar-Ilan University in Tel Aviv and Temple University in Philadelphia. He is the author of *American Federalism: A View from the States* and *American Mosaic: The Impact of Space, Time, and Culture on American Politics*.

Beverly Cigler is in the School of Public Affairs at Pennsylvania State University–Harrisburg. Her work on local administration has appeared in leading scholarly outlets.

Jeffrey Stonecash is in the Department of Political Science at the Maxwell School of Syracuse University and is the author of *American State and Local Politics*.

Peter Eisinger is in the LaFollette Institute for Public Affairs at University of Wisconsin–Madison. He is the author of *The Rise of the Entrepreneurial State: State and Local Development Policy in the United States* and *State Economic Development in the 1990s*.

Daniel DiLeo is a political scientist at Pennsylvania State University–Altoona; he writes about the impact of public opinion on gubernatorial agendas and the differences between governors' and presidents' agendas in the 1990s.

James Lester is a political scientist at Colorado State University. He is the author of *Public Policy: An Evolutionary Approach* and the editor of *Environmental Politics and Policy: Theories and Evidence*.

Emmett Lombard is a political scientist at Oakland University in Rochester, Michigan. He has published articles about state environmental policy and air quality management in scholarly journals.

Timothy Tilton is a political scientist at Indiana University Bloomington. An authority on welfare states in western Europe, Tilton has retired from politics and is doing field research on the development of national parks in different countries.

Charles Barrilleaux is a political scientist at Florida State University. He has published articles on state politics, policy, and administration in leading scholarly journals.

Index

Time for Results (National Governors' Association), 121
Towns and townships, 29
Transportation, 41, 61, 94
Turner School, 129

Ultra vires, 37
  See also Dillon's Rule
Unitary system of government, 17, 36(n1)
Universities, 59, 67, 69, 97
Utah, 127, 148(table), 150(table), 152, 190(table), 192(table)

Vermont, 45, 132, 148(table), 150(table), 152, 190(table), 192(table)
Veterans, 166
Virginia, 104, 113, 148(table), 150(table)
Vouchers, 65, 69

War on Poverty, 7, 182
Washington (state), 150(table), 190(table), 192(table)
  concurrency legislation in land-use planning, 68
  education policies, 122, 127
  regional governments, 148(table), 152
Watershed authorities, 11
Welfare, 13–14, 178–188
  driving forces of reform, 178, 197
  entitlement vs. means-tested programs, 184
  expansion of states' power, 13

local implementation of programs, 76
myths about, 187–188
partisan politics of, 181–183
Personal Responsibility and Work Opportunity Reconciliation Act (1996), 60
promotion of welfare dependency, 187–188
public opinion on, 182–183
reforms, 2, 178–183, 186–188, 197
self-reliance of aid recipients, 69, 179
spending for, 13–14, 60, 180–181, 189–196, 189–190(table), 192(table)
types of recipients, 178
"workfare," 60–61, 178, 187, 188
  See also Aid to Families with Dependent Children
West Virginia, 122, 135, 148(table), 150(table), 190(table), 192(table)
Wilson-Gentry, Laura, 146, 152
Wisconsin, 122, 123, 130, 148(table), 150(table), 190(table), 192(table)
Wise use movement, 62
"Workfare," 60–61, 178, 187, 188
World War II, 185
Wyoming, 122, 130, 148(table), 150(table), 190(table), 192(table)

Youth, demographics of, 55, 59

Zoning, exclusionary, 62, 77